First World War
and Army of Occupation
War Diary
France, Belgium and Germany

59 DIVISION
178 Infantry Brigade
175 Machine Gun Company
24 October 1916 - 26 February 1918

WO95/3025/12

The Naval & Military Press Ltd
www.nmarchive.com
Published in association with The National Archives

Published by

The Naval & Military Press Ltd

Unit 10 Ridgewood Industrial Park,

Uckfield, East Sussex,

TN22 5QE England

Tel: +44 (0) 1825 749494

www.naval-military-press.com

www.nmarchive.com

This diary has been reprinted in facsimile from the original. Any imperfections are inevitably reproduced and the quality may fall short of modern type and cartographic standards.

© **Crown Copyright**
Images reproduced by permission of The National Archives, London, England, 2015.

Contents

Document type	Place/Title	Date From	Date To
Heading	WO 3025 59th 178 1. B 175th Machine Gun Coy 1916 Oct-1918 Feb		
Heading	59th Division 178th Infy Bde 175th Machine Gun Coy Oct 1916-Feb 1918		
Heading	War Diary Of 175 Machine Gun Company From 24th Oct 1916 To 30th March 1917 Volume 1.		
War Diary	Belton Park Grantham.	24/10/1916	08/02/1917
War Diary	Aldershot	08/02/1917	17/02/1917
War Diary	Southampton	17/02/1917	18/02/1917
War Diary	Transport	19/02/1917	21/02/1917
War Diary	Transport	22/02/1917	22/02/1917
War Diary	Havre	23/02/1917	25/02/1917
War Diary	Longeau	26/02/1917	26/02/1917
War Diary	Glisy (Somme)	26/02/1917	26/02/1917
War Diary	Warfusee	27/02/1917	27/02/1917
War Diary	Mericourt	28/02/1917	12/03/1917
War Diary	Foucaucourt	13/03/1917	20/03/1917
War Diary	Estrees (Transport)	21/03/1917	21/03/1917
War Diary	Villers Carbonnel	22/03/1917	25/03/1917
War Diary	St Cren	26/03/1917	27/03/1917
War Diary	Bavincourt	28/03/1917	01/04/1917
War Diary	Bernes	02/04/1917	05/04/1917
War Diary	Flechin	06/04/1917	09/04/1917
War Diary	Bernes.	10/04/1917	19/04/1917
War Diary	Roisel	20/04/1917	30/04/1917
Miscellaneous	To H.Q. 59th Division		
War Diary	Roisel	01/05/1917	06/05/1917
War Diary	Bernes	07/05/1917	28/05/1917
War Diary	Hamelet	29/05/1917	29/05/1917
War Diary	Equancourt	30/05/1917	31/05/1917
War Diary	Metz-En-Couture	01/06/1917	12/06/1917
War Diary	Equancourt	12/06/1917	22/06/1917
War Diary	Gouzeaucourt Wood	23/06/1917	09/07/1917
War Diary	Y.6.d.0.3 (Fins) B.35.d Nr. La Mesnil En-Arrovaise	10/07/1917	26/07/1917
Miscellaneous	Signals Cpl Cockroft i/c Signals		
Operation(al) Order(s)	Transport Orders	18/07/1917	18/07/1917
Miscellaneous	Appendix "A" Officer Commanding No 1 Section.		
Operation(al) Order(s)	Operation Order No 1 by Lieut J.H. Gardner Commdg 175 M.G.Coy	18/07/1917	18/07/1917
Map	Map		
Miscellaneous	Map K		
Miscellaneous	Appendix A Officer Commanding No 2 Section.		
Miscellaneous	Appendix B		
Miscellaneous	Appendix C		
War Diary	O.35.d.	27/07/1917	24/08/1917
War Diary	O 35.d Later Aveluy Cabstand Huts W.16.b.5.8	24/08/1917	24/08/1917
War Diary	Aveluy	25/08/1917	30/08/1917
War Diary	I.12.d.4.7	31/08/1917	19/09/1917
War Diary	L.13.d.3.4.	20/09/1917	22/09/1917
War Diary	G.6.d.4.4	23/09/1917	24/09/1917

Type	Description	Start	End
War Diary	H.2.e.5.2	25/09/1917	27/09/1917
War Diary	H.2.e.5.2. And Delette (witter Up While St At)	27/09/1917	29/09/1917
War Diary	Delette Written Up Whilst At	27/09/1917	29/09/1917
War Diary	Warrington Camp H.2.e.5.2	30/09/1917	30/09/1917
War Diary	Billets North Of Boes E.9.H.E.M 4 F. 20.	01/10/1917	01/10/1917
War Diary	Boeseghem	02/10/1917	04/10/1917
War Diary	Delette	05/10/1917	09/10/1917
War Diary	Sachin At Farm N Of N In Sachin	10/10/1917	10/10/1917
War Diary	Sachin As Atone	11/10/1917	11/10/1917
War Diary	Gouy-Servins Coy. HQ At Road Hard N.W. Of G In Gouy	12/10/1917	12/10/1917
War Diary	Carency Coy. HQ. on N Side Of Carency-Souchez Road N Of A In Carency	13/10/1917	13/10/1917
War Diary	Carency	14/10/1917	13/11/1917
War Diary	Duissans	14/11/1917	19/11/1917
War Diary	Hendecourt	19/11/1917	21/11/1917
War Diary	Gomiecourt	22/11/1917	23/11/1917
War Diary	Equancourt	23/11/1917	29/11/1917
War Diary	Trescault	30/11/1917	30/11/1917
War Diary	Flesquieres	03/12/1917	05/12/1917
War Diary	Trescault	06/12/1917	08/12/1917
War Diary	Flesquieres	09/12/1917	16/12/1917
War Diary	Mq. Camp Trescault	17/12/1917	18/12/1917
War Diary	O.b.f. Line K.32e	19/12/1917	20/12/1917
War Diary	Barastre A 16a.8.2	21/12/1917	21/12/1917
War Diary	Beaulencourt N.18.a.22	22/12/1917	24/12/1917
War Diary	Moncheaux B 25.C.50	25/12/1917	25/01/1918
Miscellaneous Heading	178 Infantry Bde To HQ. 59 Div		
War Diary	Moncheaux B.25.c.50.	28/01/1918	07/02/1918
War Diary	Barly	08/02/1918	08/02/1918
War Diary	Northumberland Camp Mercatel	09/02/1918	14/02/1918
War Diary	St Leger B4.b.25.	12/02/1918	19/02/1918
War Diary	Durrow Camp Mory B.21.a.65	20/02/1918	23/02/1918
War Diary	Durrow Camp B.21.a.65	24/02/1918	26/02/1918
Operation(al) Order(s)	178th Infantry Brigade Order No. 90	06/02/1918	06/02/1918
Operation(al) Order(s)	178th Infantry Brigade Order No. 92	07/02/1918	07/02/1918
Operation(al) Order(s)	178th Infantry Brigade Order No. 91	07/02/1918	07/02/1918
Operation(al) Order(s)	178th Infantry Brigade Order No. 93	09/02/1918	09/02/1918
Operation(al) Order(s)	175 Machine Gun Company Operation Order No. 27	18/02/1918	18/02/1918
Operation(al) Order(s)	175 Infantry Coy Operation Order No. 28	22/02/1918	22/02/1918
Operation(al) Order(s)	175 Machine Gun Company Operation Order No. 29	26/02/1918	26/02/1918
Operation(al) Order(s)	Machine Gun Company Operation Order No 29	26/02/1917	26/02/1917

WO 3025

59th 17 & 1.8

175th Machine Gun Coy
1916 Oct - 1918 Feb

59TH DIVISION
178TH INFY BDE

175TH MACHINE GUN COY.
OCT 1916 — FEB 1918

WO1 & II

CONFIDENTIAL

WAR DIARY
of
175 Machine Gun Company

from 24th Oct. 1916. to 30th March 1917

(Volume 1.)

Army Form C. 2118.

WAR DIARY
or
INTELLIGENCE SUMMARY
(Erase heading not required.)

175. Machine Gun Company

Instructions regarding War Diaries and Intelligence Summaries are contained in F. S. Regs., Part II and the Staff Manual respectively. Title Pages will be prepared in manuscript.

Place	Date	Hour	Summary of Events and Information	Remarks and references to Appendices
BELTON PARK, GRANTHAM.	24.10.16	—	Company formed as part of 'B' Service Batt?. Training in this area until ordered to proceed overseas. During this time 5 Officers who did not proceed overseas with company were attached Of whom 2 went as drafts to France 1 as O.C. Coy. @ 2 as search in Command	J.M.G.
BELTON PARK, GRANTHAM.	8.2.17	3.15am	Left Camp. Entrained Military Siding 6.9 am. Departed GRANTHAM 7.0 am. Company Complete. 10 Officers, 177 other Ranks, 11 Riding horses, 47 mules, 13 Limbered Waggons, 1 Cooks cart, 1 Water cart. 33 N.C.os men left behind, 10 form new Company viz 228 B.2 Service B?. Of this number 7 were in hospital, 2 in isolation and 3 in Detention.	J.M.G.
ALDERSHOT	8.2.17	2.5 pm	Company arrived Military Siding THORNHILL CAMP. Billetted in 1st Coy: Lines A.S.C. Offices at A.S.C.H.Q. BULLER Mess.	J.M.G.
ALDERSHOT	9.2.17		Company training in stone area. T/Capt. A.P.SKEVINGTON 2nd WEST YORKSHIRE REGT. Seconded M.G.C., Commanding Company admitted to MANDORA ISOLATION HOSPITAL Suffering from Chickenpox. Command of Company taken over by Lt. J.H. GARDNER 2nd i/c. Application for replacement made to I/Comm and H.Q. ALDERSHOT.	J.M.G.
ALDERSHOT	10.2.17 to 12.2.17	—	Company training at ALDERSHOT.	J.M.G.
ALDERSHOT	13.2.17	—	Major B.H. PUCKLE D.S.O. WELCH. REGT. Att?. M.G.C. from WING COMMANDER 'C' Service Batt? BELTON PARK., assumed Command and i/c Company.	J.M.G.
ALDERSHOT	14.2.17 to 16.2.17	—	Company training at ALDERSHOT.	J.M.G.
ALDERSHOT	17.2.17	4.45 am	Left Camp.; Train left MILITARY SIDING THORNHILL CAMP at 4.25 am 1 Offr, 5 men remained behind, being medically unfit for various reasons to proceed overseas. These men to return to Training Centre GRANTHAM.	J.M.G.
SOUTHAMPTON	17.2.17	7.0 am	Arrived Berth 38 & Detrained. Waiting to for transport aboard. Arrive till 4.0 P.M. Embarked. 4.30 P.M. on MANCHESTER IMPORTER. No 8026.	J.M.G.

B. Pol Puckle Major
Comdg. 175 Machine Gun Coy.

WAR DIARY
or
INTELLIGENCE SUMMARY

Army Form C. 2118.

175 Machine Gun Company

Place	Date	Hour	Summary of Events and Information	Remarks and references to Appendices
SOUTHAMPTON	18.2.17	4:35 pm	Left dock. Having taken on board some cargo & mails we altered v'thro' anchorage off NETLEY 5.27 pm.	7.4.9
TRANSPORT	19.2.17	2:20 pm	Left anchorage & proceeded to sea. Fog again v'thro'. Anchored 3:51 pm. Proceeded 9.9 pm. Anchored again outside Boom at 10:42 pm.	7.4.9
TRANSPORT	20.2.17	9:00 am	Returned from anchorage outside Boom to NETLEY and anchored there at 4.24 am. 1 Hepl (Cdr) R.M. Clerk + 1 man reported sick, were taken off ship suffering from Measles.	7.4.9
TRANSPORT	21.2.17	2:40 pm	Returned to dock at SOUTHAMPTON. Berthed 46 at 3.36 pm. Company less Transport Personnel, animals & wagons & was entrained & proceeded to Rest Camp arr'd 6 pm. animals thus 5:30 pm. 1 man taken off ship with measles.	7.4.9
REST CAMP SOUTHAMPTON	21.2.17	5:30	Arrived. Billeted in huts. Officers in one Hut.	7.4.9
TRANSPORT	22.2.17	12:0	Left Camp. 2 man left behind in hospital with measles. Embarked 1:30 pm. Left Dock 3.8 pm. Anchored outside Boom in ST HELENS BAY 6.20 pm for night.	7.4.9
HAVRE	23.2.17	5:50	Left anchorage for HAVRE. Very smooth passage. Used Escort, boat & staff parties (Sea S/b arranged). Left anchorage 9.20 am. Berthed 11:30 am. Finished unloading stores wagons etc at 7:30 pm after as storm mails has been removed.	7.4.9
	24.2.17	2:30 am	Transport Personnel, horses billeted in HALLE 3. Wagons parked outside. Rest of Company in N°5 REST CAMP Tents.	
HAVRE	26.2.17	10:30 am	Left Camp. Entrained POINT 3. 12:30 pm. Train left 3:15 pm. Travelled via ROUEN & AMIENS.	7.4.9
LONGEAU	26.2.17	11 am	Arrived Military Siding. Detrained. Company arrived. Guns & in dugouts Head.	7.4.9

B. Nath Vickers Major
Comdg. N°. 175 Machine Gun Coy.

Army Form C. 2118.

WAR DIARY
or
INTELLIGENCE SUMMARY

175 Machine Gun Company

(Erase heading not required.)

Place	Date	Hour	Summary of Events and Information	Remarks and references to Appendices
GLISY (SOMME)	26.2.17	3.30 pm	Arrived from LONGEAU. Billeted in village for night. Left 8.0 am 27.2.17.	M.G.
WARFUSÉE	27.2.17	12.30 pm	Arrived from GLISY. Billeted in village for night. Left 9.30 am 28.2.17.	M.G.
MÉRICOURT	28.2.17	11.30 am	Arrived from WARFUSÉE. Billeted in Army huts. Thaw over. Much gun fire all day & two	M.G.

B. Dale Pickl
Major
Comdg. No. 175 Machine Gun Coy.

Army Form C. 2118.

WAR DIARY
or
INTELLIGENCE SUMMARY

(Erase heading not required.)

175. Machine Gun Company

Instructions regarding War Diaries and Intelligence Summaries are contained in F. S. Regs., Part II. and the Staff Manual respectively. Title Pages will be prepared in manuscript.

Place	Date	Hour	Summary of Events and Information	Remarks and references to Appendices
MÉRICOURT	1.3.17	—	Company Training in Camp Area. 1 Man removed to hospital with measles. Observation balloon in S.E. direction observed to burst into flames and fell at 6.25 pm, probably due to attack by hostile aircraft, as anti aircraft shells were seen bursting. Weather cold foggy	J.M.G.
MÉRICOURT	2.3.17	9.0 am	Major B.H. PUCKLE, D.S.O Commanding, aired to proceed up line to see front to be taken over by Company. Training Continues. Nos 1 + 2 Sections ordered by M.O. to be isolated from rest of Company owing to contact with measles case. Order for 4 officers & 16 other ranks to report to 151 Bgde on 4.3.17 received. Hostile Air Craft (1) Appeared about 6.0 pm. Two planes gave chase & drove off the Enemy machine, with gun fire. Some hostile shelling between 10.0 & 11.0 pm in the Henrite & Bosley, BRAY. Weather cold & foggy	J.M.G.
MÉRICOURT	3.3.17	—	Company Training. Whole Company isolated by order of D.A.M.S. 59 & 2 IV. for measles. Transport Personnel moved from Dug out & Hut in Camp. Orders for relief of trenches on 4.3.17 cancelled for above reason. Transport Driver removed to hospital suffering from Pneumonia. Weather mostly cold.	J.M.G.
MÉRICOURT	4.3.17	—	Sunday. No Parades. Various ming made Bore Re beration Cte, Company paid out. Major B.H. PUCKLE returned from 151 Bgde H.Q. FAUCAUCOURT. Fine Clear day, bright sunshine.	J.M.G.
MÉRICOURT	5.3.17	—	Training interfered with by fairly heavy snow fall	J.M.G.
MÉRICOURT	6.3.17	—	Company Training in Camp area. Coy. Route March.	J.M.G.
MÉRICOURT	7.3.17	—	Company Training in Camp Area. Coy. Route March. Very heavy & continuous bombardment for about 1 hour commencing 3.50 am. S.E. direction. Also for short time at 7.0 p.m. That E. wind. V. cold.	J.M.G.
MÉRICOURT	8.3.17	—	Medical Inspection of whole Company. Training	J.M.G.

B. Bal. Puckle Major
Comdg. No. 175 Machine Gun Coy.

WAR DIARY or INTELLIGENCE SUMMARY

Army Form C. 2118.

175 Machine Gun Company

5.

Place	Date	Hour	Summary of Events and Information	Remarks and references to Appendices
MERICOURT	9.3.17	–	Company Training. Route March.	JWG
MERICOURT	10.3.17	–	1 Opl. suffering from measles admitted to hospital. 4 men isolated on his account. 4 men met previous case also isolated. Major Ricket went up the line again.	JWG
MERICOURT	11.3.17	–	2 men suffering from measles admitted to hospital. 8 men isolated on their account. All the men in one hut. Rest of Company ordered the twenty so as to not contract. Inter supervision of Sanitary Officer 50th Div. Contact. Authority ADMS 50th Div.	JWG
MERICOURT	12.3.17	11.30 am	Orders for Company to proceed to FOUCAUCOURT at 2.0 pm. Company left at 3.0 pm. Railed FOUCAUCOURT 5.45 pm. Men in hut O/P in CAMP D'EGLISE. Waggons parked opposite Pl. BICHAT. O/P changes in village. Mules & Drivers in O/P W of ST MARTIN'S CAMP. 16 Men contacts from Measles left behind at MERICOURT. Running. Company settled by 7.10 pm.	JWG
FOUCAUCOURT	13.3.17	–	Company remained in Billets. Attached to 178 Brigade. Div. Order 115/SG for Relief of 177 Coy on nights 16/17 & 17/18 received.	JWG
FOUCAUCOURT	14.3.17	5.15 pm	4 Section Officers 16 other ranks (1 man per gun team) + C.S.M. went up to Finches for instruction purposes under 177 M.G. Coy already holding line. T.O also went up for instruction to Brump at THIEPVAL on ST QUENTIN – AMIENS ROAD.	2/1/40 JWG
FOUCAUCOURT	15.3.17		Company Training. Bgde order N:3 Cancelling Relief of 177 M.G. Coy received at 12.0 noon. 16 other rank Sgt Anchayed from Hospital to duty.	JWG
FOUCAUCOURT	16.3.17		Company Training. Preparations made to remove Coy stores etc to transport lines owing to Order of Troops in village. Report of Great French advance on front of 1st & Cdn Corps received. Returned from at 15B AMORE also advanced 30 miles N of BAPAUME.	JWG
FOUCAUCOURT	17.3.17	1.45 am	Orders received for relief of 177 M.G. Coy. on nights of 17/18 & 18/19. Preparations for moving up made.	
		12.45 pm	Order BM 45 Cancelling BM 34 for relief received. Orders for relief of 40/6 & 16 O.R. in trenches received from OC 178th proceed up to Coy H.Q in support trench, & returned stating that the German front had retired and that our troops had occupied their front line system. were advancing over the open unmolested. Later information from all rounds and intelligence report confirmed this. Division wrote. Command issued 4 days provisions learning 20 per company. Orders for advance. Advance by 1st SQN & 6th Division moving. Troops penetrated as far as VILLERS-CARBONNEL. Report that both BAPAUME & PERONNE had fallen. Report of abdication of CZAR of Russia received.	JWG

B. Hale Ruchel Major
Comdg. No. 175 Machine Gun Coy.

WAR DIARY or INTELLIGENCE SUMMARY

Army Form C. 2118.

175 Machine Gun Company.

Place	Date	Hour	Summary of Events and Information	Remarks and references to Appendices
FOUCAUCOURT	18.3.17	—	O.C. Coy, 4 Officers & 16 Other Ranks returned to Billets. VILLERS CARBONNEL, MISERY & other villages on Foggé front occupied. General retreat of Enemy forces from HAM on N. to NOYON on South. Allied advance continued. French Cavalry across River SOMME, for several miles. No rearguard. Information re poisoning of wells by Enemy received at BARLEUX wet Arsenic BO5E/34	J.H.G.
FOUCAUCOURT	19.3.17	—	Billets & Truck Advance continues. Bringing of SOMME commenced: Div 1/4th Alternary of ft strips for advance &c parade orders for "relief" S/177 H.Q. Coy. Received.	J.H.G.
FOUCAUCOURT	20.3.17	—	2 sections (20+) moved with Limbers at 7 a.m. Nos. 1 & 3 at EPPEUS WOOD T5 E 26, No 3 at N 36 C 22 No. 2 See at T 5 d 4 8, Nº 2 at EPPEUS WOOD T 5 E 26, Sw. Edition S.A. No. 4 at ATTIE WOOD T Sab. French Mob Laund, Blueb 2 East End N 24 at ATTIE WOOD mved to dugouts at ESTREES, East End. No Enemy in front. Transport FOUCAUCOURT in charge of Stores left lines west of 1 Officer left Sick at CAPPY. Mess at FOUCAUCOURT and onward.	Much difficulty in transport owing to inability to carry all stores & pack in one journey. J.H.G.
ESTREES (Transport)	21.3.17	—	Company and Transport as above stated under 20.3.17. No certain news concerning line of Enemy retirement yet to hand. Some gun fire to NORTH & SOUTH none in immediate front. 1 Officer servant star at FOUCAUCOURT Coy. Reconnoitring country round their positions. British Advance continued.	J.H.G.
VILLERS CARBONNEL	22.3.17	4.0 am	Company in same position. Reconnoitring. Transport Limbers moved from ESTREES to BACK side NE of village. Reminder of stores brought up with Limbers from Transport Lines at FOUCAUCOURT. Two journeys being required. 1 Officer & Servant at Foy (4th Coy Court Village in very bad & in very badly usecked condition. Two horses eff. Standing. No limber travel. Road ESTRÉES — VILLERS CARBONNEL very badly cut up in places. Labour Btns & Infantry repairing. Very heavy Horse drawn traffic. Motors. German lines good for the most part through some rec. then blown up. French & British Sleepers in iron & Everywhere into German esplanard found bad many Sheds (all kinds) & bombs by not about etc. very bridge over SOMME constructed for heavy traffic king used N and many enemy snow...	J.H.G. F. Black, Major ? Comdg No. 175 Machine Gun Coy.

WAR DIARY or INTELLIGENCE SUMMARY

Army Form C. 2118.

175 Machine Gun Company

Page 7.

Place	Date	Hour	Summary of Events and Information	Remarks and references to Appendices
VILLERS CARBONNEL	22.3.17	—	Company & Transport as on 22.3.17. O.C. Coy & O. Officers Recce Route to view M.G. Positions at Point 29.d.5.0 ATHIES WOOD. Digging Party of 1+4 sections also Recced being Gun Emplacements at above point. 5th Divisional Artillery arrived in afternoon. Also 1 Division of Cavalry. Enemy Reported at VERMAND making a Stand. Weather very bright but cold N. wind. Fell frost at night.	J.H.J.
VILLERS CARBONNEL	24.3.17	—	Company & Transport as on 23.3.17. Digging Party under 2 Officers proceeded as on 23.3.17. 2 Officers & Nos 2 & 3 proceeded to O.29.d.5.0 to take up position. Reconnoitred British Batteries arriving to support troops. Came down just outside transport lines in ... after bad running wheel completed owing to strong N. wind. Both Pilots thrown violent to making successful landing. Two 175 Coys, General Sothern Out O. Coy, & our preparations to accompany dump formed from Coy brought more light a-head as enough stores as possible. Weather here fine but ord. wind adopted by British Forces in France at 11 P.M. Front. Some advice continued N.E. direction. Enemy shewing gun fire TN 7 of BILLE Enemy French proposed N to SOISSONS Enemy Kirch arre. stiffening all along.	J.H.J.
VILLERS CARBONNEL	25.3.17	—	Company & Transport as on 24.3.17. Service actually early in morning. Heavy shelling by Anti aircraft batteries. Shells bursting directly over Enemy machine was brought down about two miles to North, in flames. Orders for Company to move to MONS EN CHAUSSEE.	J.H.J.
ST CREN	26.3.17	5.30 PM	Company arrived billeted. 5 limbers & 15 O.Rs left behind at Transport lines to move all Coy stores. Dow'r gen had been required to haul cores dumps as it was found impracticable to move all Coy. 10.R. returned from Hospital & joined at lines. As light as possible a dump what was not essential. Buzz over SOMME at BRIE Canal Company Transport turned right to South of Road Transport water horses returned & forming ... on no billets could be obtained at MONS EN CHAUSSEE, which has been much damaged & Coy Reserve. Enemy Coy; proceed to ST CREN. Roads blown up at cross roads Pt. P.25. R.14. also partly Craters from E of Church in MONS. All fruit & many other trees cut down. All Telegraph arms destroyed. Dug out burnt in Kirsou in Roads. Weather very wet & cold. X Trench Map Sheet 62°.5². Edition 2.A.	J.H.J.

A. Neil Field Major
Comdg. No. 175 Machine Gun Coy.

WAR DIARY
INTELLIGENCE SUMMARY

175 Machine Gun Company

Army Form C. 2118.

Place	Date	Hour	Summary of Events and Information	Remarks and references to Appendices
ST CREN.	27.3.17	—	Company was on 26.3.17 Two sections (No3) reported to Company from O.C. 29 A.S.C. with five other Bunks at Transport Lines. Completed 2 mens rations for 14 days left in charge of another with stores handed over to Company at 11.0.a.m. Remaining three, with 2nd i/c Command, Remainder of O.R. at 6.0 p.m. 2 O.Rs from Isolation at MERICOURT joined Transport Lines. 1.30 pm. approached from Company at 6.0 pm. Company ordered tomorrow to CREN to MONS EN CHAUSSEE to billets Div. HQ. tomorrow with St CREN. When was under tomorrow to BOVINCOURT at 8.0. am. Next day was to camel. Completed Major Pierre Commanding Cory; ordered proceed at 2.0 am to your line a ask Division. HQ. Position weather very bad. Heavy snow showers all day.	J.W.G.
BOVINCOURT.	28.3.17	10.30 am	Company & Transport arrived under 2nd i/c from ST CREN. Billeted alleguite in empty house & being Stables at N. end of village his ago not all destroyed. Some house reported mined, including Billet occupied by Officers of Company R.E. reported Other dangerous Cut out wires etc. Billet occupied on arrival of Company at 2/17 Sherwood Foresters. Met bie recent at 7.0 pm. Before settled orders received for 174 Section to proceed with 215 & 2/17 Foresters Regt. Billet 1 gun team per Company, and pack animals, to Fill up positions in Cruciform trench (to dug that night) on a line running E. of BERNES and FLECHIN. There moved off at 6.30 & 10. pm. No 4. going to BERNES. Guns also removed for No. 3. Section with Canadian Officers & 2 sections of the 16 located men at-. They moved off at 6.45 pm. 14 other ranks. Being the Remainder of the Company. MERICOURT moved at 4.30 pm. No notification of their arrival having been given Company also has Supply on Water supply authenticity out for were at-VRAIGNES. deep Snow on Ground Steef of rations. Company also has trough by the three daily. Pack Amm. an was for rations graph Ration by Divm. as Train with M.... did not arrive til 1.30 am. There were dumped Sections at 2.30 am. We ache, cold & rainy Snow & rain showers all night. Pack animals found any safe factory. Water was carried in Panniers from 8 wood trails to wire, which was attacked by looters to huts of packs adeleay. Each had 3 Two (Peters) teypes found becoming the purpose very well. 12 in all were made.	J.W.G.

A. Oak Webb Major
Comdg. No. 175 Machine Gun Coy.

Army Form C. 2118.

WAR DIARY or INTELLIGENCE SUMMARY

175 Machine Gun Company

(Erase heading not required.)

Place	Date	Hour	Summary of Events and Information	Remarks and references to Appendices
BOVINCOURT	29.3.17	—	H.Q. Company & Sections & transport arrived No. 1 Sec. at FLÉCHIN 9/2 Sec. united No. 3 at HANDCOURT & No. 4 at BERNES. Owing to 3.0 p.m. Trenches completed to afford 80% M.G. Emplacements made but not much else. Very little cover for troops occupying them. No dug outs. Day rainy, wet country in bad state for working. HAND COURT & BERNES Company deteriorated by enemy very few billets obtaining but being available for troops arrived in the Convent of SOYÉ COURT & pt. B.G.A. receiving covering fire alongway for above dug for the work by Gun of No.1 Sec. at FLÉCHIN. Some hostile shelling 77mm Guns of FLÉCHIN & BERNES about 5.0 p.m. Gun Sprinkler fire on SOYÉ COURT Mount at 6.30 p.m. Officer Commanding No.1 Sec. No.3 Sec. Sub Section Officer of No.2 Sec. returned to Regt. H.Q. Major & 2/c returned H.Q. 3.0 p.m. Rations arrived 12 Midnight were sent to sections at 1.30 a.m.	M.G.

M. Hal Ruehl
Major

Comdg. No. 175 Machine Gun Coy.

Army Form C. 2118.

WAR DIARY
or
INTELLIGENCE SUMMARY
(Erase heading not required.)

175 MACHINE GUN COMPANY

SHEET 1
VOL: 2

Remarks and references to Appendices

Bill Richard
Capt. 29/3/17 Vol 3

Place	Date	Hour	Summary of Events and Information
BOUVINCOURT	30.3.17		Company and Transport as on 29.3.17. Orders for attack of SOYÉCOURT received. The order on previous day having been cancelled owing to bad weather. Detail: Artillery to open fire on village at 7.15 pm to left at 7.45 p.m. of Bns. (WARWICKS) to attack at 7.30 p.m. Three guns of Nº 1 Section to open Barrage fire on front Nº of SOYÉCOURT VILLAGE at 7.15 PM & maintain till 7.45 p.m. Gun positions were manned by 2½ pm. and Nºs 1 & 3 were observed into the E. and SE. FLECHIN, as their positions in the overturn trenches had probably been spotted by the enemy. Positions of these guns was as follows. Nº 1, from S.E. village to Point Q.17.a.6505. Nº 2 in village just S. of main road to VENDELLES at Q.17.c.7679. Nº 3 gun from overturn trench Nº of FLECHIN (Q.11.C.2.5) to Q.17.c.6085. Ranges given left gun Nº 3, 1400 Barrage sights 50° Diff. giving roughly swept area of 231° from Q.18.c.02 to R.13.c.0.2. These orders were duly carried out and the village of SOYÉCOURT assaulted, occupied, ahead, with little or no resistance. Nº 2 of returns fired Nº 1 gun 800, Nº 2 gun 1050, Nº 3 gun 1000. Total 2850. On form also. While 2/L Nº 1 Section Officer were reconnoitring gun position at about 2·0 pm. Several of the enemy were clearly observed walking along a ridge running N. from SOYÉCOURT at distance of from 1000 to 1500" sniping on position of Nº 1 gun earlier in the day was reported. One small shell fell within 20' of Nº 2 gun at about 3.0 p.m. This position was hotter than previous gave away by the gun team who took no pains to conceal themselves when approaching or leaving the gun. Enemy wire (mostly but good stretch) seen running N. to S. in front of SOYÉCOURT. Both sides of the valley lying between FLECHIN & SOYÉCOURT were fully wired, in the open by gates & foot sides, no notices being taken. Nº 2 SECTION Section Commander, C.S.M & Section Sgt. having been warned of impending attack on VENDELLES on 31.3.17, reconnoitered ground & to E. of BERNES for gun positions after noon. Party of enemy observed engaged in carrying out work from factory to VENDELLES. This reconnoitring party pushed past Nº 14 COPSE until Railway crossing at R.16.03 was under observation of HANCOURT. Intelligence NIL. Nº 3. SECTION of BERNES. Intelligence. Enemy strong post heavily wired occupied. Located 200° N.E. of E. in MONDE 8.15 d. Ref. Map B. Also working party at SENAVES FARM. All four guns were fired 1 & 2 at 3.30 L.S. left, on junction road 400' N of J. in JEANCOURT. (Map 18) No ovservation. Rounds fired 360. Nºs 3 & 4 guns fired at working parties observed at Q.12.d.7.9. R.4.3.p.q. at 3.30 pm Nº rounds fired 1600. Observation difficult, no accurate results known. Enemy shelled BERNES, FLECHIN, HANCOURT & VRAIGNES intermittently during the day with 77m.m & a few 5·9"s. H.E. The BOUVINCOURT-VRAIGNES Road was shelled with 5·9 H.E. while transport was passing with rations (direction Nº damage done though shells were pretty close. BOUVINCOURT was also shelled between 9 pm & 11·0 pm. & 6·9. H.E. about 20 shells counted District in & about F. captured. Day fine. Heavy rain & hail showers at intervals. Cloudy. Wind. Fresh, Westerly. One free of them our limbs about 2.30 pm. W.9.th. Gun. Cord.

Map reference France Sheet 62.e.S.E. 1/20,000

WAR DIARY or INTELLIGENCE SUMMARY

Army Form C. 2118.

175 MACHINE GUN COMPANY

Comdg. No. 175 Machine Gun [Coy]

Place	Date	Hour	Summary of Events and Information	Remarks and references to Appendices
BOUVINCOURT	31.3.17	4.0 am	In accordance with Bgde O.O. No. 9 No. 4 Section was in BERNES at 4.0 am. Section officer in consultation with O.C. 2/6 S.F. The guns of this Section were pushed out in front of BERNES in such a position that they could bring fire to bear on village of VENDELLES & on Road E & N of that village. Fire was opened on these of the enemy	
		10.30 am	at 11 am. Guard at 1.35 pm. when information was received that our patrols had found into VENDELLES. This Section was then concentrated at BERNES ready to move up in support if required.	
		1.0 pm		
		3.30 am	No 2 Section - O.C. 'B' Coy, Capt T. Innes at BOUVINCOURT proceeded to take up position which had been decided upon by Section officer in the afternoon. The Left Sect: Sec.Lieut. 2/Lt FRIEND took up position in MONTIGNY FARM, in order to cover the left flank of the attacking Companies. This was Subsection. Capt BERNES at 10.30 am late up position on main road through Q.5.a. while about 400F from farm party of GERMANS was seen advancing on farm from direction of BOIS DE LA CROIX. They were engaged by infantry post on the FARM & by M.G. owners dispersed.	
		12.40 pm	Guns of Left Subsection No 2. in position at FARM in front of wood K.35.d. covering approaches to VENDELLES from N & NE, and on Railway N of FARM. Owing to the artillery bombardment, then the guns fired on the above mentioned.	
			O/c reported that own attacking troops were 300 S of JEANCOURT & enemy about 40 strong having retired to high ground S of LE VERGUIER had halted on our line. Without O.K. M.G was being informed, he therefore bring in without infantry protection with three forks guns to wood in K.35.a. This Sect: Section was made up to strength to VENDELLES to take up position for the defence of this village. This movement completed.	
		6.0 pm		
		8.30 pm	At Subsection No 2 Section 2/Lt HARVEY was to advance behind Raining Battery to ascending Vendelles & LE VERGUIER. On	
		10.45 pm	outskirts of VENDELLES another N. flank infantry along high ground between VENDELLES & JEANCOURT. Completion of this movement he was to take up position for the defence of JEANCOURT.	
		11.15 pm	There two guns advanced with 'A' Company attacking, four on reaching N.E. [end] of VENDELLES, O/c found that infantry were nearing to the Left, called a small group of enemy was seen on by Gd in R.2. & when engaged, the infantry being ordered to retire, M.g. was fell back on VENDELLES and took up defensive positions on N.E. & S.E. of village.	
		6.0 pm	Position of guns at close of operations:- HQ in village.	
		6.0 pm	No.1 Section guns at defensive pots at FLECHIN. R.1d.6.3, R.2.c.2.3, R.2.a.4.8 + one in reserve near R.7.6.7.7.14. Map 62E SE.	
			No.2 Section guns in positions at HANCOURT.	
			No.3 Section H.Q. & all guns in reserve in defensive positions on N.E. & S.E. of village in cruciform trenches.	
			No.4 Section H.Q. at BERNES 3 guns in defensive positions BOUVINCOURT. C.O at BERNES.	
			Transport lines E.Q.14.3 Stores orderly Room BOUVINCOURT.	
			Weather. Strong W. wind. Rain & Snow showers.	Map references France Sheet 62 E SE 1/20,000
BOUVINCOURT	1.4.17		No infantry actions. All guns etc in position as on 31.3.17 Weather as above.	

Army Form C. 2118.

WAR DIARY or INTELLIGENCE SUMMARY

175 MACHINE GUN COMPANY

SHEETS VOL II

(Erase heading not required.)

Corps: No. 175 Machine Gun Coy.

Place	Date	Hour	Summary of Events and Information	Remarks and references to Appendices
BERNES	24/7		Attack on hill in R9A & LE VERGUIER	
		3.50 am 4.10	No. 2 Section Orders. To attack and capture hill in R9A with the 2/8 Staffords. So as to bring fire to bear on LE VERGUIER during the attack on that village during the night following. The Covering Party embarked at Centre R.7.a.8.8. at 3.50 am. Moved off 4.10am. A Coy S.F. leading, 2 Section of No. 4 Section 175 M.G. Coy next. D Coy in rear. The Party passed down the VENDELLES-BIHECOURT ROAD, then turned off above Railway at R.3.a.3.3. Halted at Edge of WOOD. The two guns followed A Coy through wood to E Edge.	
		5.0 am	At 5.0 am Artillery put barrage at Page of WOOD. The two guns followed by the guns C9 am & number 2 HARVEY on left flank. D gun under Sgt BROGAN on right flank. The Crest (Ridge) was gained. C gun was dug in on left flank of line dug by Infantry facing EAST. D gun occupied breast rifle pits on R flank. At day break Friendly troops (1/4 R. Bs. ?) were seen 1000 on right. French dug in also abandoned a trench. Trenches dug facing NE. Communication being then established with Bde on our right. Both M guns were then with drawn to N. Edge of WOOD to protect left flank of Infantry. Only opposition to this whole movement was by Snipers at about R.2.a.2 & R.2.a.6.6. M. guns fired on them about in known Pill box a 1500.	
		8.0 pm	At 8.0 pm guns stood to. Guns at R.9.(c.y.1) AHWAY prepared & that time failed. Guns were ordered to hold on until they were thus above. Case altie 1 O.R. (Cpl) wounded. Position of guns after attacks N.Edge of Wood R.8.c.9.9.	
		1.30 am	No. 3 Section moved from Reserve at HANCOURT to VENDELLES to reach their day light. Met carrying party 1 NCO & 30 O.Rs from 2/5 S.F. at Cr.Rds R.16.a.8.2 at 4 am beyond which point transport could not proceed. Guided 1/pt JEFFREYS from N.o.4 Section in BERNES between met party & out bivouac at X Roads N. of BERNES at 3.35 am, also party to VENDELLES. Section was ordered to wait in VENDELLES. No operations which were timed to begin at 7.0 p.m.	
		9.30 pm	O.C. No. 2 Section reports to O.C. 2/7 S.F. at 8.30 p.m. at 9.30 p.m. O.C. Section accompanied O.C. 2/7 S.F. & staff, preceded by 4 first & 20 men to Point R.2.a.5.8 by way of VENDELLES - LE VERGUIER ROAD at Point R.2.a.1.3. Section Sgt (St. ELDRIDGE) 4 guns also waited up. On arrival at Point R.2.a.5.8 it was found that Infantry carrying party lost all 4 on duty with one of the guns, and not report. M.G. in change lost touch with the body, and has been the case. Thus bringing total of guns up to 4 instead of 3 as planned. All was then met by rapid rifle fire at short range from enemy posts forward & slightly beyond Point R.2.a.5.8 and was then followed in rear. They along took Cover. When all took cover, a Section Officer returned to warn the guns, which were turning through at R.2.a.6.8. Guns also got into this trench. The guns fire slackened, Coast returned to trench facing NE. In ordering to decrease casualty as to position of own troops in front, was got ready to fire but O.C. 2/7 S.F. refused to open fire without warning front line & being in force of S.F.R which was attacking from N.W. on fearing then retired suddenly without giving warning to the M.G. These also retired & gun Teams pt 2a53 & then back to VENDELLES, with the loss of 1 O.R. (wounded). 1 gun, 1 tray & several pairs of S.A.A. which were due to the darkness & confusion caused by the hurried retirement of the infantry. No Casualties. Run in fire & ML whole attack on LE VERGUIER a failure.	
			No. 1 Section in defensive positions at LETCHIN. No. 4 Section in defensive positions ETNE of BERNES. H.Q. moved from BOUVINCOURT, Transport Lines to BERNES Close to No.4 Sec's H.Q. 2/Lt. F.W. GEORGE (O.P.?) admitted to C.C.S. vacate. Victual, ham, lost & gave shower, stunned S.W. wound. BRAY Suffering Myalgia. Map reference France sheet 62 CSE	R M G 2.11

2449 Wt. W14957/M90 750,000 1/16 J.B.C. & A. Forms/C.2118/12.

WAR DIARY
or
INTELLIGENCE SUMMARY

Army Form C. 2118.

175 MACHINE GUN COMPANY.

SHEET 4 VOL II

Corps No. 175 Machine

Place	Date	Hour	Summary of Events and Information	Remarks and references to Appendices
BERNES	3.4.17.		No infantry action. Artillery shelled LE VERGUIER, Ridges N°5 and Wire. M.guns & personnel in same position as on 2.4.17. Guns S6 N°5 2 & 3 Sections hosted by 2/1c Snipers in R.2.d.03 & R.2.d.66 still fairly active. O.C. N°2 Section reported that Tripod etc lost by N°3 Section previous night had been taken in by enemy. Aeroplanes flew low over this area and dropped message stating Enemy trench lightly held with m.gs & a few men.	
		5.0 pm	2/Lt W.H. STEADMAN reported for duty at 5 pm & was posted to N°3 Section.	
		3.30 pm	Morale & Strength	
		10.0 pm	O.O. N°11 for general attack on LE VERGUIER on 4.4.17 issued at 7.0 am. Major Puckle Comdg. left to draw up plans for action next morning.	
			Weather - Very bad. Rain at night.	
BERNES	4.4.17		## Second attack on LE VERGUIER	
		5.30 am	N°3 Section. According to orders received this Section followed in rear of the attacking Inft 2/5 S.F. & proceeded to rendezvous at point R.8.a.82. At this point N°5 1 & 2 guns under 2/Lt STEADMAN, attached themselves to the Company detailed to go to the N° of village & consolidate the Company detailed to consolidate on Crest 120 in R.4.b. 2/Lt ELFICK with remaining guns (3 Tr) attached himself to the Company detailed to consolidate on Crest 120 in R.4.b. when it had been taken.	
		6.0 am	Battalion moved to point R.9.a. & contended for action. They came at once under the Enemy artillery fire, which was well directed by their observers on crest beyond. A percentage of our own shells also fell very short and caused some Casualties. They also came under heavy M.G. and fire in the valley in front of N°1 SAUCRIERS WOOD.	
		8.0 am	Infantry were held up by enemy trench about 800× in front of LE VERGUIER & could get no further, although several were actually reached the wire.	
		8.45 am	Orders were received for whole force to retire to Hedgerows at Pt. R.8.a.82. This was done as suggested a pause of failure of attack. (1) Our artillery was ineffective so whole operations watched by enemy observer on road running S.E. from LE VERGUIER.	
		5.0 am	N°2 Section. On orders 2/Lt HARVEY took 1 Off & 12 men & proceeded to R.3.a.65 arrived there 5.45 am. Go. now of 178 Bgde. Bomb Co. found to look this. N.W. up valley VENDELLES - LE VERGUIER Road. Artillery (own) opened on valley Road & while a R.3.b.5.3 where he waited for barrage to lift onto pt. R.3.c.88 they were caught by shells which burst on his right over no farm on the Enemy. Shells bursting shot on his right caused no casualties and owing to open ground and dropping in unoccupied ground and owing to Enemy 1st Wave of 2/5 S.F. to advance Our shells were dropping in unoccupied ground and owing to Enemy	

Map references France Sheet 62c SE 25500

WAR DIARY
INTELLIGENCE SUMMARY

Army Form C. 2118.

SHEET 5 VOL II

175 MACHINE GUN COMPANY.

B. del Pugh
Major

Comdg. No. 175 Machine Gun Coy

Place	Date	Hour	Summary of Events and Information	Remarks and references to Appendices
BERNES	4.4.17	7.0 am	Second Attack on LE VERGUIER (cont) No. 2 Section's Report (cont'd) 1st Wave of Infantry advanced followed quickly by succeeding waves. These all bunched slightly in crossing R.3.d. & R.3.b. suffered some casualties before scattering again in open ground. Casualties apparently caused by R.9. fire from village and from before on right. Our own artillery was ineffective.	
		7.30 am	Party was handed over to 08. No. 3 Section (2/Lt ELFICK) on Road R.3.b.4.2. Advance was held up at 80 am after Action. Was one of Guns was kept been relieved (later ditch) No. 2 (2/Lt TREND) relieving the left subsection (2/Lt HARVEY) in R.9.a. position in the afternoon. Gun F of VENDELLES. Two of No. 3 Sections Guns (2/Lt STERDHAN) were pushed forward. One in forward direction trench 205 W of CAUBRIERS WOOD R.2.J. about R.9.a.88 and the other in a new position in R.2.d.22. Other Guns as before. Casualties No. 3 Section: 10.R. Killed in action, 10.R. (alf Connor) accidentally killed, 2.0.Rs wounded (Section Sgt.) No. 1 Section moved from position in Aufumne line in front of FLEICHIN to dug outs & billets in BERNES. No. 4 BERNES. The weather for the attack was very bad. Cloudy very cold with heavy snow. Possibly owing to the snow the camouflets were less than might otherwise have been the case.	
BERNES	5.4.17		All guns H.Q. etc as on 4.4.17. Guns of Nos 2 & 3 Sections worked by 2/c. Day & nite.	
FLEICHIN	6.4.17	P.M. 12.30 8.30 8.45	Orders for a 3rd attempt to capture LE VERGUIER recd. Arrived from BERNES HQ & Nos 1 & 4 Sections. At B Guns of No. 4 Section (2/Lt EDKINS) moved off to VENDELLES ready for attack which was timed for 12 midnight. C & D Guns of No. 4 Section (2/Lt JEFFERYS) moved off to VENDELLES via BERNES. No. 1 Section home anna in FLEICHIN. Nos 2 & 3 Sections coon 6.4.17. 10.R. (Ormiw) to Hospital (Venereal)	

Map reference France Sheet 62 c S E 1/20,000

Army Form C. 2118.

WAR DIARY
or
INTELLIGENCE SUMMARY
(Erase heading not required.)

Army Form C. 2118.

175 MACHINE GUN COMPANY

B. Otter Bugby
Comdg. No. 175 Machine Gun Company

SHEET 6
Vol II

Place	Date	Hour	Summary of Events and Information	Remarks and references to Appendices
FLECHIN	7.4.17	—	Third attack on LE VERGUIER R4b & R5a. In accordance with Bde. O.O. 12, 6 guns of 175 M.G. Coy. were detailed for overhead barrage fire and 4 guns of the Battalion were to accompany advancing troops. The 6 guns for barrage fire were disposed of as follows. 4 guns in R9.b. to fire from 12.0 midnight to 12.30 a.m. on enemy trenches SE from L.34.a.10 to R.4.b.2.8. then left 2 guns onto Copse in L.35.b. & 2 guns onto Copse in L.34.b. 1 gun in R.3.a.63 to fire on Copse in L.35.b from midnight until artillery opened. This programme was carried out throughout the two guns with 2/6 S.F. advance beyond R9.b R9.a.6.6. of the four guns att.d to Battn. The four guns att.d to Battn. the two guns with Batt.n at 12.30 reached a point R.4 c.7.5 in line to late up a position behind left flank "B" Coy. hung 100' in front. The two guns with the 2/8 S.F. advanced with Battn. "O" Coy. "A" Coy hung 100' in front. At 12.30 a.m. they advanced to a position about R.4.d.4.8 where they came under heavy fire from our own artillery and ? Coy. started digging up in 8. the M.G. Officer advanced his two guns onto their left flank. & began making preparations to protect flank in co-operation with the Lewis Gun Officer. Gun Barrage lifted at 12.40 a.m. & German activity was continuing to crowds of high swinging M.G. fire & discharge of VERY Lights, one of which fell right behind guns position. About 3.30 a.m. an H.Q. Coys. Runner reached areas "M.G.s will return O.B. Bay" by the time the guns had got back to D Coy's position the infantry had retired and as form of the att d carrying party had retired with them; the M.G.O. was forced to advance 9 left ?. Section then withdrew to VENDELLES. At a lapse to recover lost kit (none). Present position of guns are R.9.b.42; R.9.a.9.5; R.3 a 5.3; R.7.6.98; R.1.a 6.3; 2 guns in support at VENDELLES. 8 guns in Reserve at FLECHIN. No.3 1 & 2 sections. Casualties Nil. Weather for attack very not—Cold. O.C. 14 Section reported that all his Gun teams has done very well under most trying circumstances & especially mentioned his Section Sgt. (Sgt SPEARMAN) who although stunned surrendered for some 30 minutes carried on afterwards in a very plucky manner.	

Map references Franco Sheet 62cSE 62cNE ½ 20000

Army Form C. 2118.

WAR DIARY
or
INTELLIGENCE SUMMARY

(Erase heading not required.)

175 MACHINE GUN COMPANY

Army Form C. 2118.

SHEET 7 VOL II

Comdg. No. 175 Machine Gun Coy.

Place	Date	Hour	Summary of Events and Information	Remarks and references to Appendices.
FLECHIN	8.4.17		No Infantry Action. The two guns of Nos 2 & 3 Sections were relieved at 6 am & 7.30 am respectively by No 4 Section. No 2 Sections reserve guns were relieved by No 2 Section. All 4 guns of No 3 Section were relieved after dark by No 1 Section. Nos 2 & 3 Sections returned to FLECHIN. Again W.O. No 13 for ground attack by 59th Division on LE VERGUIER received.	
FLECHIN	9.4.17		W.O. No 13 Cancelled. LE VERGUIER evacuated by Germans & occupied by our own troops. Also PONTRU. Orders received for relief of whole Company by 174 M.G. Coy. Telephone messages received in Coy O.R. announced taking of VIMY RIDGE & Canal [?]. Captain [?] of 11500 prisoners & rapid advance N of ARRAS. Command [?] 2/Lt EDKINS reconnoitred ASCENSION FARM. and was killed by Divisional General for the way in which he had performed this task.	
BERNES	10.4.17	7.0pm 11.0pm	H.Q. & Nos 2 & 3 Sections arrived, taking over old Billets from 174 M.G. Coy. CQMS Stores and Transport Lines at BOUVINCOURT. No 1 Section reached BERNES from VENDELLES. 2 O.Rs (Drivers) admitted to Hospital.	
BERNES	11.4.17	2.15am	No 4 Section arrived from positions in front of LE VERGUIER. Whole Company in rest billets. Fairly good accommodation. Company training. Owing to snow fall in Evening. Heavy snow fell in Evening.	
BERNES	12.4.17	pm 3.0	Company training. 2/c & 6 limbers went to VILLERS CARBONNEL and removed all Company Stores, which had been dumped there 27.3.17, returning with the 2 O.Rs who had been left in charge. Day very bad, heavy rain, followed by heavy snow fall in Evening. Very cold. Inspection of whole Company by Brigadier Gen'l & in Full an Ballots. Strength increase 7 O.Rs (1 Sgt 2 Cpls & Hcplo). Map up to FRAMES Sheets 62 c SE Edition 2.a Sheet 62 c NE Edition 3.J 2 extra.	

2449 Wt. W14957/Mgo 750,000 1/16 J.B.C. & A. Forms/C.2118/12.

Army Form C. 2118.

WAR DIARY
or
INTELLIGENCE SUMMARY

175 MACHINE GUN COMPANY.

(Erase heading not required.)

Army Form C. 2118.

SHEET 8 VOL 2

Place	Date	Hour	Summary of Events and Information	Remarks and references to Appendices
BERNES	13.4.17		Company Training. Company paid out.	Comdg. No. 175 Machine Gun Coy. [signature]
BERNES	14.4.17		Company Training	1 O.R. admitted Hospital [signature]
BERNES	15.4.17		Divine Service for all denominations. C of E Service at 3.0 pm followed by Celebration of Holy Communion. Considerable artillery activity on both sides. Guns churning the afternoon air. In the early morning Enemy's very heavy about 10-10.30 pm apparently about ASCENSION FARM & LE VERGUIER Ridge. Our artillery replied vigorously till about 10.50 after which fire on both sides slackened. Strong searchlight (Enemy) from N.E. direction from BERNES. Traversed all around. Several times many very lights being fired by Enemy. A strong searchlight in a more Easterly direction showed work twice afterwards and entrance to play most of the night. Our artillery was again very active from about 11.15 pm till 1.00am when fired into BERNES. Think bombs 10.45 pm about 3h 45min. Second was a few minutes later & was reported to have landed in a house in BULLETIN. This was running twice at 12.45 am. Other two shots were fired at 2 & 5am bursting close to Coy. Billets & causing puff craters. These shells are of high velocity & low trajectory and annoyed. Sent out to search the same area in this 18th Relief. 12 to 12.30 midnight. 3 - 3.30am. Provoked from a house hospital. Weather dull, some rain. Wind N to NE. Gas sprayed annoyed at high. 2 O.R. admitted Hospital	[signature]
BERNES	16.4.17		Company Cleaning camp & roads. No 1 Section had firing practice from 2 - 4pm. At Sugar Factory NW of village. 2 O.R. admitted Hospital.	
BERNES	17.4.17		Company Training continued. No 2 Section firing practice. Fatigue party found for No Mg Coy who are on divisional rest. Company. Men warned of chance of French attack E & E of RHEIMS. Progress made reported good. Bgde W.O. No 15 for billing of 117 Bgde or left section wounded. Bay mostly wet - very even. Strong N wind. Some snow. 3 O R admitted hospital.	[signature]
BERNES	18.4.17		Company Training. O C Coy & Des. No's 1 & 3 Sections proceeded to reconnoitre position to be taken over. OO No 76 for relief of 117 Bgde on 20/4/17 received. Map Map to France Sheet 62 & SE Edition 2A 1/20000 62 NE 3 O.Rs admitted Hospital.	[signature]

WAR DIARY or INTELLIGENCE SUMMARY

Army Form C. 2118.

175 MACHINE GUN COMPANY.

SHEET 9 VOL 2

Comdg. No. 175 Machine Gun Company.

Place	Date	Hour	Summary of Events and Information	Remarks and references to Appendices
BERNES	19.4.17		Preparations for moving to ROISEL to relieve 177 Coy. T.O. 2 2/c took over Billets at ROISEL own Billets at BERNES handed over. Some Coy. Stores from BOUVINCOURT moved to ROISEL & front dumps at VRAIGNES. 1 O.R. admitted hospital.	JHG
ROISEL	20.4.17	1.0pm	Coy HQ. No.2 Section arrived at BERNES at 10.0 am & relieved No.3 Sec 177 Coy in Coy Section. No.2 " " No.1 Sec 177 Coy " 11.0 am No.4 " " " at HQ. ROISEL. 9.30 am No.2 " right — Transport Lines & C.Q.M.S Stores moved from BOUVINCOURT to ROISEL. Men Coy: Stores from then & from BERNES Sent to Bgde dump at VRAIGNES. Positions of various guns on front as follows. No.1 Section H.Q. L2d 63, No.1 gun L4c12, No.2 gun L4e85, No.3 gun L10a 55, No.4 gun L3a10. No.2 Section H.Q. 4 guns at ROISEL. Guns doing Anti Aircraft duties. No.3 Section H.Q. L2d 63, No.1 gun L10 636, No.2 gun L10 a 24.3, No.3 gun L16a78, No.4 gun L2d62. No.4 Section H.Q. L22 e 1.9, No.2 gun L17c33, No.2 gun L22a 62, No.3 gun L22cc09, No.4 gun L22e1.9. Of the above guns No.4 } No.3 Section was on anti aircraft duty over } No.1 } No.2 } & firing on gaps in Enemy wire at 93° No.2 } " No.3 " 22°. No.3 — Anti aircraft only & No.4 gun No.2 Sec in Reserve. No. 2 Section HQ. were on fatigues all day as Billets were found to be in very bad State owing to recent thunderstorms in Salling & destroying what remained of Huaduins in the Coy: area & to prevent attempts being done by Observation Balloon over ROISEL. The Some Enemy aerial activity chiefly on our Arti Craft batteries by M.Gs of own Coy, but they were not brought down, mychain was were hourly shots Some killings were completed without accidents. Weather improved.	JHG
ROISEL	21.4.17		Company as on 20.4.17 Fatigues continued. Quiet day. Some Enemy activity in the air. A few Shells (chiefly 6"naval) fell in ROISEL about 11 pm. One near T. Emin. No damage. Day fair. Cloudy. Wind N.E. All Maps refer to France. Sheet 62C N.E. 1/2000. Edition 3	JHG

Army Form C. 2118.

WAR DIARY
or
INTELLIGENCE SUMMARY

(Erase heading not required.)

175 MACHINE GUN COMPANY.

SHEET 10 VOL 2

Instructions regarding War Diaries and Intelligence Summaries are contained in F. S. Regs., Part II. and the Staff Manual respectively. Title Pages will be prepared in manuscript.

Place	Date	Hour	Summary of Events and Information	Remarks and references to Appendices
ROISEL	22.4.17	—	Company a.a on 21.4.17. Enemy aeroplane brought down our observation balloon over HERVILLY at about 10.30 am. It was heavily fired on by A.A guns & our M/Gs but got away safely. There were no Civilian Scenes Fatigues were continued a. Fire was opened by Several guns on gaps cut in Enemy wire at L5.d 47 & L5.d 45 & L5.d 81. Fire was not too spread. Before 2.30 am as our patrols were out. Rounds as fired 1000. 750 rounds were also fired on Enemy shelter in ridge running 9.19 a 39 to 9.13 b 92. N°3 Section HR moved from L2.d 63 b 62 to a 56 took over emplacement made at L16 b 7526. N°3 Section was known at L2 a 63 to manage both our strein known at L2 a 63 to manage both. Much Aring disturbance by Fork side in afternoon — Enemy took 1. O.R. admitted hospital. Much Aring disturbed our shrein — Enemy O. Balloon before they brought AA guns here fully to bear Reported we brought down Enemy Scouts as above reported. Day being clear but cloudy. Wing N.E.– Exra enough. Shum atoms as above reported. Day being clear but cloudy. Wing N.E.– Exra Some Artillery activity during the night. 1. Gpt's to Gas Course at VRAIGNES. D/W– Gas School	J.M.S
ROISEL	23.4.17	— 8.45 am 10.15 am	Company a.a on 22.4.17. Operations 1000 rounds fired on gaps in L5.d 47. L5.d 45. L5.d 63. L6c 57, after infilling patrols had come in. Another gun was placed in new Gun from 2.17 c.14 was moved to new position at G.14 a 62. position at L16 b 75.26. Enemy activity was noted at G.14 a 66 & working parly at G.14 a 62. Artillery. Enemy activity. Very numbers of our planes were up during the evening (about 18) They were met by 3 enemy aircraft at a great height. Some fighting took place one enemy machine fell in flames, but was thought to fall under control though both occupants were injured. Another of our planes apparently had a collision in mid air. Both fell, the occupants being killed It was impossible to say which became of the Enemy machines. Plane apparently Enemy flew over TEMPLEUX in Westerly direction showing yellow light. Same plane unlighted flew over TEMPLEUX in a like direction. Seen a Enemy plane unlighted flew over. Same in a like direction. N°2. Section under 2/Lt HARVEY moved from ROISEL to TEMPLEUX and took over dugouts vacated by N°3. Section & S6 whose guns were moved to positions as stated above. Day – fine & clear. Wind N.E. Be-came "Bangrions" by 9gd order	J.M.S

I.O.R. admitted hospital.

Map u/p to France. 2/Lieut 6/2 E.M.R

2000 [illegible] 3

Army Form C. 2118.

WAR DIARY or INTELLIGENCE SUMMARY

17B/1 MACHINE GUN COMPANY.
SHEET 11 VOL 2

(Erase heading not required.)

Instructions regarding War Diaries and Intelligence Summaries are contained in F. S. Regs., Part II. and the Staff Manual respectively. Title Pages will be prepared in manuscript.

Signed: Alfred Roche
Comdg. No. 175 Machine Gun Coy.

Place	Date	Hour	Summary of Events and Information	Remarks and references to Appendices
ROISEL	24.4.17		Positions of Company unchanged. Operations. Harassing guns opened fire on gaps in wire during the night after patrols had gone in. Rounds fired 1,250.	
		9.40am		
		3–4 pm	Between three times VILLARET – BOISSON GAURAINE FARM was under sniper observation. Enemy movement of any kind was observed from L.2.2. × 7.2. Dense black smoke was seen on fire bearing 35° distant 6–8 miles. During night no Very lights were fired from vicinity of Quarry, but from further E. in N. of COLOGNE FARM. Reporting found 4 metal poles in N. of GRAND PRIEL WOOD by No. 24 Section. Supports of belts to floating up our wire. Details as follows. Length 10 ft. diam. 3 in. Our No. 3 played other End has a smaller hole (?) but automatic fire safety pin as in Mills hand grenade N°5. This was reported to No. 2 Section Rt. Half under 2/Lt. HARVEY left ROISEL & proceeded to reserve in TEMPLEUX two guns found gun positions further E. Some aerial activity by both sides during day, especially towards dusk. No lights were lit by A.A. batteries on either side. Use of Artillery guns on both sides. OB 80 enemy shells fired into TEMPLEUX. One man failed to report. 1 O.R. admitted to hospital.	
			Day. Clear. fair, a warm. wind Northerly	
ROISEL	25.4.17		Company positions unchanged. N°1 section— Operations. Fire opened after during night on gaps out & settling in wire L12 a 08 & L11 B 20. Our other gap as above. Rounds fired 1,250. O.C. N°1 Section/Lt–HOBSON also reconnoitred for gun positions in sunken road L4C 74 85 L4 b 19 as follows. L10 a 35. L4 e 93. L4 e 93, L10 e 26 also possible positions in sunken road L4C 74 85 L4 b 19	Map ref. to FRANCE Sheet 62c N.E. Edition, 3A + Trench map N° 4 "HINDENBURG LINE"

WAR DIARY
or
INTELLIGENCE SUMMARY

Army Form C. 2118.

175 MACHINE GUN COMPANY.

Robert Paik (?)

Comdg. No. 175 Machine Gun Coy

SHEET 12 VOL 2

Place	Date	Hour	Summary of Events and Information	Remarks
ROISEL.	25.4.17	4.0 a.m.	2/Lt HARVEY went up to VILLERET to reconnoitre & select gun positions. 2 positions were selected by him in L12.a.08 & L12.a.28 but these gun & ammunition dumps were shelled by the enemy & were seen about Railway in L12.6 Central, in road from L6.a.54 - 9.7.a.50, some in Estrée G.1.c.04 to Rd. G.1.a.37	
		5.0 a.m.	but most along trenches L6.a it half, in a S.E & E direction.	
		5.30 a.m.	Gun artillery Shelled L6.d.02. Enemy unknown. Road in L6.a.55.15 to L.12.39 in aux. & ammo. & gun road corner on W. front. Probably occupied by M.G.s.	
		3-4 p.m.	3/Lt HARVEY + 2/Lt FRIEND observed COLOGNE FARM from O.P. in Sunken road L10.b.33 & O.P L.4.6.12. Very little enemy movement was observed except in trenches W. of FARM.	M.G
		4.0 am	2/Lt ELFICK reconnoitred ground in L11 for new gun positions & reported that such positions could be made, 2 area 20.10 Corse L11.c.20, & 2 in road at L11.c.18 & L11.c.19.	
		3.0 p.m.	No. 4 Section withdrawn. Enemy Firing Artillery action, was observed over our right of BUISSON GAULAINE FARM. true bearing 80° Range estimated 3000'. Distribution of M.G.s unchanged. Any but dull with poor observation till the evening. Weather. Any but day was very sunny. for the rest of day was very good. O.O. No 20 for attack on QUARRY Trenches E8 j 4 + COLOGNE FARM Received. Time of attack 3.30am 27.4.17	
ROISEL.	26.4.17	1.0 am	Company as above. 2 Sections of No 2.00 Company moved from camp at BEAUMETZ to HQ of 175 Coy for a share in moving up to position in further support of Infantry for the attack. They two Section moved up at 3.0 pm & 9.0 pm, No 1 Section going to position on left Bank of River Front, Half No 2 to VILLERET to join No 1 Section of 175 Coy. The Guns of 2.00 Coy moved to positions in Sunken Road in L4.6. where L10.a.47 at 10.30 pm. These two guns of 2.00 Coy moved in position @ 11.30 pm	
		4.0 am	Miluiyuo (?) These gun in wood were reported by B.5.a. Other 7 were fired on during the night at L10.a.55 was moving up after patrols had been in. Rounds fired 3000. The gun in tree any L10.a.55 was moving up to L10 b.3.6 for above work. The seven gun engaged were at L5.0.47, to L5.0.45, L6.C.33, L6.4.2 L.5.8.6015, L11.a.88 & L12.a.08. Lifted from wire to COLOGNE WOOD, were arranged on and rate. Guns at L4.6.12 & L.4.c.85 Railway 1700 Elevation 2° 26' Further N than L6.a.57	C.M.G
		10.30 p.m.	All No 1 Section Guns were laid on COLOGNE & the two SB No 2 Section 3.00 Coy on tank in L.6.C. B.O.R returned from Hospital. Weather. Dull, poor observation. Reinforcements taken on Strength. With a difficulty in Sketches. Map up France Sheet 62 ° N.E Edition 3A + Trench Map Sheet N° 4 "HINDENBURG /24000 LINE".	

Army Form C. 2118.

WAR DIARY or INTELLIGENCE SUMMARY

175 MACHINE GUN COMPANY

SHEET 1B1 Vol 3.

(Erase heading not required.)

Place	Date	Hour	Summary of Events and Information	Remarks and references to Appendices
ROISEL	27.4.17		ATTACK ON HIGH GROUND TO EAST OF COLOGNE AND SO TO OBTAIN DIRECT OBSERVATION ON HINDENBURG LINE. REPORT ON ACTION AS AFFECTING THE MACHINE GUNS EMPLOYED. The Operation ordered in Nos 20 and addendums as to Artillery Barrage etc were to summit of that the various objectives etc were set forth as under. 1st Objective To capture the line running along Roman Trench L5d 59 to L5d 56, then N & NE of QUARRIES to L12a 49. 2nd Objective German trench running from L6c19 – W of COLOGNE FARM to L6c72. 3rd Objective German trench running from L6c69 E of COLOGNE FARM to L6c93. Preliminary Operations. During the five days previous to Operation the Artillery cut gaps in enemy wire at various points in the three objectives. In all 7 gaps ranging in width from 10′ to 30′ were made and the M.G.s were detailed nightly (while these gaps open) do attacks on previous days in diary. These guns fired from positions in Sunken Road in 14 Sub 6.2 to L10.6 at Ranges from 1200 to 1500. During the night the 7 gaps were kept open. The remaining gaps it was thought could be leapt on by the guns and the guns laid at dusk. Six out of the 7 gaps were kept open day and a wrap map reference was given by the Artillery. During this night firing it was found advisable necessary for the M.G.Ös in charge of the guns to keep in Tel direct touch with the 183rd coy Commanders as patrols were constantly going out and it was found difficult for M.G.Os to get information as to their return. This Roan was Soho factory, maint arrived. The disposition of the guns on night previous to the attack were as follows. On the day previous to attack the T.O.P. 175/M9 Coy lent 2 Sections /89 run/ of 200 M.G. Coy. These came under the orders of O.P. 175/MG Coy & he had therefore 24 guns at his disposal. Of these 6 remained in the same position on the Southern Crest of the Bde Front. The remaining 18 were disposed of as follows:— A. 4 guns behind Crest of Ridge in F28d – F29a Enfilading 2nd & 3rd Objectives. B. 4 guns in Sunken Road in L4 to fire on trench running F & N through L62. C. 2 guns in road running S through L10.6 to fire on QUARRIES, COLOGNE FARM, & small wood E of L6i G10 D. 4 guns on N outskirts of VILLERET to barrage trenches running S.E. from COLOGNE FARM through B72 & 2. E. 2 guns in L17 b to enfilade M.G. fire and especially to deal with counter attacks. F. 2 guns in leave in QUARRY L10a to go forward on trenches in G12d & G8a. Of the above:— A. These guns were able to get into position in daytime behind the crest. It was possible for all (their taking fire from a forward position and guns were kept under cover on their target the previous day. B, C. Were all to be laid on their target the previous day. D,E. had total up positions which had been previously reconnitered by night. M.L.P. Ref: France Scale 20v E 1/40000 526 NW 1/20000	249

2449 Wt. W14957/Mg0 750,000 1/16 J.B.C. & A. Forms/C.2118/12.

WAR DIARY or INTELLIGENCE SUMMARY

Army Form C. 2118.

SHEET #2 195 M.G. Coy
VOL 3

Place	Date	Hour	Summary of Events and Information	Remarks and references to Appendices
ROISEL	27.4.17		**ATTACK ON HIGH GROUND EAST OF COLOGNE FARM.** (cont'd)	A. Hill Vickers Coy 1

Action during Operations.

Zero hours was at 3.55 a.m.

A. These guns fired according to programme and at Zero + 22 switched two guns onto MALAKOFF FARM range 1500x + 2 guns onto COPSE in G 2a range 2100x. When it was known that only the 1st Objective was being consolidated these guns were turned back onto 3rd Objective and fire was opened during the day. A hostile M.G. firing from F 30 c 7.1 (approx) was silenced.

B. These guns put up an intense barrage till daylight and after that fired occasional bursts. Their target was under direct observation.

C. These guns fired according to programme.

D. These guns kept up barrage during Zerohour and then ceased fire in order to prevent their position being spotted. About 7.45 am a party of about 20 Germans were observed in SUNKEN ROAD L 6 c 4.5 0.0 forming through hedge in direction of the QUARRIES. One gun opened on them. Range 600x and they dispersed over burst to N.E. Two bodies were left lying on road. A hostile M.G. firing from G 7 a 7.1 (approx) was silenced.

These guns encountered hostile trenches running S. through G 7 a + c until daylight.

F. About 6.15 am the O.C. B'de gave orders to O.C. 195 M.G. Coy to move the two Reserve guns to the QUARRY to avoid injuring who were consolidating the 1st Objective. By this time the situation was such that guns were sent to it at once. They reached the QUARRY at about 7.30 am when they reported to the Senior Officer present and at once began digging in on the Eastern edge of the QUARRIES. They were subsequently shelled out of their positions and retired little Reserve dugout of waste dump. They took up position firing to the flank. At dusk on one gun was moved to position in trench at L 5 a 66, 6 the other went forward to S.E. edge of QUARRY in L 6 c 195 when suppression was made. During the night a hostile Battery of 7 men was observed moving along trenches at L 6 a 27. Fire was opened on them and 3 men killed their bodies being plainly seen at daylight.

General.

As far as can be ascertained the M.G. Barrage was a success. German prisoners explained how the QUARRY staking that they suffered heavily from M.G. fire. The Country was clear for M.G. work, excepting the gun firing at close range during the operation at its target, and about 3000 rounds were fired, each gun 120 rounds during the previous night and at hand Belts were filled by hand with ammunition found taken back from our positions 3 to 5 times at a time an opportunity occurred. Moves S/b

MAP ref. France Sheets 62 F NE 1/2 (ground
62 F NW Sketch)

WAR DIARY
INTELLIGENCE SUMMARY

Army Form C. 2118.

175 MACHINE GUN COMPANY.
SHEET No 3   VOL 3

Place	Date	Hour	Summary of Events and Information	Remarks and references to Appendices
ROISEL	2.7.4.17		REPORT ON ATTACK ON HIGH GROUND EAST OF COLOGNE FARM (Cont'd)	

Gun positions were located but by special stalking by the Bosche and the keeping of A group, the remaining stalked exposed themselves on the skyline. It may be taken for granted that nearly all other positions were spotted.

Eventually gun crews were done in by 2/Lt D.P. HARVEY in command of No 2 sections guns which were sent forward to the QUARRY. This Officer although wounded in the knee carried on his guns with great ability until every shell fire. The moral of these guns on our own infantry was & always great. Our casualties were approximately Eight Officer wounded (See sheet 3a)

During action Enemy sent up signals lights as follows:-
Green & Red c = warning to infantry not to advance Red lights = call for barrage. Green rain = meaning unknown.

Other act into of Circumstances for attack as follows.

There was a searching party of 2/7 Rd S.Fs who pushed to K-2 See at TEMPLEUX about 9 a.m. (B.6.1.4.1.7) a second gun up to VILLERET.

No 200 M.Gs guns were taken up to forward guns of No 1 sec (17.500) from X roads in L.10.a.4.7 at 4.30 pm (26/4/17). That took 200 Boxes guns to Sunken Road in L.4.b.

Communication all messages from Section Officers were sent by runner to the H.Q. No 3 Section in the Quarry in L.10.a where a copy was taken to the message phoned through to advanced Bat H.R.

Officers Reports (Details)

No 2 Left half 2/Lt FRIEND. BARAGE. VILLERET at 11.30 p.m. 26.4.17. Fired on Sunken Road SE of COLOGNE FARM
at 5.30 a.m. 27.4.17 fired on Enemy Seen in SUNKEN ROAD L.12.a.3.8
at 6.30 a.m. Saw own Troops in QUARRY - digging in Rd. L.12.c.0.9 to L.12.c.3.8
Very little Communication in Villiage found heavy enemy shelling R.8. front 2500 Camulets N.W.

No. 2 Section Rt half 2/Lt HARVEY
Took two guns to QUARRY. Reported Capt TOMKINS D. Coy 2/6 S.Fs as Senior Officer present
B. Co. sounds very weak, may be Bt. there were 5 Lewis guns in QUARRY. Very accurate and concentrated shell fire & Very heavy trench mortar also by enemy batteries 2/Lt B.S.F. leaving advanced line met Enemy working Parties N. "B" posts in the Rd Know infantry supports disorganised. 3 mg Fire was withstood alone at dusk.

Amongst E Artillery found Missing Sunken Road, myself slightly wounded & other wounded at dusk.
2. O.Rs. reported from Hospital 1.O.R. 5 others C.C.S. HEILLY. 1 Officer Wd & 3 others Wd around at dusk.
2 O.Rs. Missing 1.O.R. 8 miles C.C.S. HEILLY.

MAP REFS. FRANCE. Sheets 62 c N.E. & 62 S.N.W.
1/20.000

WAR DIARY
or
INTELLIGENCE SUMMARY

(Erase heading not required.)

Army Form C. 2118.

175 MACHINE GUN COMPANY

SHEET 4 VOL 3

Place	Date	Hour	Summary of Events and Information	Remarks and references to Appendices
ROISEL.	28.4.17	6.0 pm	Orders given to guns after attack were as follows:—	
			No 1 Section position as before	
			No 2 — left half 2/Lt FRIEND was ordered to lay guns on line L6 c 47, L6 a 55 at	
			the time during night on of our SOS went up.	
			No 3 Section as when was ordered to remain at BRESSLE wood with 2 No 2 section apart from Posn Instructions	
			No 4 Section in the morning of an SOS going up. These guns were in L.17.	
		6.10 am	No 1 Section & 200 Coy were ordered to train guns on French running S from F 30 a 40 to L 6 a 47	
			No 2 — as for No 2 (left half) section of 175 Coy above	
			Extracts from Sec 8/p Report	
		6.30 am	No 1 Nil	
		9.6 pm	No 2 left half 2/Lt FRIEND (L17e 05 60) laid guns as ordered	
			Saw our SOS (left gun) fire a SOS guns taking up firing up.	
			Enemy shelled VILLERET at 8-10 pm, between 12 am.	
			Sunken Road in L12 a 3 8, gun occupied by Enemy Rfle fire 15:00	
		6.0 pm	Rt Half 2/Lt HARVEY in QUARRY	J.H.Q.
		(1st April)	Enemy shelling of QUARRY Gun. Amongst 1st COS SO 2/C 2/L of & SFS as to dispositions	
			for the night. The infantry of these Bns were out in front of the QUARRY and in the	
			Sunken mille Fifth. It was arranged that a patrol should visit the UNNAMED FARM & at	
			8 pm SOS. to lease the gun. We moved into trench in front of UNNAMED FARM, Quarry	
			& 2 G.S's to lower them in front & at flank, the MG groups in front of QUARRY	
			Very heavy shelling of QUARRY started at 8.0 pm. The high dumps were rendered untenable and	
	22 April	9 pm (on)	the garrison entry, retired down steps making for entrance to QUARRY, They were however invited	
			to take up this positions on top of dumps again after shelling had somewhat abated.	
			Two hours later there was a repeat, some of the garrison going on the top SOS trenches occupied	
			by the 2/6 SFS. The shelling of the front wood was incessant, the MG gun pit in front of UNNAMED FARM Fus	
			at 8 pm by a heavy Gerg (hop Grose) FARM over the top, the fire over our boundaries SAA land	
			was splashed by 2 feet a few telephones making a few wounded men very shaken by the fire attending is	
			all night.	
			No 2 Section Nil.	

Map Ref France
Sheet 62 NE 3/8
62-b-NW 5 20000

(san)

2449 Wt. W14957/M90 750,000 1/16 J.B.C. & A. Forms/C.2118/12.

WAR DIARY or INTELLIGENCE SUMMARY

Army Form C. 2118.

175 Machine Gun Company

B. McNab Capt.
May.

SHEET 5 VOL 2

Place	Date	Hour	Summary of Events and Information	Remarks and references to Appendices
ROISEL	28/4/17		**(Cont.) Officer Reports (Belnoff)** No. 4 Section. Quiet during the day. On enemy working parties, and on our S.O.S. going up at 1.10 p.m. also at troops during the night in trenches running through C 9, 7 & 8. At 1 a.m. SB No.3 section on amm. gun N. 22 z 62 methods firing during day. It was notice that machine guns hostile shelling rounds fired 8000 which methods previous day. The wood was much hostile shelling of plates such as HARGICOURT, VILLERET & the QUARRY. There was a subdued, possibly Loss SB battery on the Eastern side. **Information from Russians Captured on morning 28/27th** They were observed their positions at all costs. BOLOGNE FARM was held by 1 Coy 43, 2nd B2 10th RI This was so far as they knew about IMQ. They stated the Battn. of Bovery about 150 yds to 10 [illegible] the remaining 3 coys on tour. HQs Bevron. Felt now trying to catch up their losses. They were very glad to be brought up. The HINDENBURG Line was situated by their personal said they were 3/4 & 6 officers an H.M. Battle of the day. Their men at about 900 stations with own artillery arty M.Q. Fire was accurate & caused them losses. No attack in this district to be expected. This Ration was good & plentiful, dug outs etc. But that M.Q. & T.M. Equipments were in complete. There was yet no order own men found rations in the QUARRY which they had rations it was food for wagons trains than our own. Seats of Rations German were as follows — 2 per able for men. Bread ... 1½ lb. Coffee or Tea ... 3 cigars. Biscuits & Cigarettes 2 each of Bacon 109 Meat ... ½ lb. Butter 21 oz. Quarterly Bev (out of line only 5 othr) or 8 men. Sausage 75 grams. vegetables.	JAG
			General: Roisel was bombed & ROISEL during the night by the C.R.R. construction employed. ROISEL was shelled by long range H.V. gun from 5 pm onwards. At dusk consisted yellow light observed on ridge SE of ROISEL about 8.30 pm. But rocket following explosions of yellow light observed on ridge SE of ROISEL about 8.30 pm. 1 Rpt returned from O.W. Gas Course Weather fine Warm.	
ROISEL	29/4/17	6 am 7.30 am 7.15 pm	**Intelligence:** The 2/4 & 2/18 & 2/5 S.Fs. holding front line were strengthened by 1 Coy. each of the 2/4 Wm. Sher. Regt. Of small enemy party attempted to rush the QUARRY but were shortly blocked. Some movement of enemy returned E of MARAKOFF FARM. Minimum 30 mins & gifts signals was sent by enemy meaning unknown. Movement of A. A. gs. During the day the following changes of position took place. 2/4 Z2 Section. 2/19 FRIEND was relieved from line, returned to Billets at ROISEL. 3 Guns of N°1 Section. 2 teams of N°3 was relieved & returned to Billets at ROISEL. 2 guns of N°2 Sec 200 Coy & 2 guns of N°2 Sec 175 Coy (each) were ordered the relieved by N°4 section 200 Coy & N°0 of 1/6 Q. Wm. Arthur Beng. **Officers Reports:** N°1 Section. 3 left guns were returning by 3 guns of N°2 Section 200 Coy. The relief was complete by 11.30 pm when 3/S Hudson returning with 3 teams to ROISEL & took stabilized. Drawing N°1 Gun under Spt. HOWLEY Rommel fired 200 Rounds fired 2.00. (cont.) Map Ref. France Sheet 62E NE & 62S N.W. 1/250.	JAG

2449 Wt. W14957/M90 750,000 1/16 J.B.C. & A. Forms/C.2118/12.

WAR DIARY or INTELLIGENCE SUMMARY

Army Form C. 2118.

175. Machine Gun Company

SHEET 6. VOL 3.

Place	Date	Hour	Summary of Events and Information	Remarks and references to Appendices
ROISEL	29.4.17		Slip Repub (cont'd)	
			No 2 Section. Was relieved as stated above. Relief complete by 2 am. Arrived Quarry L10.a at 4.40 am & reached ROISEL via TEMPLEUX at 6.0 am.	
			No 3 Section. Teams 1 & 4 relieved by 2 O.Rs on night of 28/29. Relief complete at 10.30 pm. Teams went via BROSSE WOOD. Brought a limber. Enemy shelled heavily Gdn to ROISEL.	
			No 4 Section left 2 O.Rs on 2/4 JEFFERYS in QUARRY. Reported slight shelling by Enemy. 2/7 relieved 9 2 S.E's at midnight. 2/8 only 20 strong. 5 large HE shells on left, at L5 d67 were in consequence of	JHQ
			left unrelieved - for ends of M.G. Sections. Reb force 50.	
			There were identified 5 guns left in the line disposed of as follows.	
			No 1 Section 1 gun in SUNKEN ROAD L10.b.22	
			No 2 Section R+half returned from QUARRY L.5a. + remained night at TEMPLEUX.	
			No 3 Section 2 guns SUNKEN ROAD L10d.25. L16a.86	
			No 4 Sect. 2 guns in QUARRY L5a. 2 guns at BROSSE WOOD L22	
			General:	
			ROISEL was shelled lightly again during the morning & again in the evening a good many 'duds' Some hostile shelling of front areas. Hostile aircraft fairly active. Heavy shelled 8 two A.M.'s but one hit. Much cloud activity on our front. 1 O.R. wounded to duty. Four admitted hospital. 8 O.Rs evacuated to base. Weather very fair at 1st. Clear.	
ROISEL	30.4.17	am 1.30	General. Enemy shelling 8 front line area. Some hostile aerial activity. HA brought to action. 2/Lieut PADFORD sent forward & relieved Lieut to brings of Goo Schools. Obtained a hang fire immediately 2/Lt D.P. HARVEY evacuated to C.C.S. 55. He would. Leaving Rifleman BROSE. Other wounded may pass clear & he. Message fwd. Wind Gram going. Teams on alert on Rt half No 2 Section. Lieut Capt ALLEN returned from TEMPLEUX to PAIN to ROISEL.	JHQ
			Map Ref. Frame. Sheets 62 C NE 1/4	
			62 & N W 3/20000	

M.G/K/219.

To. H.Q. 54th Division.
From. O.C. No. 175 Machine Gun Company.

The War Diary of the Company for
enduring April 28th has been brought up
to date as owing to the operations on the
27th it was found impossible to complete it to date in time.
The Delay in searching it has been also caused
owing to the latter having endeavouring unsuccessfully to
obtain the signature of the Officer commanding the
Company before the morning of the 29th. A.G. arrives the O.C.

J.A.G Major. Comdg. No. 175 Machine Gun Coy.

WAR DIARY or INTELLIGENCE SUMMARY

Army Form C. 2118.

175 Machine Gun Company

SHEET 7. Part II. VOL-3

Place	Date	Hour	Summary of Events and Information	Remarks and references to Appendices
ROISEL	1/5/17		**Change of Positions** No 4 Section and No 9 Coy were relieved by the Left ½ Section of No 3 Sec 175 Coy at VILLERET. 2 guns of No 4 Section South of L21 6 33 & L21 a 95 and post at X Roads in G.14. Information: The front line system South of L21 6 33 & L21 a 95 and post at X Roads in G.14 was taken over during the night 30/1 by 177 Inf. Bde. Coy H.Q. Guns in GRAND PRIEL WOOD had 2500 Rds during the day along ridge at about G.13.d.93 where enemy movement was observed. No 1 & No 9 in QUARRY fired 1500 Rds into COLOGNE FARM during the night. Enemy artillery: Behaved quietly. Shelled VILLERET at av. rate of fire 26 rds per hour also LG L2s apparently. They also shelled HARGICOURT & the QUARRY. N° 9 concentration. Change of Gunner from Bellus Left half of No 2 Section 2/Lt Ex-FRIEND went up line again. General activity: Many hostile machine guns busily looking for our Red Lees & Brun gun positions in ROISEL. Our heavy artillery was actively boring on villages in enemy back areas in retaliation for shelling of ROISEL which was in receipt again of a few 5.9s. Enemy flivels Lt ALLEN & 8 O.Rs during gas school at PONT NOYELLES. Weather: Fine h.S. Fine Gas alert on. CO N°23 seeing working with observation of B.E.s having studies of infantry B.E.s in line.	J.A.P.
ROISEL	2/5/17		**Officers Reports** 2/Lt ELFICK N°3 Sec Lt ½ in QUARRY L.19a 2 at 9 ams laid as following— N°1 gun on wire at F.30.c.50 & F.30.c.40/15. Range 1800x N°2 gun on Trench at L.6.a.50 to L.6.a.27 traversing north. Range 1850. 2/Lt STEADMAN No 2 guns in VILLERET reported that his age hung slightly killed in entry only by 2 two guns and about 80 men under a Sgt. They were relieved on August 30 1/2. the Officer during the night returning with the party having. The our skies the village however the Sonets in stated an only time 100x from heavy branch and from the position of his our guns it would be impossible owing to the trenches of trenches to prevent this from that heard into the village. Information & Enemy Barrier: Our snipers 6 Enemy Notes Suspicion of Enemy in occupying to the Colonic Wing of only 16 & 17 Jan over the Railway (Hostile) was active. The QUARRY & HARGICOURT being shelled intermittently all day until 775 9 5.95. Change of guns Left ½ Sec No 4 2/Lt JEFFERYS returned to billets in ROISEL divided to No / Dam No 21 Elfin. General v great day No Shooting of RESBE, Vray Little actual activity on either side. Weather: Very h.S. & Else. Fine. Gas Alert. On 10 OR returns onwaid.	J.A.P.
	10 pm			

Map ref. France Sheet 62 P.N.E 7.½ & HARFLEUR & COLOGNE FARMS on nght of B/4. 62 B.N.W.S 20000

WAR DIARY
or
INTELLIGENCE SUMMARY 175 Machine Gun Company
(Erase heading not required.)

Army Form C. 2118.

SHEET 8
Vol 3

N Malakoff Map

Place	Date	Hour	Summary of Events and Information	Remarks and references to Appendices
ROISEL	3.5.17		ASSAULT ON MALAKOFF AND COLOGNE FARMS, AND TRENCHES ROUND THESE POINTS.	

The Assault obtained in Bgde O.O. Nº 24, was by the 2/5 SHERWOOD FORESTERS. Two Companies were detailed for this operation. 177 Bgde were ordered to demonstrate and were BUISSON – GAULAINE FARM. The same time, & the 42nd Division on the left of & round the Enemy strong point N of MALAKOFF FARM.
1. The 1st objective on attack on MALAKOFF FARM was the trench running W & E from L6a 28.65 & F30 e 38.25
2. The 2nd objective was road running on N.E side of MALAKOFF FARM from F30 c 91 to about F30 e 70.45
When this battle was taken it was to be held by 2 posts of a platoon each. This Remainder of platoon for 1st & 2nd were to be objectives.
To forming up place for the attack was SUNKEN TRENCH in L58 & F29a.

For attack on COLOGNE FARM
  1st objective was trench SW of the farm from L6 e 52 to L68.26.
  2nd objective was trench E of the farm at L68.4 & L68.57
  Posts were in objectives were to be cut by hand L1 2/8 S.F on N.G.W. 2/3
Artillery & T.M. barrages were arranged. 175 Coy 82 a T.O. were held in readiness.

178. T.M. Battery was parted (the 2/5 S.F. formed a strong patrol &c). After the Capture a strong patrol was to go forward & mop up the valley & 1/8 Railway cutting & were also & 12 to 80 all Coy Leaders would be informed by Capt W.C.S. commander, whose business to sort & get to the sunken trench, & he would get further instructions by orders.

175 MGs Coys Guns were assembled as follows:—
(a) 4 Guns at F30 e 92 as W.Z. [B?]
(b) 4 Guns at G7 c 92 as WZ G7 b from zero to zero trs after had to lift to an other targets.
(c) The barrage taken in F & G 1 b from zero 5 zero trs 2 guns.
(d) After the Sing zero to zero trs one gun then lifter.
(e) The lifting in L1Z 2 b & zero T/15 then lifter.
(4) Indirect Barrages through G7 a & G7 c & A2 central & through G7 a & G7 c permanently.
The M.G's of 1/5 Coy in left & 2 pm Bey On right went to Buffalo at 6 AM. They were up anticipating of 1/5 Bde H.Q. ROISEL at 6 PM. Zero hour was 11.30 pm May 3rd.

Preparations for covering out the above programme on commencing the covering were made during the day and evening. Report on action marker 4.5.17

During night of 2/3 M.G. gun fired 500 rds on working parties near L6.a,W. & F29a.
Enemy's [?] MICRET was obvious during the day.
TEMPLEUX was fired between 8.10 + 9.30, 100 & 200 rds.
It was noticed that the 1st line in the district German aircraft were showing up into our position within a Search Light which was not our own.

For orders of ST QUENTIN Summer Time Saved by perennial to permanent body. 750 more to Kentish hospital
The M.G. was never active.

Att Nº 2 Section 2/st Hobson proceeded from ROISEL to positions in SUNKEN ROAD N of MAPPLECROFT.
Mitchell Cards Forward H made places with spare engine carriers turned about lashing forward at 10.40 p.m. & 1/2 & 3 Repeated horse round in the command of MORTEL
Sorted E.A. HUERON in tractor by foot cut was in trouble.
Sect Serjeants 2/nd & 7/st CARRUTHERS when the SECT 4th reported to Nº 1 Sect in tub Gurdu & he remained of MORTEL. The journey Sir STEADMAN, the hand pressed Sect 3 OP 2 wd, 100 Was evacuated hospitalized Sir to G.S. Smiles himself actively and other Hunders 1/ Sgt Pan & 2/Hufts promoted to Corporals to Half hazand.
Weather fine, very hot. gas alert on Mgs Rifle Flares. Flwb. 52 L/15 + G2 fb/n 5.050.

Maps Ryton

2449 Wt. W14957/Mgo 750,000 1/16 J.B.C. & A. Forms/C.2118/12
STEADMAN Ltd. 2/nd 7/st CARRUTHERS

Army Form C. 2118.

WAR DIARY or INTELLIGENCE SUMMARY

175 Machine Gun Company
B Att. Pickle Coy.

Place	Date	Hour	Summary of Events and Information	Remarks and references to Appendices
POISER	4.6.17		Report on attack of MALAKOFF & COLOGNE FARMS, as affecting Machine Guns. On night of 3/4. The attack on attack was carried on by M.G. fire as follows:- 1 Section of 125 Coy (2 Guns left) fired an intermittent barrage along F30a92 - A25a81- from position at F23d. 2 Sec. No 1 Sec. 175 Coy on Pippin F30C98 from sunken road L4b. 3 Sec. No 1 Sec. 175 Coy on E end of Embankment trench & SUGAR FACTORY lifting onto Coops q.2a at zero +1.25. 4 Sec. No 2 Sec. 175 Coy on cutting in L12a, lifting 100' at zero +15. 5 Sec. No 3 Sec. 175 Coy + 2 Sec No 2.00 Coy, firing barrage through Q1.7a & 9.78. 6 Sec. No 2 & Sec. No 2.00 Coy, firing barrage through Q1.7a & 9.78 — about 2000 ads per gun. The war spent and mounted. OPENING to team — about 2000 ads per gun. The attack on COLOGNE FARM failed, but the two Companies on the left succeeded in establishing themselves in front of MALAKOFF FARM. The situation was however so unlettered in (?) it was deemed inadvisable to send forward any guns so they remained in their old position.

General intelligence
During the day HQs fixed 1000 ads on Painter N. of COLOGNE FARM. The ROARER L58 was shelled with shrapnel at 9am to 3 pm. (Painter fired up by Enemy who suspected the destruction of his O. balloon.) Observers observed in parachute. Some aerial activity by Enemy. One enemy plane very shelled by our A.A. shelling. One of the enemy planes was burnt down in flames. Later in the day an enemy plane. The plane was also descended in parachute & a novel spectacle being burnt by the Gun O. Balloon at HERVILLY. The plane was also descended in parachute & a novel spectacle being burnt by the enemy man after balloon was hit.

O/p reports
4/6/17 Moved to Ruins q. 10a at 8.45 pm Spent guns in sunken road L4E74 to L4 B.18 at an enemy MG Section learned by 4.11 pm. (This before the op was known for the attack.) Opened fire, zero. Zero + 25 end on sugar factory left of COLOGNE from 200 +60. Crews were learned at 8.45am to fire on SUGAR FACTORY Reserve garage. MG of MALAKOFF FARM. Fire opened at 3.55 am. artillery (enemy) retaliation. Victorias.
No. 2 W.E. L10 a 2/4 FRIEND. Guns laid on NO.E. of COLOGNE FARM q.211. Spent fire at zero. Rang 2300 at zero + 15 lifted 100 to 2700. Guards fire at zero + 40. at 4.15am 4/5/17. 80 enemy observed firing air to fall Crows at 4.30am of 5.55am fires NO Balloon was observed losing downs during L10 a 45 south it was impossible to see the red fed. 15C8.
B.a.W.D. 11.255. Guns. Teatads 8 bedaf of 17b Psc9 & 176 Rsc9 12 enemy 175 MG fire returned on morning 5/6/8 by Lt. the Coy to ac go with no in service.
Martin fair hot. Cumulus nil.
Man R/R Fermes shut 62C NE + 62 C NW 20000 | J/49
|

Maj R/R Fermes Sheet 62C NE + 62C NW 1/20000

WAR DIARY or INTELLIGENCE SUMMARY

Army Form C. 2118.

175 Machine Gun Company

SHEET 1/0. VOL 3

A. McNeill Major

Place	Date	Hour	Summary of Events and Information	Remarks and references to Appendices
ROISEL	5.5.17		**COUNTER-ATTACK BY ENEMY ON MALAKOFF FARM & UNNAMED FARM**	
			As a result of our attack on the night 28 3/4 we had MALAKOFF FARM and the Cherry Trench E & W it. This time was held by 3 sections who were in The remainder of the CW. occupied jones on this part of the recaptured occupied and evacuated the German trench The attack on COLOGNE FARM. had been held up by M.G. fire the farm remained in Enemy hands. UNNAMED FARM. had been occupied by us on the afternoon 27th without opposition. a post established and Lewisburg Flocks at Junction. 26 NEW TRENCH & ENFILADE TRENCH AND IN NEW TRENCH at about L.6.S.4.	
		2.0 pm	The day was quiet till about 2.0 pm when report was received that Enemy were massing for an attack in dead ground in A.25d, E of the positions occupied by us. E of MALAKOFF FARM, and in wood A.26 Central. Our artillery was notified of this on their boundaries.	
		3.0 pm	Gun S.O.S. was put up from positions E of MALAKOFF FARM. Enemy barrage shells fell from L6.9.0 to F.29.9.9.0. At this hour also the Enemy put down heavy barrage about L9 & stella heavily all and as far as L28 in L9.	17.4.9
		9.30 pm	Enemy advanced on UNNAMED FARM. L6.a.2.0, in strength. opened our post there to withdraw. Enemy occupied in swarms on our position in MALAKOFF FARM. Attack was chiefly against our night. The 3 reasons leading thither E of the FARM had to fall. (the support line (Switch TRENCH) with the FARM. The Enemy pressed their attack down (Long wood) had been forced thro further (was SUNKEN ROAD in L.6.a.s.59. Doing the day they were seen further withdrawn to the shelter trench in L.5.G. as our position was untenable.	
			During the attack Enemy made use of all kinds of shells. including gas, over whizzed our front line arose. & forward Communications wire cut almost at once.	
			Details from Sec. Off. reports	
			No. 1 Section 2/Lt. HOBSON. 7:15 pm about 15 Enemy (?) seen entered also 23 UNNAMED FARM. Returned 2 guns at M.3 to E. in SUNKEN ROAD L.6.97.4 - Let L.Cpl. OAKE'S. Comd. 7/7 S.F. El. Patrol. Was ordered n.c.o. to fire on counter-attack had to be relieved to undernourishable. Saw L.Cpl. DIBBIN & horn Pete. when following firm. for recapture of lost ground price operation. Was overcome. Saw some Artillery coverage on UNNAMED FARM and BOLOGNE FARM. 11/10 - 11:25 am. Enlisting Took to Dun with 1 am to 1/100 am. Artillery Coverage on UNNAMED FARM & BOLOGNE FARM. attack at 11/10 am. 2 m. of of This Enemy were to fire on our SUGAR FACTORY and the other on COLOGNE FARM during about 26 minute. Howitz. no artillery bent up. 2/Lt. HOBSON walked till 1:5 am when obtained tad at about Long'sh, w trivers. Placed till 1/25 am. 2/Lt. CARRUTHERS attended to duty at QUARRY L.15.d. & Rec'd new Enemy firing from the front 2 pm.	
			No.2 Section 2/Lt. FRIEND. Commun. a VILLERET. 10:0 pm. W/5/17 found our gun had been withdrawn. & proceeded to find new position in d- VILLAGE was relieved. Shelled at 9.0 pm Army Spent. til 12 2.0 am. Learnt company flying from QUARRY L.5.d. was at VILLERET. Made Rifle France. Sleb. 62c N.E. & 62b N.W. 57.00 (South)	

WAR DIARY or INTELLIGENCE SUMMARY

Army Form C. 2118.

175 Machine Gun Company

SHEET 11 VOL 3

Place	Date	Hour	Summary of Events and Information	Remarks and references to Appendices
ROISEL	5.5.17		(Cont'd)	
		9.0 pm	No. 4 Section 2/Lt EDKINS. Traced N° 3 Quarry (L.5.d) bombarded by enemy for an hour, at dusk (4.5.17) accompanied apparently by gas or smoke discharge. Patrol with Lewis gun fell back from UNNAMED FARM. Fired at what was apparently during strafe. Later moved gun to shell hole half way to road from valley portion and fired on trenches in front of COLOGNE FARM. The S. gun teams were untouched, but N. gun had hole huge in top of barrel casing but remained in action. No casualties, but ration party lost. Preparations were made from 7.30 pm to 9.0 pm. Two other close but covered that gas was in Malta discharge but the fumes from so great a number of shells, some with tear gas, emulsion with human fires gave similar. Enemy bombardment on other section from front or repulsed by the officer on being headed at 4.0 am to 4.30 am.	J.A.9
		2 am	General service activity on both sides common. At work also 2 teams of No. 3 Section returned as above (1.5.20) arrived in billets at HP ROISEL. Warning order for Relief by 174 M.G. Coy received. B.W.O. No. 25 Weather very hot a close, high wind. Wounded brought with slight rain. Artillery heavy firing heard in direction of TEMPLEUX & HARGICOURT. C.O. No. 25 & O.C. N°26 attached for relief. Gunning details for relief of 83 Sec. received MALAKOFF & COLOGNE FARM. Remained static. Casualties. BATTLE OF ARRAS. (Gas wind tin)	
ROISEL	6.5.17		Intelligence Enemy made two attacks on the night of the 5/6th inst. They were repulsed with fear to advance on the night was also attached to young Gagnies Infantry who were established on our second extreme trench soon N° 5 MALAKOFF FARM reported much damage by our shelled by very light sent up by hour N.? found behind this was reported told. Many very light sent up by hour N. C.M.G. 5 and 6 over RP during night to our 80 COLOGNE FARM. Gun T.M. Battery Discount gun M.G.5 and 6 over RP during night to our 80 COLOGNE FARM also on BEARNES. Enemy Artillery quiet as well on HARGICOURT VILLERET & TEMPLEUX. Enemy troops by reg. 8th Div. Where was opposite HARGICOURT. The 20.4.17 relieved by 32 234 Div. has been indicated in the fighting round ARRAS. From Enemy bombed attacks which although take place on ground which overlooks the HINDENBURG LINE, it is assumed that he intends to hold that line strongly & works to prevent quiet observation on it by us.	J.A.9
		11.30 pm	Orders from S.C. O/c Roberts. No. 1 Section 2/Lt HOBSON. Moved from Quarry in L.5.d to relieve 2 guns of No. 24 Section in QUARRY in L.5.a.32. Relief complete by 1.0 am. Unable to fire owing to wounds attached teams being our our sight very good. No. 2 Section 2/Lt FRIEND (VILLERET) Put on one gun in new position in L.17.c.26. Reports all very quiet in front of No. 3 Section. 2/Lt FRIEND had changed two guns of N°3 Section, owing to 2/Lt SEADMAN having gone down sick wounded. Map Ref France Sheets 62NE, 626 NW. 20000	

WAR DIARY or INTELLIGENCE SUMMARY

Army Form C. 2118.

SHEET 12 175 Machine Gun Company
Vol 3

Place	Date	Hour	Summary of Events and Information	Remarks and references to Appendices
ROISEL	6.5.17	—	(Cont'd) No 2 Section & No 1 Section 2/Lt PARRUTHERS Guns as follows 1 gun No 2 in QUARRY L10a, 1 gun No 2 in SUNKEN ROAD at L14c. Both East mountings guns firing on gaps in wire showing the night. Rds fired 1050 Pannellen M.G. L10 B 33. 1 M.G. 1 No 2 gun No 1 Sec in SUNKEN ROAD of M No 1 Section Nil report ex night as filled by No 1 Sec completed at 10.00am. R.M.G. Emplacements (Enemy) No above by Sec Sgt reported on by T.M. Bde.	J.M.C.
		—	Opened (?) Ammunition sent to for having are gun positions shown of Hd related to T.M. Bty. Their Shelaive arranged. Light casts. Battalion went to relieve in BERNES with Coy's T.M. Message for relief sent to Shelaive in time. Some ammo brought by our Planes but they generally very good. No artillery activity.	
		10.15	NCs alpha member stretcher but fine. I.O.R from Hospital to Coy RELFORD returned from Duty Coy school with I.O.R. on reporting work done.	
BERNES	7.5.17	2.0 pm	Arrived from ROISEL HQ Transport all No 4 Section slept N°2 & N°3 Section Batt'n HQ 1/2 Pdr HQ, taken over. Men in the some huts Good. Guns and ammo to some huts used scarce in Room huts. Pipe and ammo made for BERNES & Section emplaced from the time. Gunter guns mounted & Sunken in Infacen post Tot B.6.	
			Heavy rain commenced to fall about 1.00 pm. 2/Lt JENKINS proceeded to TENPLEUX & 2/Lt JEFFERYS to QUARRY in L10 & thence over then to 17th Bay Co Reconnised of HQ ROIsel by relieving UNNAMED FARM tenants the Wins occupied by day.	D.7.3.
			Coy Reports Battalgone NU on report Quiet day.	
			General Some ammo brought by fort Sides obtained. Quiet day Weather — fine warm & dry Nil work. Some over obtaining main cable as above at storm. V warm night.	
			I.O.R. Returned from 10 days leave to U.K.	
BERNES	8.5.17	12.30am 1.30am 2.50am 6.35am 21.00am	2/Lt PARRUTHERS with 2 No 1 & No 2 Sections arrived at BERNES. C.O Sind EDKINS & 2/Lt JEFFERYS arrived from QUARRY in L10. 2/Lt Hodson and 2/Lt SKELT arrived from VILLERET 2/Lt FRIEND and 2 No 3 Section arrived from VILLERET. The return of Confection which by code word "TIN" was sent to Bde. Durning most of the night Heavy rain fell and the men arrived soaked toto skin Tr huts put up by the R.E.s were also leaking but waterproof. Day spent in Cleaning up guns stores & little orientating new mess. In spite of the weather & fatigue the moral of the Men was good. Some arms getting baggu. This was an pouring(?) our had Section Sine immediately or arrived Wire of artillery & anti aircrft (?). I.O.R Shilling killed Denby from Hospital to Duty. W.U.D. Weland left. Map ref France Sheets 62eNE & 62bSW.	J.M.C.

2449 Wt. W14957/M90 750,000 1/16 J.B.C. & A. Forms/C.2118/12.

WAR DIARY or INTELLIGENCE SUMMARY

Army Form C. 2118.

175 Machine Gun Company

SHEET 13 VOL 3

Place	Date	Hour	Summary of Events and Information	Remarks and references to Appendices
BERNES	9.5.17	—	Company refitting and training at Bernes. Enemy Gun Shelling & hit up a Rey Dump Company paid out. Gas Alert on. On attack by 176 BS Bde on the NEW TRENCH, only succeeded on a Small Scale. The use of the attacking troops having been held up by Enfilade M.G. fire. The party which delivered an attack & Bayonet was subsequently withdrawn.	M.A.G.
BERNES	10.5.17	—	Company as above. Work done: Training as per programme. Cleaning Guns, rifles etc. Members indulged in 3 Football Matches, mainly Bay Easily fund. Some abroad in an Early ar ROISEL was Shelled 6-7pm. Guard & Safety Factory with 2/7 S.F. M.G. Personnel consisting of Men Coming on Ward, Safe at 4.30pm. 2 O.R's rejoined from hospital (Stretcher no.1 was Sgt Suffering from Shell Shock 2.O.R admitted hospital 2. O.R's hospitalized taken to Stretcher, near Bury 2.1/5303 L/Cpl Signaller Reported wo... B. O.R's hospitalized. Taken to Stretcher will carry Kits at own expense Safely. Q.M.S. McCann taken on Strength on that gls of 8.O.M.S. Will carry Kits at own expense Safely. Sgt J.A. WATSON taken on that gls up as to No. 3 Section.	M.A.G.
BERNES	11.5.17	—	Company as above. Stone work & rifle inspection by cmdg at 10am. M.G. kit Inspection by cmdg at 10am. Enemy AA's active. Bns of our aeroplanes was hit at 7.30pm & brought down sch of Jalons. Schwein MENTIGNY FARM. ROISEL was again Shelled & Enemy OVENDELLES. BSR occupants being killed. Weather very fine but wind Safe.	M.A.G.
BERNES	12.5.17	—	Company as above Training & Refitting in the morning. In the afternoon Sports (Football) v 24 S.F. in field near Sugar Factory. Robin Spin PO. M.G. Coy declared winners by having Scored over etc 17's Coy. Put in a fair entry to well up M.G. Coy declared winners by having Scored good efforts and from the enemy. Commencing the Shot was the enemy throughout in numbers etc. Given fire & Coy. So By the was men Cheaters in numbers given given for a Coy. So By the was men The attack was followed. Wind Conditions glass alarm on. Meanies as Lt. J.H. GARDNER & 154 L 9/12/84. Manner for M.G. Course at CAMIERS cured for T Div (158 & 30 OR's). Manners as Lt. J.H. GARDNER & 154 L 9/12/84. Gentle Some activity early on. wind Shelling by Horse Artillery. 1 O.R returned to duty from hospital.	M.A.G.

Map Ref. Sheet 62cNE & 62eNW 1/20000

Army Form C. 2118.

WAR DIARY or INTELLIGENCE SUMMARY

175 Machine Gun Company

SHEET 14   VOL 3.

(Erase heading not required.)

Place	Date	Hour	Summary of Events and Information	Remarks and references to Appendices
BERNES	13.5.17	2.0 a.m.	Company in training as before. Very quiet day. O.C. 2/½ Co. 2 P.O. reconnoitred 2 Gun Defensive posts from Railway N.E. of RUISEL to BERNES. Enemy at Balloon hung active indeed. Reconnoitred shelling of our aerodrome which was fairly active, also activity at ST QUENTIN. Weather dull - no rain. Range firing test resumed. 118" from Off. gun. Observed all rounds probably OK. Cpl. will report. B Coy at 10.30 am. 2/4 Jt MacLELLAN joined for duty & was posted to Coy and No 2 section. 2. O.Rs. evacuated to C.C.S. R.P.M.	J.M.G.
BERNES	14.5.17	—	Company as above. Improvement of billets etc carried on. R.J. inspection of whole company. All unfit clothing supplies led. Men into close for return to D.A.D.OS in order to equip company as far as possible. Heavy thunderstorm continuing till about 6.0 P.M. with one of which a high wind & heavy heavy rain. All ranks suffered considerably from drenching kits. 2 Officers practised 2 day scouts at AMIENS. 1 Sect (Cpl ...) reported for duty & were accordingly taken over wef. 2 O.Rs. admitted to hospital. 2 Intelligence notes. At Battalion Hqrs. again very active. Gun machines were very ... for an open ... . Gun obs. appt appeared to mark so ... an advance. Enemy patrols from VENDELLES & BERNES & harbouring over to G.55 ...	J.M.G.
		3.0am (approx)	A & MS 596 Cav 00 No.5 withdrawing to advance position from VENDELLES & BERNES & harbouring over to G.55 Cavalry Div. rejoined.	
		10.0pm	... Bde 00 Re 27 Recd. stating that 17/8 Inf. B.de will from 9am 16/5/17 come under orders of 57 118 2nd Bde HQ to continue at VRAIGNES as 17's Bdy. Cavalry Division who relieved the 59th Division on that date. Bdy HQ to continue at VRAIGNES as 17's Bdy.	
BERNES	15.5.17		Company training. In accordance with Bde. order 2 1/6 fall machines played in afternoon, in order to select two good teams to represent the Company in the Bde. "knock out" matches. Very quiet day till 11.0 pm when guns on the Rt. of Corps front became active. Very little general activity. Weather morning dull, wet after noon but would sat. Many explosions reported in JEANCOURT, & a field up shafts was found under Roadway by VRAIGNES CHURCH. 1 O.R admitted hospital.	J.M.G.
BERNES	16.5.17		Company as above. Inter Competition between teams starts. Between some Secd to eat close. Recreational training in abeyance in afternoon owing to inclement weather, but arrangements for G by sports enter are, I H too supposed, & at last special, Rt. Lutton groups gun stores left in bunkers by as told in the line off, to be surfied cleaned, tea etc. one man for section in readiness solid for 1 day to a Permanent ... brighton and Bankhave after leather's artillery & patrol of 6. One 1 O.R. left to hospital find Bernes Frame to U.K. Weather dull cold rain. Afternoon - heavy rain. 2 O.R admitted to hospital	R.A.B

Map Reference France 62c NE v NW 1/20,000

War Diary / Intelligence Summary

Army Form C. 2118

175 Machine Gun Company

Sheet No. 15, Vol. 3

Place	Date	Hour	Summary of Events and Information	Remarks and references to Appendices
BERNES	17-5-17		Company training. Route March; preparation for Bde. Revolver Competition & practice match for Brigade Football Competition. 1 O.R. admitted hospital. Brigade Band played from 6.0 – 7.30 p.m. Weather; Rain showers – cool. Wind Safe.	(Recd)
BERNES	18-5-17		Company Training. Revolver shooting preliminary round Bde. Competition. Finished 1st round mountings in emplacements 1,3,5, & 6. BERNES FLECHIN, HAMELET defence line. Played (off 2nd Bde. Football Competition 2nd in Command 2nd Gardiner succeeded to BARIERS for a wound came tuching in on defence of Fasting) to the present district. Cloudy – showery – cool. 1 Officer. 2 O.R. CARNETS – CAVNES. 2 O.R. returned to duty from Hospital.	(Recd)
BERNES	19-5-17		Company Training as usual. Whole Company on parade morning. Nos 1,2, & RT's set off preliminary at Bde. Revolver Comp.	(Recd)
		6.30 p.m.	shooting in afternoon from 2.0 onwards a day occupied Company Sports meeting was carried out. The Brigade Band played at around the pits attendance was heavily contested. On event for men was billed at 1.30 p.m. which was MV Gunshots 3 & 4.5 clerk in and MV gun dashes are attempted of the front Scruffy, for jointly decided by an enemy Kite Balloon observer who E. Paraschop was subsequently recovered at 7.0 and promptly established by Nos R.Os MacR,R.M. D.S.O. the excellent competition was enlisted in the artillery front being attacked for 9.0's (heads & check. Randall 3 Section 12 Pk., 2 Section 10 Pk., 1 section and HQ. last Pk.	(Recd)
		9.45 p.m.	About 4 a.m. an enemy was exploding in regularly showing on from 9 Kit Battery who continued KH Batteries were up all the tra. all day. Approximate in Pl. 2 returns showed what Bohe. Evacuated for casualties. Weather Fine Cool. Wind Safe. Secret Code No. 98/92/06 – Defence Scheme received during day.	
BERNES	20-5-17 Sunday	11 a.m.	Inspection by C.O. annual satisfactory. Aircraft and antiaircraft guns very during morning. Bcn. A repeated Company preceded to BARRIS to shoot off to second round of Bell. Revolver Competition. Barks by two of 9th Stewart Hausten Leur Gunners but standard of shooting disappointing. Played the 172 M.G. Coy football ownway 2-0. It has to be stressed that a great deal of	(Recd)
		5 p.m.	Recreational training is being carried out in addition to the regular training; the effort of this in the Company is very evident and obtainable a sense of completeness and "esprit de corps"; and of devotion as well as Players friends a highly valuable for mind and body. 11 hrs off hours used with an absence of to be fritted away in games of Monna. Weather Fine cloudy and rainy HH. Wind safe.	
BERNES	21-5-17	6.30 a.m.	Company Training Gun drill, I.A, P.T, J.D, Village attempts & Vickers (defects), 1 Officer & 27 other ranks promoted to JEANCOURT area under aeroplanes, & RE. on hand-referring Recall "Howeuvre," & Evening, 2 Lt. from Bde HQ team & 2nd ch 3 bde Comp. & O.R. transferred as 122 MG Coy, 2 O.R. rejoined from Hospital. Weather, fine; pleasant, cloudy.	(Recd)
BERNES	22-5-17		Company Training. 2 Officers proceeded to Base & Argonne. (12 hrs.) Renewed and artillery activity nil. Weather heavy rain all midday Fine fine. DECORATIONS: 2nd Lt. D.P. HARVEY 175 M.G. Coy. (D.S.) Section at forward in English UK.) Extract from D.R.O. 334:- "ON 27th April at the QUARRIES infront of COLOGNE FARM. This officer when in charge of two machine guns showed great courage and determination in getting his guns into position under heavy shell fire. Although wounded he continued to command his guns with the greatest coolness and ability by his action hours of shelling he also dug out and removed the wounds of a number of men who had been buried by Shells. The fine example set by the greatest fruits of his gave all the troops in the vicinity in the usual performance these officers has shown great courage and resources." Awarded the MILITARY CROSS.	(Recd)
BERNES	23-5-17	6.0 p.m.	Company Training – Route March, Arms drill, Village Clearing. As 2 Man Cemtry Regmnt, Recent Fours, the village. Brigade Band played in evening. Weather Fine. Map Reference 62c NE & SE. 20000	(Recd)

Map Reference 62c NE & SE. 20000

WAR DIARY or **INTELLIGENCE SUMMARY**

Army Form C. 2118.

175 Machine Gun Company
Vol 3.
Sheet No 16

Place	Date	Hour	Summary of Events and Information	Remarks and references to Appendices
BERNES	24.5.17		Company Training. Instead of Classes. Formed 173rd Ode. Machine Gun Coles 28 & moved to EQUANCOURT than no 14 29(?) of this month. Major demand Bombers which seem to indicate he means first and probably a certain confidence (and carelessness in clearing all in 61st with Euancourt in pale into patrol league with Erristhun. Weather magnificent.	(Pass)
BERNES	25.5.17	10 a.m.	After a attempt a landing an hospital former aircraft repulsed by anti aircraft guns. Company training Firing on 30° range and ½ hr. work. All ranks first interesting (??) Football Euranis magnificent.	(Pass)
BERNES	26.5.17	9.0	R.W. Allen who was a member of the 2nd Battalion Ordnance Recreational training in afternoon. Lectures football. 1 O.R. to Hospital. Pall Company.	(Pass)
		3.0 p.m.	Weather fine, held still nice — Operation orden No 29 received, detail and march table of move to EQUANCOURT on SHEET 57C.COURT 11.SW — 21/5/14. 173 Brigade will relieve 178 Ode on 14 night 31st May/1st June and this company will take over the machine gun position of 178 Bde recto on the night 21/31st June Barraconnel front (apparently), for manning with 28) R 2.c.30.5 K3.b.b.15.	

Map Reference $\dfrac{1}{40,000}$ $\dfrac{1}{20,000}$ 57c NE & SE. 62c NE & SE.

Army Form C. 2118.

M9/X/546

B Hel Vieill hay
175 Machine Gun Company
Vol 5

WAR DIARY
or
INTELLIGENCE SUMMARY
(Erase heading not required.)

SHEET 1
Vol IV

Instructions regarding War Diaries and Intelligence Summaries are contained in F.S. Regs. Part II. and the Staff Manual respectively. Title Pages will be prepared in manuscript.

Place	Date	Hour	Summary of Events and Information	Remarks and references to Appendices
BERNES	27.5.17	10.30 a.m.	Church parade. Church of England 10.30 a.m. R.C.'s 8.30 a.m. Rags Wachhouse. Played 2nd M.G. Coy at football in evening. Weather fine, hot.	(Pl. A)
BERNES	28.5.17		Checked contents of Limbers, inspected gas masks and cleaned up camp against move off. C.O. mounted foot line. Weather fine but breezing. 2 I.O.R. returned to duty from Base U.K. 1 O.R. evacuated C.C.S.	(Pl. B)
HAMELET	29.5.17 4.45 a.m. 12.0 noon		Company moved off to HAMELET arriving 7 a.m. H.Q. at K.36.c.7.9. Camped in centre of village, allotted 13 tents for purposes and made dust out well trench covers. Found road to POTTE in splinter. 2 army dropped a few rounds H.V. 4.3 shell on railway at S.W. corner of ROISEL and Ramequel. No harm done though shell nearly in my lucky turned with three times of the Camp by Corps Sports football in afternoon. Weather retied provided rain came. Sunday yesterday released. Upstream. Bd. O.O. 9.30 received, details of relief. A white Very no/rocket at BERNEY at 11.0 a.m. and took 14 gun store through 16 P28.C.27 m. HAYETTES WOOD. In addition to the M.Q.S. supply waggon brought rations to HAMELET. Packs were carried in Limbers, and Blankets on Leys. so that 14 men were mounted under very possible conditions. Advance party preceded as usual under C.Q.M.S.	(Pl. C)
EQUANCOURT	30.5.17 6.0 a.m. 4.30 p.m.		Company moved to EQUANCOURT arriving 11.0 a.m. H.Q. at V.16.b.1.O. Q.M. Store remain at P28.c.2.7 where transport will attest weakly arrive when Company goes in line. Bde. H.Q. received EQUANCOURT completing the concentration here. We are now in the XX corps and Coffre corps. Gave attendance changed in consequence. Breakfast before move off and dinner by 12.30 p.m. No man took place without incident in perfect weather. Found 12 bell pickets by advance party and drew 8 more subsequently.	(Pl. D)
EQUANCOURT	31.5.17		Physical & Camp, and packed fighting limbers. Deflector gun application handed into line for onslaught. Against Card. Journal to METZ en COUTURE ack with Lieut Col. MARTIN C.O.'s conferences of Bde. 7.0 p.m. At 1st HOBSON v. 1st MAPILLAN ack. 1 N.C.O. and 4 O.R. from 1 v 2 Sections proceeded to line the 7.0 p.m. A/Lt Lt.'s MAPILLAN with & stay at the to machinery, transport officers accompanied under CO peg armies. Officers & Lieutenants ammunition, & water supply. Bde H.Q. moved to NEUVILLE BOURJONVAL, party to 5 and givens of rations ammunition, and there are taking the place of our and men in connection with Weather continues unusually and dust and there are taking the place of our and men to report any comptence or that the day. One line is until reached by Lt Pittenoo, who ran up in his a pair to report any comptence or that activity. 1 O.R. to depot. In approach of plan of ditto of Surry 1 O.R. to Rft Bde PERONNE. Infantry battalion carried out with during day and night of 31.5./1st June.	(Pl. E)

Map Reference 1/20,000 62c Edn 5/c

Army Form C. 2118.

WAR DIARY
or
INTELLIGENCE SUMMARY
(Erase heading not required.)

13th Bn. Tuckey Major
Sheet 2 175.B. Machine Gun Company
Vol. A.

Instructions regarding War Diaries and Intelligence Summaries are contained in F. S. Regs., Part II and the Staff Manual respectively. Title Pages will be prepared in manuscript.

Place	Date	Hour	Summary of Events and Information	Remarks and references to Appendices
METZ-EN-COUTURE	1-6-17	7.30 a.m.	Escaped at EQUANCOURT. Advance party proceeded to METZ EN COUTURE to take over billets and prepare camp. Found METZ (thereafter) a village not so badly demolished as many we have passed through, most of the houses still standing, but no fire buildings left intact at time for the men (not pitched moved out scheduled to large Bdy. Cpy for H.Q. & N.C.O.s billet in HAVRINCOURT d N of the village. The Bdre allotted me two rooms, which served for Officers Mess & Sleeping quarters, a floor below which served as kitchen, finally our home — Same 100 men to sleep Orderly Room. E. of that I found a small and separate scrambled area. Same 100 men to sleep & that area of the main buildings shelter (14) got one cooked his meal and his kit. There were no lights on top, possibly exposing what remained could carry a reasonable supply of water. Cooks tent was erected the C.O., who rejected somewhat reluctantly refusal by pitch tent for cooks & sleep in. Cooks tent was erected the C.O., who rejected somewhat reluctantly refusal by ridgepole hold, most comfortable and sufficient thought there more but would have been sufficient for sufficient & 9 sections made the officers company situated by all banks and laying trenches. See at the ground up to put his billing arm for the 1st M.G. Coy, 3rd Division occupied Reserve Transport lines and Comp. Stores turned at VALLUART WOOD.	(Rec'd)
		10 a.m.	Summary of Positions taken over: H.Q. 9.11.d.6.1	
			9.5 V Section H.Q. Q.11.d.6.1 No. 2 Section H.Q. Q.15.b.8.3 Company H.Q. Q.25.5.3.3	
			2nd Lt HOBSON Guns at { Q.12.a.3.4 / Q.11.b.6.6 / Q.11.d.6.3 / Q.11.d.2.6 } 2nd Lt MacLELLAN 2nd Lt FRIEND Guns { Q.11.b.6.2.8 / Q.15.c.a.7 / Q.11.a.3.2 / Q.15.b.8.3 } Transport & C.Q.M.S. P.27.d.1.0	
			There was a certain amount of enemy artillery & M.G. activity during relief, which however was lodged without accident. Two days behind were taken up by Coy, in the rain. Now station is on road. Weather unexceptionable. Ground dangerous from E.G. am.	
METZ	2.6.17	7.10am	Relief complete. Animal activity by Company in reserve at RT village improvements. There spells of work & 6 days relaxing. Company to be well fortified near the banks. Section 1 & 2 on the lower barrel the day without event, and settled to their new quarters. In the village walk in on the 2/5 SHERWOOD, a 9/10 N.F.T.M.R, a bty of 18 pounders, and a C.F.F. Canadian Field Engineer Company laying Decauville Tracks. On A.A. gun (to a front post N of Camp during day) and a section of heavy Batteries flank the village & my Headquarters by their banks, & when fire a few places flank no Metz a M.G. to follow. Informed on 5 torpedo Moreno. Weather fine. Map Reference 57.C.	(Rec'd)

WAR DIARY
or
INTELLIGENCE SUMMARY

(Erase heading not required.)

Army Form C. 2118.

B. HQ. Fourth Corps
176th Machine Gun Corps
Vol. IV

Place	Date	Hour	Summary of Events and Information	Remarks and references to Appendices
METZ	2.6.17 (cont)		Artillery attention are afforded in any defences can for gun positions taken over by O.C. 9 Section. Section HQ Q.18.a.9.5. It will be seen that only 2 & 3 gun recesses at the Gun 1 Q.5.d.a.3 position hauled in. The remaining positions were changed for " 2 Q.10.c.9.3 tactical considerations and were administered upon them at once. " 3 Q.11.a.3.3 " 4 Q.16.a.6.4 The photo of the line particularly the front line in this area for a long time & since (taking bomb attacks & the of strafing) and has not suffered cable a number state as it was on the 12 (TERQUIER - HARGICOURT) last. The front line in this area cannot for her defence (viewed (abet (depth) actually is also maintained at night so it has a accessed no & discover any possibility of advancing the front line in any critical portion.	(P.B.)
METZ	3.6.17 SUNDAY BIRTHDAY OF H.M. GEORGE V.G.V.	10 a.m. 11.30 p.m.	Church parade voluntary good attendance. Certain in our front did full work in gun positions, dugouts, blow etc. Enemy shelled HAVRINCOURT WOOD heavily during day. There was some He. shell but [?] two at from a gun (probably a '5") this is of & the [?] a 5½" lights and also a good deal of work & to down. Enemy aeroplanes over. I the number of big flame flame the enemy from at great altitude, nightly, Enemy prepared or much by fine flare excellent was carried in METZ and as for back to HAVRINCOURT WOOD, but formed down or much by fire flame very low and in number. They coming flem at great altitude, nightly came to a point not far on Runs. An aeroplane fight emerged over TRESCAULT, & enemy plane and watched our artillery to come on their lines. by a half suffered loft cable, Leave up of ground apart and noticeably attacking 2 flights 19 19 our lines. by a half suffered loft cable, Leave up apparently without damage. A few Jno. [?] were compelled by hour shelled HAVRINCOURT WOOD and passed up and down the line. Enemy attacked a convent of & golden rain, and a white Sunday and numerous balls of various colours, so formidable or much by fire from exitement in sector, as fir back as HAVRINCOURT WOOD, but we could All by midnight the position in the other had was quieter of the whole affair. We a personnel that most in the artillery SE of HAVRINCOURT WOOD, continued till 3.15 but the sound, though slight, was to given give rise to the alarm.	(P.B.)
METZ	4.6.17	7.a.m. 30 A.30 a.m.	Our enemy gun chaser 77 on shell in HAVRINCOURT WOOD at about 3 minute intervals, [?] Later on our TRESCAULT ROAD near 2 Section HQ was damp dent. Visual improvement by Enemy section in line improving quietly and constructing some single cement and shelter. 3 Gun steady morning Enemy O.P. up at dawn at 2.15 Map Reference 57 c 1/10,000	(P.B.)

WAR DIARY or INTELLIGENCE SUMMARY

Army Form C. 2118.

B. Bath (Lieut.) Major
1/5th Machine Gun Corps

Sheet 4 Vol IV

Place	Date	Hour	Summary of Events and Information	Remarks and references to Appendices
METZ	4.6.17 (cont)	5.0 a.m. to 10 a.m.	May; it is 10 a.m. now. 2nd Lt Elston fired 11 makes burst at M.G. occupying houses & way back, at Dup man and a dog were seen to Gun. BOAR COPSE and Dauffsur were safe in trenches of German line. Machine gun emplacements were definitely located by us & though at K36 a 3.2 & K36 a 45.18. 1 OR reported for Boar. Weather great; light west-to-pass. The system of standing two days at a time works well. It carry on turns and twelve men is not great burden and units have all the rest of day. All meet and have as world in METZ. Rest and real attained days. This is much appreciated in this line when how men posted at again in village & c c. Very found bottom our men is full working order, and old lectures cleared out, I. Tour there was a flashlight only. A mine that is in process of sapping out trend with new cart flow on the front of latrines. A stoke bar has been cleared of mines to a depth of two feet. After O.R. fire was found and the mines were placed on gardens round HQ. SUNKEN ROAD L31.c.03 - L31.c.33. Pm. Gun in Q11.c.62. During night field 300 rds into SUNKEN ROAD.	(Pas 7)
METZ	5.6.17	6.0 a.m. cont	Enemy dropped a few shells on A&I SECTION HQ at Q11 d 65. This no doing. Observed by aeroplane at great height. Britain in line carried a usual work; improved dugouts, building pontoons at 3 & 2 Section carried on with twenty and village cleaning. G10c B11 and no usual walking and were pleased with our progress in this respect. Weather appears, hot and very unit changeon. Three enemy were again observed in a gap in BOAR COPSE. A white flag was seen at of K36 a 3.3 moving in back p. Light was from 19.2 H and 3th Lieut. Jefferys combatted only one 9.1.G. Pak 22 and 23 at Q17.c 30.35. Q17.c 35.54. During night fired 1500 rounds on sunken road, and on sunken road in K36.c central. Very little artillery activity. 3 GR. To Hospital.	(Pas 8)
METZ	6.6.17	10 am to 10 p.m.	Sections in line carried on with establishments at Section in METZ training and village cleaning. Heavy clouds hung in the German line throughout day so that no enemy O.B's was hostile and lightly in few of own aeroplane activity. Our balloons were up all day, and aeroplanes extra ordinarily active. Artillery slackest 24 hrs. Internally hot, heavy scored to E. & N. Weather fine. No retaliation.	(Pas 9)

Map Reference 57c 1/40,000

2449 Wt. W14957/Mgo 750,000 1/16 J.B.C. & A. Forms/C.2118/12.

Army Form C. 2118.

1/5th Oxon Bucks L.I.
175th Machine Gun Corps

WAR DIARY
or
INTELLIGENCE SUMMARY
(Erase heading not required.)

Vol IV Sheet 5

Place	Date	Hour	Summary of Events and Information	Remarks and references to Appendices
METZ	6.6.17		No. 3 Section relieved No. 1 Section. One gun of No. 4 Section silenced gun at Q.16.a.0.7. Tunnelling Engineers commenced work on small dugouts at Q.5.c.8.4 and Q.12.a.3.6. Labour provided and material carried by M.G.C... No gun at Q.12 Vickers which was relieved moved up to new position at Q.12.a.6.5. Night firing 90 box shoot × 1500 rds on sunken roads. Flares and Verey again observed in BOAR COPSE. A 2 inch mortar was active against BETHLEM FARM. No Aerial act. 1 OR transferred to 174 MG Coy. One OR from base.	(R&B)
METZ	7.6.17	10.30pm	No. 1 Section rested during day. No. 4 Section on village cleaning. No. 3 resting in line. No. 2 carrying on in line. Weather fine but overcast later, then dim showers, evening fine. No. 4 Section relieved No. 2 Section. No. 1 Section provided working parties for small dugouts and also giving up position 24 and 25. These are to be manned forthwith which will necessitate three sections in this material drawn for officers + N.C.Os shelter at Q.12.a.3.A. Night firing on sunken roads— 1000 rds. Endeavour to bring establishment of ammunition in trenches to 5000 rds per gun. 250 rds ammunition to be drawn for N.O.1 and line guns but not forthcoming. Reported on late establishment of ammunition took up and proving of check lines and shelterbelt line tables. Transport lorries worked and in progress. Permanent shelters for personnel, RAM store and ammunition. Brick parry for transport lorries. Hypnosed latrines. Incineration for manure. Ordered to strengthen ted banks of Lisbon by cutting a triangle of wood inside them, Sent antichars, who both measurements material in school for. An enemy plane with advantage of clouds to appear over METZ at 8.30 p.m. was quickly sent to H. night about Off accurate AA fire. This was a very fast machine.	(R&B)
		10-10.15 pm	Artillery on B/L bombarded FLESQUIERES and neighbourhood heavily for 1/2 hr. Hun retaliation took place	
		10.45-11.10 pm	half an hour later on HAVRINCOURT WOOD which sector reliefs was in progress.	
METZ	8.6.17	9pm	Artillery activity during remainder of night. Learnt 2nd Army had launched attack. General activities during day. At night No. 1 Section moved into Algedery position 22, 23, 24 and 25 — intermediate line. Gun only manned at night, and of 11 men per gun. Progress on small dug.out shelters for MG. Plenty of material carried and carried to position in front line.	

Map Reference 57c

WAR DIARY or INTELLIGENCE SUMMARY

Army Form C. 2118.

B. Hd. 105th Machine Gun Company

Sheet 6 Vol IV

Place	Date	Hour	Summary of Events and Information	Remarks and references to Appendices
METZ	8.6.17		Review of position. Two sections are now in the line and with 5 guns in front line and support. A third man from Villyodry M.G. Junction in the intermediate line. No 2 Coy. moves two guns behind no 1 line of trenches running Way S end of HAVRINCOURT WOOD. Gun positions HQ. are now as follows:-	
			No 1 Section / No 3 Section / No 2 Section	(Ra B)
			HQ. Q15c 9.0 / HQ Q11d 6.1 MINED DUG-OUT / HQ. Q15a 8.5	
			OMGP 22 1 Gun Q17a 70.35 / 1 Gun Q12a 8.3 / 1 gun Q5d 1.1	
			23 2 " Q17c 25.65 / 2 " Q12a 6.5 / 2 " Q5c 9.3 MINED DUG-OUT	
			24 3 " Q16c 90.25 / 3 " Q11c 6.6 / 3 " Q11a 3.3	
			25 4 " Q16a 9.7 / 4 " Q11d 4.6 / 4 " Q10 2.1.3	
			/ 5 " Q11d 6.2 / 5 " Q15 6.9.7	
	2p-4p 6am		There was very little work actually during day. Some fighting at great altitudes took place. An enemy plane fainted brown arcated and was covered with white circles approached our line & aeroworks. We were flying our own tanks. Wind Dangerous 2 OR. L injured from shrapnel. Very fine. Unit's shortly later, were cut. Warning Order No. 93 at actif received.	
METZ	9.6.17		Because as usual, the section out of the line provides fatigues and working parties. In the line observation and heat continue to make work in the day difficult. Good progress can been made at night. There was a particularly quiet day. 6 trench mortars which have met been satisfactorily located continued active	(RaB)
	9.20 pm		against first line near BILHEM FARM. The Divisional artillery made good play in a 10 minutes strife in the evening and machine guns co-operated firing on the targets allotted with success & preventing temporary withdrawal of C.Coy. Yorks & this day was dull, close, and hot. Wind still dangerous. An officer of the Lancashire Fusiliers, returning from a working party, recommoitred with 2 Lieut Jefferys in that the truck of the party had been severely shipelled by his B gun from Q.10 £.1.3 on sunken road K35 a.0.5. "to man could have stood it with file 2 of chances. An officer & the 98th SF, recomoitering NW. of BOAR COPSE passed the work of this gun as specking a beneficial effect on the moral of his patrol. 1 OR. 6 hospital.	
			LIEUT. GARDNER and 2 OR. Recorded from course at SAMMERS K.36 d.75.00 and K.36 £.90 - K30 £.8.0. Hostile arrived day with Q5. 9.3, 7 and 8 guns Q12 a 6.5, 7 and 9 Reconnected. Map Reference 57c 1/40.000	

Army Form C. 2118.

WAR DIARY or INTELLIGENCE SUMMARY
(Erase heading not required.)

175th Machine Gun Company

B. Ech Such ayo

Army Form C. 2118.

Instructions regarding War Diaries and Intelligence Summaries are contained in F. S. Regs., Part II. and the Staff Manual respectively. Title Pages will be prepared in manuscript.

SHEET 7
VOL IV

Place	Date	Hour	Summary of Events and Information	Remarks and references to Appendices
METZ	10-6-17 SUNDAY		A quiet day. Village deaning and voluntary Church Parade. Section in line carrying on with construction of emplacements and shelters. No. 4 commenced work on a new Section H.Q. near front line. Two rifle grenades or trench mortar shells	Par 8
		11 a.m	were thrown over near Q.10.b.13 in morning. Explosion broke that of Hills parade. Right trying as usual 2500 ids on road 13.b.6 76.00 and northwards. 750 rounds on Q.6.c.65.75 and NE. This target was given by the Bde. Intelligence Officer Lieut. HANS, who reported that it effectively hampered the work of a	
		4.30 pm & 11.30 pm	German party man the road. The artillery of divisions on right and left were very active. Lieut. BURTON, 2nd in Comd. and of NY 174th M.G. Coy came to METZ to reconnoitre took a new to taking over During night 10/11. 10 and 11 pame were completed in the shafts of mined dug out at Q.12 a 8.3 and 10 and 12 in the day and at Q.5.c. q.3. A splinter proof shelter was completed at Q.12 a 6.6 Day overcast	
METZ	11-6-17	2 am	A violent thunderstorm raged over METZ making it culmination at about 3 am, from when on it rained heavily till 10 am. This proved a severe test for the Company billets and shelters, most of which admitted water freely. Repairs	Par 9
		11.15 am and 4.0 pm	were executed during the morning, and all roofs made weatherproof. The transport lines and Q.M. stores suffered more heavily, and the camp at EQUANCOURT was reported flooded. Captain BENN and S.O.E. Lt. 1/174 Company went round the lines reconnoitering for the relief. All arrangements completed for relief. Some trench mortar and enemy M.G. activity reported during day and night. Weather fine, but wind dangerous	
METZ	12-6-17	9 am	Transport lines and Q.M. Stores moved to old camp at V.16.b.10. on reaching during day by 174th M.G. Company. Section in line carrying on. Those behind engaged in cleaning up billets and flagstones in boundary with areas and surr. up. Town report NMIZ. expressed himself extremely pleased with condition of billets & gave certificate same	Par 8
EQUANCOURT		5.15 pm	Company moved off 4.0 p.m. platoons advanced party of 90 in lorries ahead. Section on the line relieved during night, and marched back independently to EQUANCOURT. Found the camp very much as we left it, with some slight improvements by 174 M.G. Coy. Weather fine but wind dangerous	
EQUANCOURT	13-6-17	1.30 am	All reliefs complete. All Sections needed camp by 3.30 a.m. Spent day respectively, cleaning and finishing Weather fine. Very hot.	Par 8
EQUANCOURT	14-6-17	7.30-8.30	Company training :- 7.30-7.30. Route Parade (men by N drill). 8.30 - 12.30 Training under Coy Commander's instructions, and no limber decay after noon. Billeted 100 off units at V.32 a.B.6. Baths are also nearing completion at this camp Weather very hot. 1 O.R. (Att B) to hospital OR retired from hospital.	Par 8

Map Reference 57c 1/40,000

Army Form C. 2118.

WAR DIARY or INTELLIGENCE SUMMARY
(Erase heading not required.)

Army Form C. 2118.

Place	Date	Hour	Summary of Events and Information	Remarks and references to Appendices
EQUANCOURT	15.6.17		Company Training. An important change inaugurated with a view to forging the practice of M.G. Coy. training and fire with the tactical theory as taught at the M.G. Base CAMIERS. It has been found that to meet here has been too little coherent mediation between the tactical teaching of the guns, so that O.R. are apt to look on a use of the of Officer concerned the instructor, and to lose sight of the great tactical possibilities of this weapon. The daily programme is therefore divided into two parts, one of which on request for special classes with an Officer. The following subjects are dealt with in this manner:— Visual training, Fire Control, Map reading and Topography (Scouts), Theory of Indirect and Control Fire (Clinometry) and its tactical application, Immobility — this N.C. Teams may be fully instructed in it, matters of secondary Interest — Camouflage, Cambrai, Musketry. Reconnoitre are included as occasion serves. Indirect Fire Barrage fire & coöperation with other arms in attack and defence are explained and illustrated. The history of the M.G. change is a correct medium for points to that of Artillery. Recreational training. Sub. Unit competing with 116 about preparation on material for a Bde. Sports meeting to be held on Fu 195, and a technical display on 16 205, and training of Coy's teams commences. 10.R. Reported from Bde. 10.R. admitted to Fd. Ambce. Weather. Fine Very Hot. Weid Dangerous.	Plans
EQUANCOURT	16.6.17	2.30 pm	Company training and camp improvements. The batten consisted of cleaning up have been underway for orderly in Company's construction of new latrines, a continuance O.M. stores and rifle racks, knives laid through camp for drawing off the heavy dry and a portion of ground NE of camp marked out for east section and transport as a calling place. Training for sports furnished. Coy. tea tea & Coy Team of 29/5 Sherwood Foresters third round of Brigade cup. (chiefly NSBRENCH) — 2.8 putting up a very good fight Lifted by Brig. Egerton of the RFC. & Officers and NCOs in "Aeroplane" & Infantry Coöperation. 1 NCO. to course at Divisional Gas School EQUANCOURT. This will bring establishment of Gas NCOs to 4 per section. Weather. Fine. Very Hot.	Plans
EQUANCOURT	17.6.17	9.30a 8.30a 10.30a 5.30p	Brigade Church Parade in field on Bde. H.Q. V.10.6.8.0. R.C. parade EQUANCOURT Special consecration service of the Allied Armies. United Board church parade. Preliminary agreement written re relief of Battalion of Bde. in right sector O.C. and 2/c. Command inspected right sector.	Plans

Map Reference 57c 1/40,000

Army Form C. 2118.

WAR DIARY
or
INTELLIGENCE SUMMARY
(Erase heading not required.)

Army Book __B Ack Iack Tuelv__
175th Machine Gun Company
Vol IV

Instructions regarding War Diaries and Intelligence Summaries are contained in F. S. Regs., Part II. and the Staff Manual respectively. Title Pages will be prepared in manuscript.

Sheet 9

Place	Date	Hour	Summary of Events and Information	Remarks and references to Appendices
EQUANCOURT	18/6/17	8.0 a.m	4 Officers reported at Bde H.Q. and proceeded to Tanks H.Q., WAILLY, in motor lorry for instruction in Tanks. Company Training as before. Classes under Section Officers. An Officers class is also held daily by 2/Lieut. GARDNER, refresher course and series of CAMMIERS course. The walking those in the evening. These three platoons having gone close at intervals. 2 horses went through full days journey for estn. Wind Safe	(R.6)
EQUANCOURT	19/6/17	5.0 p—	Company Training. Bugles sports a go in Ork H.Q. Torrential rain alone forced on the camp during the morning and afternoon. Lapon at 6.30p.m. hindered the complete success of an otherwise well arranged meeting. The Coy obtained the first prize in the grenade mule race, and second in the relay race, and obtained the award for best turn out with their limber which reflected great credit on this N.C.O. in charge Pte Work was commenced on the new Transport and grenade track there lines at VEDOS, where permanent horse lines and camp are to be erected and Transport consolidated under Divisional arrangements. The Battalion will move than Transport etter on the 24th and the Company on the 25th. Served Relief of 177th Bde in right sub sector by 174th Bde	(R.7)
EQUANCOURT	20/6/17	11 a.m	This day was allotted to Bde. competitions of a class that would bring out the efficiency of the Bde in the handling of its various weapons, endurance of the man etc. This Company performed will up from our own. The Lewis Gun Team competed, and with one limber for section. The Lewis competed, packed & galloped of an N.C.O. and any men in section complete, with one limber for section. The Lewis competed, packed & galloped into action. The team arrived at the woods for tea, and a team of 3 took a gun into action, firing a burst. The gun was then stripped and reassembled so far as a blight wound a could from 1 of 2 ten came into action with exploded mounting, also being a bonet for the signal by their N.C.O. this Lewis was led their officer came forward and all the guns and ammo were returned. W being given who and the team had fallen in behind the limber. Points were given on speed, accuracy of fire, correct 1A per formance (Sceyand). The Lewis performance from "action to up" occupied 6 minutes. 2nd Section not go for (Sceyand). The Lewis performance from "action to up" occupied 6 minutes. 2nd Section (2nd LIEUT. LEPICK) first 1 . 4" took for second place (2nd LIEUT. HOBSON & JEFFERYS). The display was judged by Officers of 2nd M.G. Coy. A working party carried on wth new Transport lines. The Company also competed on Rifle Shooting, and Revolver shooting competitions. 1 OR from Hospital. 10R from leave. Wind Mod West. Fine Dry. Got hot abt 7.30 p.m MAJOR B. HARE PICKLE D.B. appointed G.S.O. 2nd D.M.G.O. 2nd Lieut LETHBRIDGE proceeded on leave to UK for 10 days. Map Reference 57c 40,000	(R.8)

Army Form C. 2118.

B. Lt. Col. Tubb [cap?]
1/3rd Machine Gun Company

WAR DIARY
or
INTELLIGENCE SUMMARY
(Erase heading not required.)

SHEET 9
VOL IV

Instructions regarding War Diaries and Intelligence Summaries are contained in F.S. Regs., Part II. and the Staff Manual respectively. Title Pages will be prepared in manuscript.

Place	Date	Hour	Summary of Events and Information	Remarks and references to Appendices
EQUANCOURT	27/6/17	11.30 am 4.30 pm	Cleaning and checking contents of limbers preparatory to relief. Work on new transport lines continued. O.C.s 1, 2, 3, & 4 sections proceeded to line to reconnoitre positions. O.C. & a/OC 6 Coy H.Q. at Q.28.a.0.3 to reconnoitre. Uncertain weather, some showers.	(R a 8)
EQUANCOURT	28/6/17	9.30 am	Cleaning camp. QM Stores and transport moved to new lines at V.6.d.0.3. 2nd Lt. HOBSON appointed acting T.O. during absence on leave of T.O.	(R 8)
GOUZEAUCOURT WD	29/6/17	4.30 pm	Coy HQ moved to Q.28.a.0.3 & relieve 177 M.G. Coy. Weather uncertain. Cabin fire.	
GOUZEAUCOURT WD	29/6/17	2.30 am	Relief complete. Section guns on the whole line intermittent shelling. Pte Inman sligtly & Pte Warner slightly wounded. 4 Pte MARSH all carried from 2/6th SHERWOOD FORESTERS killed by a shell splinter. 1 G.F. slightly wounded. N. 3 AP repaired its own. Enemy planes (8) approached LA VACQUERIE about 11am and all aerial activity. Weather very fine. armed AA defences very active against our planes. Enemy shelled Q.28 central intermittently with tear gas. Section in the line as follows:	(R 2)

FRONT LINE	- 3+2 SECTION	INTERMEDIATE LINE	1+2 Section	BARRAGE GUNS	2+2 Section	COMPANY H.Q.
SECTION HQ	R.13.a.05.70	SECTION HQ	Q.18.a.4.1	SECTION HQ	Q.12.d.6.0	Q.28.a.0.3
Gun N° 1	R.d.7.5.9	Gun N° 1	Q.17	Gun N° 1	Q.18.d.92.30	TRANSPORT LINES & MN STORES
2	R.7.c.92.95	2	Q.17	2	Q.18.d.4.4	V.6.d.0.3
3	Q.12.b.7.2	3	Q.19	3	Q.18.c.93.55	* These guns belong to N° 3 Section
4 *	Q.12.b.47.32	4	Q.20	4	Q.18.c.6.7	+ All barrage guns shown then
5	Q.19.a.35.65	5 *	Q.21	5	Q.18.a.1.5	

1 O.R. returned to duty from Gen. Hospital. 3 O.R. Hospital. B.O. R° 36 received.

| GOUZEAUCOURT WD | 30/6/17 | 7.15 pm | Section in line at work on dug outs and emplacement. 9.0: Section in reserve working at bomb proof shelter. An enemy plane dipped only of both clouds and flew silently towards our O.B. near HUDECOURT. Observer descended in parachute and place opened fire with M.G. It was heavily engaged by AA guns and forced to retire as quickly as it came. Enemy bombarded GOUZEAUCOURT WOOD with battery fire. No damage. Weather fine. None wounded. | (R 2) |
| GOUZEAUCOURT WD | | 8.15–6 pm
11.0 pm | 2000 rounds fired from guns at Q.12.d.33.95 on cross roads in R.1.8.16.80. An enemy casualty is observed in heavy enfilade no° from Q.16.d.95.10 Map Reference 57C 1/40,000 | (R 2) |

WAR DIARY or INTELLIGENCE SUMMARY

Army Form C. 2118.

J H Garner Lieut
175" Machine Gun Company

SHEET 10
Vol IV

Map Reference 57 C / 40,000

Place	Date	Hour	Summary of Events and Information	Remarks and references to Appendices
Gouzeaucourt Wood	25/6/17		Trench routine. Section H working on new emplacement Q.17.b.85.60 a narrow gauge to emplacement. No 3 completed position at Q.18.c.5.6, with shelter. No 2, trench improvements and overhauling belts.	(Ross)
		4.30 pm	Enemy dropped 10 shells near Q.12.d.6.0	
		6.30 pm	A number of 77 am were dropped on edge of wood in Q.29a and commencement of LINCOLN AV. C.T.	
		6.20 pm	8 Enemy planes hovered over LA VAQUERIE but did not appear to am down.	
		8.30 pm	Slow bombardment of BEAUCAMP and over surrounding country	
		9.30 pm	No enemy aerial light was again observed on a bearing of 130° mag. from Q.18.d.05.50. Another observer gave it location as R.21.d.9.7. It appears to be brought down this coast by motor. During the night 2000 rds. were fired by No 17 gun from R.13.c.5.5 a western bend in L.31.d.1.1.	
		11 pm	Trench fire, flares. Showers during night B.B. R.O. 37 received.	
Gouzeaucourt Wood	26/6/17		Trench routine. No 1 Section in reserve at Coy HQ worked on wired dug out. Artillery actively normal to quiet. A large down mnging pursued much cared work, but when the full out the day closed about 5.10 pm. a number of planes were up on both sides. One E.A. found our GOUZEAUCOURT WOOD II	(Ross)
		9.40 pm	gun, Hugh U and plane towards own L.F.C. Woodwards, shrapnel, but ineffectually protected by A.A. guns. 4. late on, another E.A. flew over VILLERS PLOUICH and distant return of after 8 minutes a T.M. funded against an advanced front-line trenches at L.31.c.0.4 and L.21.d.1.1 during night 17 and 19 guns fired on areas north m. B.B. aros 98 and 39 received Weather fair, fresh breeze, late calm.	

Army Form C. 2118.

WAR DIARY or INTELLIGENCE SUMMARY
(Erase heading not required.)

175th Machine Gun Company

Sheet 1 Vol V

Place	Date	Hour	Summary of Events and Information	Remarks and references to Appendices
GOUZEAUCOURT WOOD	27.6.17	2 am	Practice S.O.S. sent up by night and left Battalion.	
		4 am	Enemy bombarded GOUZEAUCOURT WOOD with 10.5 cm. shell ranging on an average of 1 shell a minute. This continued for 3 hours. The target seemed to be Battalion 300x SE of Bn HQ and certainly was concentrated and accurate. No 1 Section worked on emplacement at Bn HQ pulling in top pieces and top trees of place R.1.b.11 wall of entrance. No 4 emplaced new emplacement in BEAUCAMP VALLEY 1330 yds from Bn HQ. very night a serious road of hostile machine gun fire from this direction was noticed by the first patrol at R.1.b.1.9. : a German machine gun emplacement and did not fire again during night. Weather very fair, hot. Wind dangerous. Very little aircraft activity.	(Rod?)
GOUZEAUCOURT WOOD	28.6.17		A quiet day. Working on new camp at V.6.b.6.3, moved about 6 officers and guard over Coy HQ before we were working in dug out. Vincit improvements, C.T.s to emplacement &c at 7.30 pm c new installed their directions. Flew up from the W and rain continued till about 4:30 pm wringing everything below moved emplacement and taking smoke out of trenches. No night firing. Conal activity below normal. Enemy shelled front line at intervals and S M G was active from support. Front line heaps of night 2nd Friend returned from reconnaissance around FOURCROFT. 2.O.R. to hospital sick, 1 O.R. returned to duty. 2nd FRIENDS are sick. Batt is not Brigade was anxious to know what is being done about gun positions in front line. Here are alot. Battalion would be against principle of M.G. work to place guns on the front line except as urgent recent. The line is not continuous - thinly defended by posts (as yet), these deep in mud and weak rifleman. and in the forward advanced left C.T's an eventually aided against that part of the line. But it will be found that M G firing is not always the only saving factor in deciding the fortunes of the guns.	(Rod)
GOUZEAUCOURT WOOD	29.6.17	8:30 am	19th? Lieut CARRUTHERS to 157th Artillery Bde for instruction until July 3rd.	
		5 pm	Very calm aerial activity.	
		12:45 pm	A large party of Huns observed at R.9.7.11. apparently constructing a field work.	
		1 am	Enemy made an unsuccessful raid on our right and killed and took a wounded VILLERS-PLOUICH & another hard area. This search plt were found in operation on true bearing of 1080 from Q.18 c 6.5-5.5. Gun guns fired 1000 rnds on area aware at L.31.d.1.1. during night. Carried on during day and night with bursts improvements at 1142 and in line.	(Rod)

Wrath. drive. aterial. ports. Wind Safe

Map Reference 57c 1 : 40,000

WAR DIARY or INTELLIGENCE SUMMARY

Army Form C. 2118.

175th Machine Gun Company

Sheet 2 Vol V

Place	Date	Hour	Summary of Events and Information	Remarks and references to Appendices
GOUZEAUCOURT WOOD	30/6/17	10.30 p.m.	Steady rain until 6.30 p.m. O.C. went round front line with C.O. inspecting the positions of guns in advanced front line and considering proposals in effect instead. Capt. S. GRANT & C/Sgm. DOD. O.Sgt. Cross & Cpl. BATES of Major PICKLE D.S.O. & O.C.S. with these turnt. An E.A. visiting ground close behind HINDENBURG LINE flew on and fired on as far as SUNKEN ROAD at a height of some 300x only; his immunity can be ascribed to the unexpectedness of the feat; aeroplane was altogether unknown or even been previously to necessitate being rescued. 9 my unknown unescort. 2 O.R. proceeded to CAMIERS for course. 3 O.R. evacuated O.C.S.	R of B
GOUZEAUCOURT WOOD	1/7/17 SUNDAY		Intermittent rain. Very little activity of any kind. Received notification of relief by 58th Division. A short party from the Bde. will proceed to 0.35d to prepare camp. No.1 Section relieved No.2 Section to Front Gun. No.2 came to Cp. H.Q. 1 O.R. to HOME on 6.61. 1 O.R. evacuated sick.	R of B
GOUZEAUCOURT WOOD	2/7/17	2.30 a.m.	Relief of No.2 Section complete. No 2 now in reserve in this wood. Heavy rain during morning. New front line position definitely settled. A very good day. City me IS.A.a.c during afternoon. No. 3 and 4 section changed places from Quinchatt line to S. position in front gun barrage gun positioned. 2nd LIEUT. FRIEND attached from Vintex service GOUZEAUCOURT.	R of B
GOUZEAUCOURT WOOD	3/7/17		Received B.O. 41's standing orders on 8/4th met by 58th Division. Prepared for offensive action against German relief on may 11 of M/S. 2 guns left for prepared positions. Evening night 2 sections consolidated M4.P and M4.R.P. left gun advanced and 9.2 section advanced P.4 and 4 position in same line. Low casual mornings included in 9.2 position present line.	R of B
GOUZEAUCOURT WOOD	4/7/17	5.30 a.m.	Take gas alarm. From 3 E.A. & m heavy rain. O.R.rate account to fine. 2nd LIEUT. JETHERIDGE returned to duty from line UK. O.R. 108 M.G.Cp came to successfully. This is attached to 174th Bde. which relieves the Bde. At 9.30 and 11.15 p.m. Coys installing carried out a two minutes shoot on enemy acts, no enemy was observed to be relieving. 5 M.G. of this company also engaged two other M.G. sunken road M L31 c, from specially prepared position in the support line. Enemy retaliated with a good deal of T.M. activity and kept up a show tombardment during night. Barrage on our left covered BOAR COPSE and source No1 BOAR COPSE during night. 2 O.R. to hospital. From our right sent up practice S.O.S. signals at 2.30 a.m.	R of B

Map Reference 57c NW.5040

MACLAGAN C/O 1st May 1917

WAR DIARY or INTELLIGENCE SUMMARY

Army Form C. 2118.

175th Machine Gun Company
Vol. V.

Place	Date	Hour	Summary of Events and Information	Remarks and references to Appendices
GOUZEAUCOURT WOOD	3/7/17	12.1 a.m.	Enemy aircraft bombarded form at Q.32.d.20.45. Until 11.0 a.m. Work on 7 front line positions completed. 4 battle and 3 alternative. During the day we were quiet, and the enemy retaliated with some counter shrapnel & trench mortars all for yesterday's activity. E.A. came over our lines at 1.15. and 9.15 p.m. and were engaged by our anti aircraft gun - 800 rds. Working parties were seen at R.8.b.9.7. and R.15.b.9.7, and a fire was then seen as of smoke at 3 p.m. in LA VACQUERIE. Walker fine. Wind dangerous. Reliefs of gun positions, etc. —	(P.A.8)

	(A) FRONT LINE	(B) SUPPORT LINE	(C) RESERVE LINE	(D) INTERMEDIATE LINE	COMPANY H.Q.
1	Position @ Alternative P.	R.7.b.2.6 R.7.b.65.33	Position Sec. H.Q. R.7.d.27.90 R.13.a.05.70 R.7.c.9.9	4. Sec H.Q. Q.12.d.6.0 Battery Gun	3 Sec H.Q. Q.18.a.4.1 17 Left Position Q.28.d.95.25	A gun in reserve Q.28.a.0.3
2	Position	R.7.a.05.24	Position	1 Position Q.18.b.60.47	2 18 Q.18.c.60.70	TRANSPORT
3	Position	Q.12.b.35.78	"	Q.18.b.50.06	19 Q.18.b.55.85	
4	Position @ Alternative P.	Q.6.d.1.0 Q.12.b.20.94.5	" Position B.5 v D.5 manned by this section	2 Q.12.c.45.25 Q.12.a.95.50	20 Q.18.a.0.4 5 21 Q.17.b.85.50	6 G.M. Station V.6.d.0.3

(A) Position only. (B)(C) and (D) one manned. B.2 is manned for AA work. This gun and B.5 have ammunition firing SAA to repel attack by armoured cars. Barrade (C) 1+2, (D) 1,2,3 v 4 are laid at night in direction SOS lines. To strengthen artillery barrage it will be noticed that the 7 front-line positions have been constructed by this Company, also the positions C.1 v 2 and the new position D.5, which necessitated a reconstruction of this line. Took on new transport lines and preparation for a permanent camp for the whole Company, and work on mined dug out and sand bag shelters has increased concurrently with the above. The revised system of improvements to shelters and dug outs in the line has also been carried out. Special attention has been directed throughout to the guides / communication.

B.O. 42 reference relief received.
B.O. 43 reference relief received.

| GOUZEAUCOURT WOOD | 6/7/17 | 10.30 a.m. | Movement was observed at R.8.b.9.7. During day engaged E.A. at 6.30 v 8 a.m. and 5.40 v 6.5 p.m. 1000 Rds. E.A. brought down on O.B. over FINS at 6.20 a.m. Night firing 16.00 rds on ground believe R.1.a v R.1.c. Central. 6A/9.95? relief received. | (P.A.8) |

| GOUZEAUCOURT WOOD | 7/7/17 | 4 p.m. | O/c F. FIRTH died of wounds at 4 p.m. at station & H.E. burst through our night light outside B's line. Field 1000 rds in E.A. during day, and too rds. Nachtang from R.12 to R.4.2. Central during night. Few rds observed artillery activity during the day. Amended to B.O. 41 (actual) received Ref.7 LETHBRIDGE and 1 O.R. admitted to Hospital. 2 v 3 B.A.B. Code received. | |

Map Reference 57c NE v S.E. 20,000

WAR DIARY or INTELLIGENCE SUMMARY

Army Form C. 2118.

175th Machine Gun Company
Sheet H Vol V

Place	Date	Hour	Summary of Events and Information	Remarks and references to Appendices
GOUZEAUCOURT WOOD	8/7/17 SUNDAY	3.15 p.m.	A very quiet day. Fine hot. 3 hostile blew up in rear of our H.Q. Slight enemy artillery activity in BEAUCAMP VALLEY. During night fired 1450 rds on R 3 c 3 3. 174th Bde Infantry relieved 173rd Bde Infantry in line. Officers of 198 M.G. Coy reconnoitred line to be over from 175th M.G. Coy.	(Ptd)
GOUZEAUCOURT WOOD	9/7/17	9 a.m. 12 p.m.	Preparation for relief. Stood H.Q. camp and moved to V 6 d 03 when it was overlooked for the night. 175th M.G. Coy relieved by 198 M.G. Coy and 4 Vickers guns. Found Sites handed over. Withdrew 5 guns for undamaged lit inches relief. The 28th Division Company will occupy the hole below.	(Ptd)
			Weather hot on 11, 11½ inst. Thirty mins rain late pm.	
V 6 d 0.3 (FINS) O 35 d Nr LA MESNIL EN ARROUISE	10/7/17	1.20 am 7.30 am 10.30 am	Enemy watching activity. Relief complete. Co relieved when proceeded independently to stop captain V 6 d 03. Company proceeded to new camp in O 35 D. Rear party obsvd up camp and followed in, reaching new camp by 1.30 am. Found 19 huts in site and work in progress on 2 NISSEN huts & officers Mess Shelter. Air Transport Lorries 10 pickaxes and officers bunks, and two small tables, 3 stables, bakers, incinerators. The whole camp is very cramped, and closely squeezed with old huts. Gun hardship were the whole. In surrounding country open and undulating. Bde. H.Q. at LE MESNIL.	(Ptd)
			Weather fine hot. 2 O.R. to Hospital. 1 O.R. to Base.	
O 35 d	11/7/17	9 am	LIEUT. MORRISON BECAME SECOND IN COMMAND. 2nd LIEUT EDKINS Acting T.O. Adjutants conference at Bde. H.Q. on training programme. Company overhauling equipment, guns, kit; cleaning, weighing, camp improvements in progress. Fine, very hot.	J.Y. Mac.
O 35 d	12/7/17		Company cleaning & overhauling guns, ammunition and equipment. Inspection of No 1 section with guns and all equipment by O.C. Coy. — Weather very hot. Camp Improvements continued.	J.Y. Mac.
O 35 d.	13/7/17.	2-30 p.m. 6.30 p.m.	Company continued cleaning & overhauling. Inspection of Nos. 2 & 3 Section with guns & all equipment by O.C. Coy. A Demonstration Attack was carried out by Capt. Charlton Pay, 2/4 S.F. The Attack illustrated very clearly the organization and method of advance of an infantry coy. in trench to trench fighting, and the working of the Artillery Barrage. All Officers & Sergeants went forward. The Company attended a lecture in the Quarry V 6 c 6.9. on Physical Training & Bayonet Fighting. There was also a demonstration by C.S.M.J. Atkinson & Coldstream Gdt. Smith. Weather very hot. Hot weather. First names see other papers C.S.M.J. Atkinson, 2.O.R. returned to duty. 2.O.R. signed from base. Map Reference 57 c	J.Y. Mac.

Army Form C. 2118.

WAR DIARY
or
INTELLIGENCE SUMMARY
(Erase heading not required.)

Month S[?] Vol V

145th Machine Gun Company

Place	Date	Hour	Summary of Events and Information	Remarks and references to Appendices
O.35.d.	14/4/17		Company Training. Inspection of No.4 Section with all guns & equipment by O.C. Coy. Weather fine & hot. 2.Lt M.J. Ellish & 2.a.R. proceeded to IVth Corps Infantry School, BOVES. 1 O.R. evacuated to C.C.S.	J.J. Mack.
O.35.d.	15/4/17		Church Parade in Quarry (V5 & S.9) during morning. Party of Officers went on tour of SOMME Battlefield from BAZENTIN-LE-PETIT to the BUTTE DE WARLEN-COURT. Interesting explanations of the various attacks were given by the G.S.O. III 59th Division. Weather fine, cool. 1 O.R. to hospital.	J.J. Mack.
O.35.d.	16/4/17		Company Training. Construction of Emplacements at SAILLY-SAILLISEL and reconnaissance of ground preparation for Brigade Tactical Exercise. 2 Sections fired on 30 yd range. Weather fair. 1 O.R. admitted for duty. 1 O.R. returned to duty.	J.J. Mack.
O.35.d.	17/4/17		Company Training. 1 section fired on range. Company at Divisional Baths in afternoon. Weather warm. 1 O.R. on leave to U.K.	J.J. Mack.
O.35.d.	18/4/17	4 P.M.	Company Training. Special instruction in Bayonet fighting. Gas Inspection. Lecture to officers & sergeants on "Cooperation of Infantry with Artillery" by Major Bates 59th Div. Artillery. This dealt with the methods and difficulties of the artillery in barrage work. Weather wet in morning, dull later. 1 O.R. to hospital.	J.J. Mack.
O.35.d.	19/4/17	8 a.m.	Brigade Tactical Exercise. Company operation orders for this are attached. Its operation was carried out twice, the 2/6 & 2/4 Sherwood Foresters being the attacking battalions. In the first attack the weak points were (a) too much movement obtained in assembly trenches prior to attack. (b) unequal synchronisation of watches, causing 2 minutes difference between units forming up. Transport Competition at BARASTRE. (Divisional). 1 O.R. to course. 2 O.R. to U.K. to join cadet battalion. Weather dull but fine.	J.J. Mack.
O.35.d.	20/4/17	8 a.m.	Brigade Tactical Exercise. The same operation was carried out twice with the 2/5 & 2/8 Sherwood Foresters as attacking Battalions. Special attention was paid to intercommunication and correct sending of messages. Weather	J.J. Mack.
O.35.d.	21/4/17		Company training finished at 11 A.M. DIVISIONAL SPORTS at BARASTRE. This company winners of one event, the three-legged race. The weather was good and the sports altogether a success. 1 O.R. to Hospital.	J.J. Mack.

Map Reference 57 E 1/40000

WAR DIARY or INTELLIGENCE SUMMARY

Army Form C. 2118.

M[?] Somme[?] 6 April [?]
M[?] Sodau[?] hill
175th Machine Gun Company
Vol I

Place	Date	Hour	Summary of Events and Information	Remarks and references to Appendices
0.35.d	22/4/17		Church parade and in the afternoon company at Baths. During the forenoon enemy aeroplanes were active over the back area of our line; our anti-aircraft guns replied actively. Weather fine & warm. 1 O.R. to hospital.	J.J. Mack.
0.35.d	23/4/17	8 a.m	Company engaged on Brigade Tactical Scheme over the same ground as previously at SAILLY SAILLISEL. Zero hour was 8 a.m. and on capture of 1st & 2nd objectives, two hours was spent in consolidation. A section to officers on Counter-Battery work was given at BARASTRE by Col. Kelly R.G.A. 2/Lt ROBERT WILLIAM M°INTYRE joined this coy for duty. 1 O.R. returned to duty from hospital. Weather hot.	J.J. Mack.
0.35.d	24/4/17	5.30 p.m	Company Training. A lecture was delivered by Capt Robinson R.E. on wiring and consolidation at 5.30 p.m. in the Quarry. A conference re billetting for rations was held at 5.30 p.m. at BARASTRE. Weather warm. 1 O.R. to hospital.	J.J. Mack.
0.35.d	25/4/17	5.30 a.m	Company Training. A demonstration of wiring was given by a section of R.E.'s. Lieut Col Peter, the 123rd[?] first application of "rapid fire". DIVISIONAL RIFLE MEETING at BARASTRE. Cpl Sheer 2nd in aggregate 1 O.R. to Base Camp. 1 O.R. to hospital. 1 O.R. returned from course.	F.J. Mack.
0.35.d	26/4/17		Company training. Lg Bayonet fighting under Brigade arrangements. Digging and construction of emplacements for Divisional Tactical Scheme. Reconnaissance of ground. (2/Lt A. HOBSON 2Lt) (2/Lt W. R STEFFENS) Weather still warm. 2 O.R. reinforcements. 1 O.R. came to O.R. 1 off. on course 1 off.	J.J. Mack.

Map Reference 57.c 1/20000

SECRET

SIGNALS

CPL COCKROFT i/c SIGNALS

(1) Detail signallers as follows:—
   1 to each Sec H.Q. Yourself at Coy H.Q.

(2) Wire diagram below.

(3) Signaller at H.Q.
    will pass messages from N° 2 also. Use switch if possible

(4) Take 4 instruments & Earth pins, 1 pair per signaller, spare reel wire. Trench discs & flags These will all go in N° 3 secs limber.
   No cycles required.

(5) Code letters as follows:—
   N° 1 sec   J.A.
   N° 2 sec   E.F.
   N° 4 sec   (if any distance from Bde H.Q.) K.G.
   Coy H.Q.   E.X.

N° 2   N° 1

                              N° 3

WIRE DIAGRAM (PARA.2)

Comdg. No. 175 Machine Gun Coy.

SECRET

Transport Orders

2nd Lt. T. EDKINS

(1) Four limbers + teams required one to limber and pair.

(2) Route to be followed.
To LE MESNIL VILLAGE
   Road Junction V26 b 7 3
                    V26 b 9 0
                    V 20 d 15 10
                    V 14 b 9 9
                    V 14 b 9 ent
                    V 14 a c 9
                    V 8 c 35 00

After unloading limbers will proceed to Road Junction V14 c 2095 + along Sunken Road V13 b a to V13 a 37 & pack about V13 b Sunken Rd. where they will await further orders

(3) Nos 1, 2 + 3 limbers go direct to V8c3500
   No 4   do   do   V13 a 37

(4) Details as to time of starting later.

J.H. Gardner Lt.
Comdg. No. 175 Machine Gun Coy.

SECRET

Appendix 'A'

Officer Commanding Nº 1 Section. 2/Lt HOBSON
CHEESE SUPPORT TRENCH.

Positions of Guns

Nº 1. at U 8 C 63 03
Nº 2. — U 8 C 62 16
Nº 3. — U 8 C 62 37   } & Sec. HQ at U 8 C 60 31
Nº 4. — U 8 C 65 50

These guns are dug in for defensive purposes.
The infantry advance at ZERO.
At +5 Rt Bn should be in enemy front line ie POTSDAM TR.
at +9 Left.   do   do
at +13 2nd Wave of both Bns should be in second
       objective ie in PLANET TR.

Guns going over

1. At +10 You will have the two guns which are to
go over, dismounted and everything got ready
for the advance

At +15 You will go forward with the 2 guns
to the 1st objective ie. POTSDAM TR., have your
guns mounted & loaded — using auxiliary mounting
while you reconnoitre the trench for gun positions
These guns are to put up bands of fire if required
between 1st & 2nd objectives to repel any counter-
attack. One of these guns should be about
U 8 d 6 2 giving flank fire to right front and
the other about U 8 d 4 4 giving fire to the left.
Use your Nos 1 & 4 guns for this advance
As soon as you have selected positions commence
digging at once (Not on 1st two days)
Inform O.C. Infantry holding POTSDAM TR. what
you have done and get into touch with Advanced
Bn. HQ as soon as possible

Report:—
① Your own position, i.e. Advanced H.Q.
② Positions of guns
③ Progress
④ Casualties
⑤ Requirements, S.A.A. stores

to Coy. H.Q. by runner to your old H.Q. thence by 'phone to Coy H.Q. as soon as possible.

As soon as the digging etc. is complete go on to 2nd objective & reconnoitre for gun positions there, and also alternative positions in 1st objective.

If you consider that more guns can be usefully employed in the captured positions in 1st objective you will inform M.G. H.Q. but will not move up additional guns without orders from there.

Notes ① In advancing, as ground is very bad use the C.T. to the left of your No 4 position as far as our own Front Line, then over top.

② Go over in open order concealing as far as possible what is being carried.

③ Load table is attached hereto.

② <u>Guns remaining behind</u>

Before ZERO you will give the following orders to the two gun crews.

(a) They will stand to until the operation is over, in order to repel any counter attack or cover the retirement of our own troops should the attack prove a failure.

(b) That if one or both of the advanced guns gets knocked out, they must be prepared on a written message from you to advance to replace them.

(c) That they must also be prepared to send up reinforcements to replace casualties on receipt of orders.

③ <u>Section H.Q.</u>

(a) As you will only take 4 gun Nos, 1 runner & 1 N.C.O. per gun, the surplus men will remain in H.Q. dug out. They will be used as reinforcements, carrying parties etc. as wanted

(b) Your supply of bulk S.A.A. (5000 Rds) will be here. also reserve of oil & water for guns & drinking.

(c) Spare belt boxes from evacuated gun pits at No 1 & 4 will be brought here & sent up as required to captured line.

(d) Arrangements will be made for belt filling.

LOAD TABLE

Officer	carries	1 Belt box
NCO		
No 1	"	Tripod & Oil case
No 2	"	Gun with light mounting
No 3	"	Spare parts box with wallet on back & 2 belt boxes & condenser tubes.
No 4	"	Pick & shovel & 2 belt boxes.
Runner	"	2 Belt boxes.

Total S.A.A. 1750 Rds.

(Runner brings on 2nd trip 1 tin of water for gun)

5. **Communications**

(1) You have an instrument & trained signaller at your H.Q. You must make him understand that he will not only have to pass on your own messages but also those of No 2 section on left.

(2) He will keep a copy of all messages received & despatched.

6. All your N.C.O. but especially sergeants must know as much as you do yourself so that he may be an efficient understudy should you become a casualty.

2/Lt Carruthers will be at your Sec" H.Q. & after you and 2/Lt Friend advance, will be in Command of all 4 guns left in CHEESE support.

7. Zero time is 8 am 19/7/17

8. S.O.S. signal is Rocket bursting into 4 blue lights.

9. Enlarged scale map is attached.

[signature]
Comdg. No. 175 Machine Gun Coy.

SECRET

OPERATION ORDER NO 1
by
LIEUT J.H. GARDNER
Commdg. 175 M.G. Coy

18.7.17
In the Field

[Stamp: No. 175 MACHINE GUN ORDERLY ROOM Date 18 JUL 1917 MACHINE GUN CORPS]

Ref. Map 57 C. S.W.
1/20000

1. (a) On the 19th inst the 59th Division will capture & consolidate the first line system of the German Trenches in U 4 d 95 85 to U 8 b 20 45

   (b) <u>Attacking troops</u>

   The 2/6th S.F. are holding the right sector
   2/7   do   do   left sector
   HQ. of 2/6th S.F. are at U 8 c 65 45
   HQ. of 2/7   do   U 8 a 80 10

   (c) <u>Supporting troops</u>

   The 2/5 S.F. are in support at SAILLY SAILLISEL with HQ. at U 8 c 55 80
   The 2/8 SF are in Reserve in NORTH COPSE U 7 C with HQ at U 7 c 65 15

   The 178 Inf Bde is on our right
   177   Do   is in reserve in SUNKEN ROAD U 18 a & b
   The N.d Division is attacking on our left

   (d) <u>Objectives</u>

   The 178 Bde will attack :-
   (1) The system of trenches in U 8 b & d known as POTSDAM TRENCH. This is their 1st objective
   (2) That part of PLANET TRENCH between the Co-ordinates U 8 d 65 25 & U 8 b 20 45. This is their 2nd objective.

   (e) <u>Boundaries</u>

   The 178 Inf Bde boundary runs through U 8 c 95 00 — U 8 d 72 to U 8 a 75 35 — U 8 a 52
   The Battalion boundary of the Brigade runs through U 8 c 95 80, U 8 d 35 85, U 8 d 45 90

f. **Barrages**

   ① **Artillery** The 178 Bde front is divided into 2 sectors. That on the right is covered by 'A' barrage group.
That on the left is covered by 'B' barrage group. The Corps Heavy Artillery will also barrage strong points & back areas (for details see Appendix X)

   ② **Trench Mortar Battery** will barrage the two Communication trenches known as GOTHA and BRUNSWICK, till bombing blocks have been established

     (For details see Appendix X)

   ③ **Machine Guns** will put down a barrage on BULGAR TRENCH and also give harrassing fire on SUNKEN ROAD in U3c & d

     (For details see Appendix X)

g. **Enemy Forces.** (supposed information)

The enemy trenches are known to be strongly held by BAVARIAN TROOPS, and there are strong points at U14b 95 85, U2 C 55 10. A hostile M.G. also is known to exist in trench at U8d 25 80 (approx) which sweeps along enemy wire in front of POTSDAM TRENCH, and another is suspected at U8d 30 45. He is known to have numerous Field Guns and some Heavy Artillery in rear, while Trench Mortar emplacements exist in U8 b & d.

2. **ACTION OF MACHINE GUNS**

The guns of 175 M.G. Coy will support the attack. They are divided into three groups as follows:-

   ① **Defensive Guns** There are 8 guns (2 sections) in emplacements in CHEESE support trench.

These 8 guns are divided into 2 groups.

(a) 4 guns which will go over and take up positions in the captured positions

(b) 4 guns which will remain behind for defensive purposes until the line is thoroughly organized and the tactical situation quite clear.

(For details see Appendix 'A')

2. Barrage guns

There are 4 guns in this group doing overhead covering fire & later, harrassing fire.

(For details see Appendix 'B')

3. Reserve Guns

There are four guns in this group which will be held in reserve at the disposal of the G.O.C Brigade

(For details see Appendix 'C')

3. Communications

(a) Company H.Q. are in dug out in U 8 c 35 00
    Nº 1 Section's H.Q. are at U 8 c 60 31
    Nº 2   do   do   U 8 c 80 80
    Nº 3   do   do   U 8 c 35 15
    Nº 4   do   do   U 13 a 70 95

(b) Telephone System

Wire runs from Nº 2 Section's H.Q. to Nº 1 Section's H.Q. Thence across BAPAUME – PERONNE RD. to Coy. H.Q. It is here connected with ~~the~~ a Brigade wire ~~which runs between the H.Q. of 2/7 S.F. in U 8 a 81 and Brigade H.Q. in V 13 a 70 95~~ Nº 3 Section will use runners as their H.Q. are close to Coy. H.Q.

(c) Guns advancing will use runners to their respective H.Q. whence messages will be forwarded by 'phone to Coy H.Q.

(d) Runners from the two sections in the support line will report to the Bn HQ in whose sector they are, so as to be constantly in touch with the Infy Commanders.

(e) On arrival in the captured positions, communication with the Senior Infy Officer holding the line must at once be opened up and a runner who knows such Infy H.Q. detailed to keep in touch with Infy movements

<u>Note</u>. The greatest care must be taken by all ranks concerned that :— (1) Only necessary messages are sent back
(2) That sender's name, position, time, date, address and as precise information as possible are correctly written.
(3) Ambiguity is at all costs to be avoided.

4. <u>Medical Arrangements</u>

a. These will be under arrangements with the infantry.

b. All casualties will be evacuated to the nearest Infy. advanced dressing station if possible.

c. In certain cases of men too badly wounded to move the nearest aid post or group of stretcher bearers will be informed as soon as possible if the situation allows.

d. On no account are men to be allowed to accompany any wounded man to the rear, as this practice depletes the gun teams to a serious extent

e. Advanced dressing stations are situated at V 8 ....

5. <u>S.A.A. Supply, R.E. Dumps, & Grenades</u>

a. There is a reserve of 10,000 at Coy H.Q. where a belt filling machine will be in position to assist Barrage guns.

Should it be impossible to keep belts filled by hand Empties may be sent to Coy H.Q. for filling.

(b) Each Section H.Q. will also have a reserve of 5000 Rds. at their H.Q.

(c) If more S.A.A. is required there is a very large supply in QUARRY in U.13.a.35.50 (Dugouts)

(d) Bn. S.A.A. dumps are at _ _ _ _ _

(e) R.E. dump :-
   This is at U.14.a.5.9

(f) Grenade dump.
   This is at U.8.c.5.4

Note.   If further supplies of R.E. Material are required they can be brought up from QUARRY in U.13.a by party of Section in reserve.

6. <u>Synchronisation</u> of all watches will be done at Bgde HQ in U.13.a.70.95 at ZERO -60.

7. <u>ZERO</u> time is 8 a.m.

8. <u>Acknowledge</u>.

Sent by Cyclist Orderly at
Copies to
   1 War Diary
   2 Coy Office
   3 ⎫
   4 ⎬ Section Officers
   5 ⎬
   6 ⎭
   7 ⎫
   8 ⎬ Infy Battns
   9 ⎭
   10 178 Bde
   11 Bde HQ
   12 CRA
   13 178 TMB

Appendix X

Barrage Artillery Field

A.
    (1) At Zero A & B Barrages will be put down on Enemy front line

    (2) At Zero + 5 'A' Barrage will lift on to PLANET TR.

    (3) At ZERO + 9 'B' Barrage will lift on to PLANET TR.

    (4) At ZERO + 13 Both 'A' & 'B' Barrages will lift on to WAGNER TR.

B. **HEAVIES**

    (5) ZERO to ZERO + 30 strong points U 14 b 95 85
    ZERO to ZERO + 9 .... { U 8 d 65 25
                                           U 8 d 50 55
    ZERO + 9 to ZERO + 30 lift to   U 8 d 49 80
    WAGNER TR. that part on right sector

    (6) ZERO to ZERO + 30 strong point in U 2 c 55 10
    ZERO to ZERO + 9 { strong pt in U 8 b 00 50
                                     "   - U 8 b 30 40
                                     "   - U 8 b 35 15
    ZERO + 9 to ZERO + 30 lift to WAGNER TR. that part on left sector.

    All guns cease firing at ZERO + 30 unless specially required by G.O.C.

C. **T.M.B.** 178 Trench Mortar Battery will bombard GOTHA & BRUNSWICK TRENCH to cover party who will make a bombing block in these trenches.

D. **MACHINE GUNS**

    4 Guns will put down a barrage on BULGAR TR. from ZERO to ZERO + 13

From ZERO + 13 to ZERO + 30.
Harrassing fire will be carried out on BULGAR TR.
2 guns.
SUNKEN RD. in U 9 c.d & b. 1 gun.
WOOD in U 3 c & d 1 gun.

  Details in Appendix 'B'.

         J.H. Gardner Lieut.
         Comdg. No. 175 Machine Gun Coy.

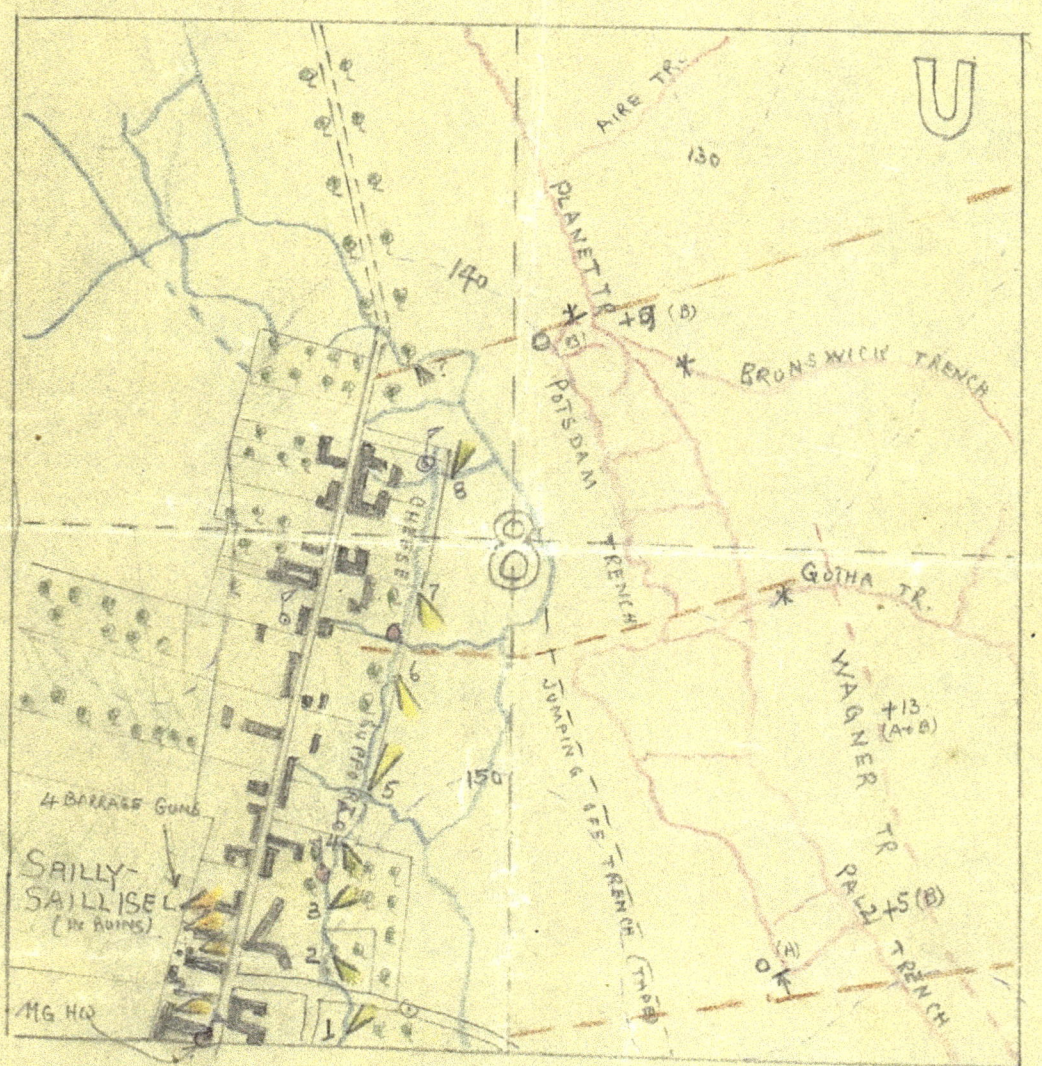

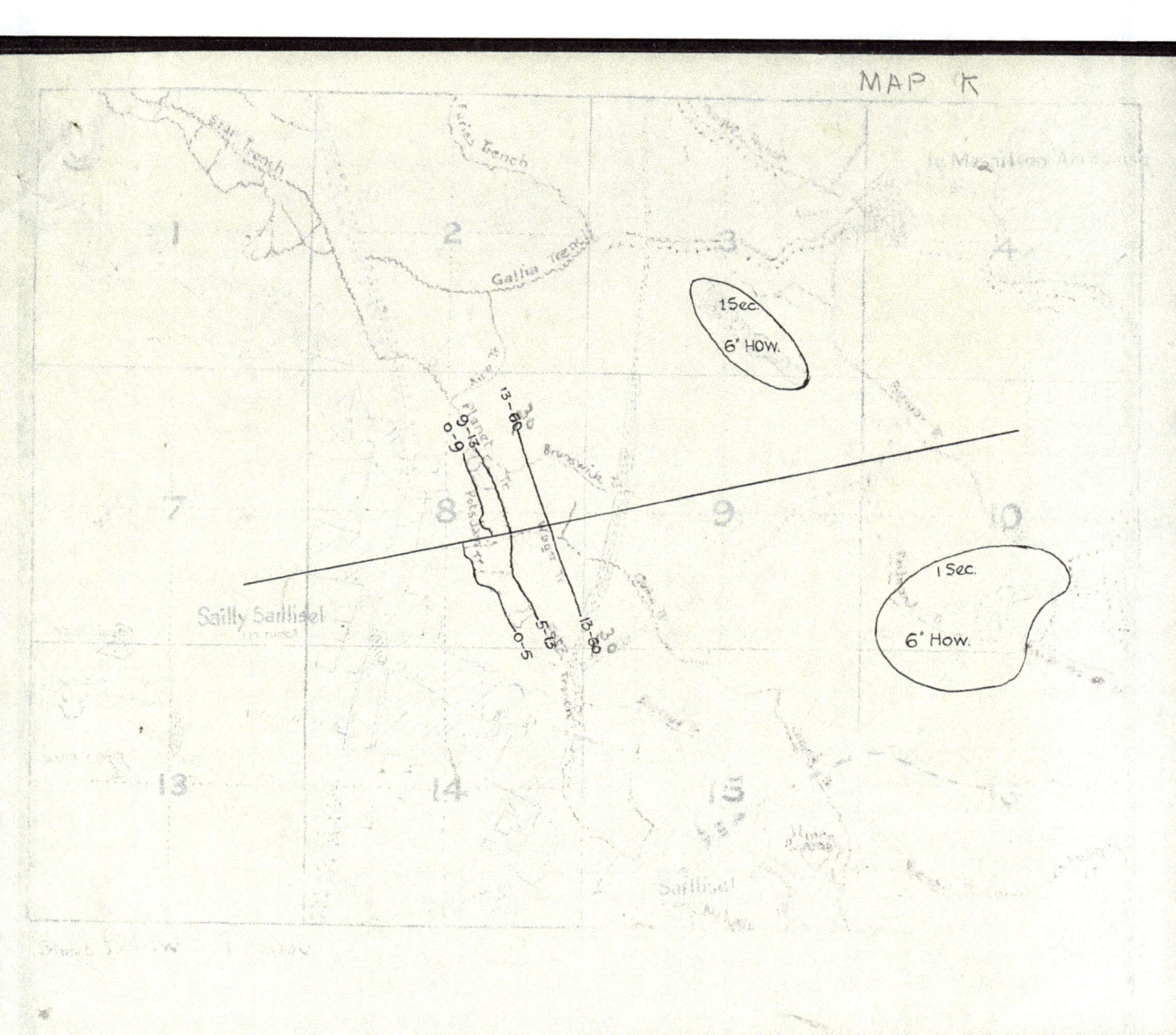

SECRET

Appendix A

Officer commanding N° 2 Section 2/Lt FRIEND
                                  CHEESE SUPPORT TRENCH

Positions of guns

N° 1 at U 8 c 68 50
N° 2 - U 8 c 75 70 } Sec HQ. at U 8 c 73.50
N° 3   U 8 c 78 88
N° 4 - U 8 a 85 10

These guns are dug in for defensive purposes.
The infantry advance at ZERO
At +5 R¹ Bn should be in enemy front line ie POTSDAM TR.
At +9 Left   do   do
At +13 2nd wave of both Bns shd be in 2nd objective
          ie in PLANET TR.

Guns Going Over.

1. At +10. You will have the two guns which are to go over, dismounted & everything got ready for the advance.

   At +15. You will go forward with the 2 guns to the 1st objective ie POTSDAM TR., have your guns mounted & loaded - using auxiliary mounting, while you reconnoitre the trench for gun positions. These guns are to put up bands of fire if required between 1st & 2nd objectives to repel any counter attacks. One of these positions should be about U 8 c 38 giving fire to the right at the other at U 8 d 25 95 (approx) giving fire to the left.

   Use your 2 centre guns for this advance.

   As soon as you have selected positions commence digging at once (7.1 or 1.7 days).

   Inform O.C. Infantry holding POTSDAM TR. what you have done, and get into touch with Advanced Bn H.Q. as soon as possible

Report:-
(1) Your own position re Advced HQ
(2) Positions of guns
(3) Progress
(4) Casualties
(5) Requirements (S.A.A., Stores etc)

to Coy HQ by runner to your old HQ thence by phone to Coy HQ as soon as possible.

As soon as the digging etc is complete go on to 2nd objective & reconnoitre for gun positions there & also alternative positions in 1st objective.

If you consider that more guns can be usefully employed in the captured position you will inform MG HQ but will not move up additional guns without orders from there.

Note (1) In advancing, as ground is very bad use C.T. which passes your Sec HQ, as far as our own front line then over top.

(2) Go over in open order concealing as far as possible what is being carried.

(3) Load table is attached.

2. <u>Guns remaining behind</u>

Before ZERO you will give the following orders to the two gun crews.

(a) They will stand to until the operation is over, in order to repel any counter attack or cover the retirement of our troops should the attack prove a failure.

(b) That if one or both of the advanced guns gets knocked out, they must be prepared, on a written message from you, to advance to replace them.

(c) That they must also be prepared to send up reinforcements to replace casualties on receipt of orders.

3. <u>Section HQ</u>

(a) As you will only take 4 gun Nos, 1 runner & 1 NCO per gun the surplus men will remain in HQ dug out. They will be used as reinforcement carrying parties, etc as wanted.

(b) Your supply of bulk S.A.A. (5000 Rds) will be here also reserve of oil, water for guns & drinking.

(c) Spare belt boxes from evacuated gun pits at N°s 1 & 4 will be brought here & sent up as required to captured line.

(d) Arrangements will be made for belt filling.

LOAD TABLE

Officer carries	1 Belt box
NCO	} Tripod & Oil case
N° 1	} Gun with light mounting
N° 2	} Spare parts box with water to back &
N° 3	2 belt boxes, condenser & tube
N° 4	Pick & shovel & 2 belt boxes
Runner	2 Belt boxes

Total S.A.A. 1750 Rds

(Runner carries on 2nd trip, 1 tin water for gun)

5. <u>Communications</u>
(1) You have an instrument & a trained signaller at your H.Q.
(2) He will keep a copy of all messages received & despatched.

6. All your NCOs, but especially your Sergeants must know as much as you do yourself so that he may be an efficient understudy should you become a casualty. 2 LT CARRUTHERS will be in command of your 2 guns after your advance, in CHEESE SUPPORT.

7. Zero time is 8 am 19/7/17

8. SOS signal is Rocket bursting into 4 blue lights

9. Enlarged scale map is attached.

J.A. Gardner Lt.
Comdg. No. 175 Machine Gun Coy.

SECRET   Appendix B

No 3 Section and four guns under 2nd Lt. WATSON

① Your section will be used exclusively (unless other orders are given you) for barrage work.
② The attached table gives you full details as to time targets etc.
③ You will have a signaller with you who will act as runner when required.
④ S.A.A. 10000 Rds are at Coy H.Q's with party and belt filler to supply your requirements in filled belts.
⑤ Attd is map showing gun positions etc.
⑥ Zero time is 8 a.m. 19/7/17.
⑦ S.O.S. Signal is a rocket bursting into four blue lights.

Comdg. No. 175 Machine Gun Coy.

No. 175 MACHINE GUN COY.
ORDERLY ROOM
Date 18 JUL 1916
MACHINE GUN CORPS

No of Gun	Map ref of Gun	Target	Mag Bearing	Traverse	Range yds	Cont of Gun	Cont of Target	VI	QE	R of F.T yds	Cont F.T	Cont Target	Remarks
1	U.8.c 25/45	U.8.c /46	52°	6°	2200	150	120	33°	271	400'	150	29.7	Zero to Z+13
2	U.8.c 31/90	U.8.c /90	77°	6°	2100	150	130	22	241	400	150	25.2	Rate of fire
3	U.8.c 35/30	63.A 55/2	71°	6°	2000	150	130	22	218	400	150	23	Long bursts until start of Traverse
4	U.8.c 30/24	U.8.d 55/65	65°	6°	200	150	130	22	218	400	150	23	One gun should always be firing
1	As Above	Road U.8.c to U.8.a	84°	—	1700 to 2000	150	125	28	130 to 208	400	150	12.7 / 23	Zero +13
2		Trench U.3.d N200 to N200.51	77°	10°	2150	150	125	25	261	400	150	27.7	onwards
3		Trench U.3.d 12/95	70°	12°	2050	150	130	22	230	400	150	24.7	to Zero +30
4		Wood U.3.c d	67°	16°	1750	150	140	11	168	400	150	17.31	Bursts of 20-30 about time fire 100 M.P.S

Comdg. No. 175 Machine Gun Coy.

SECRET   Appendix 6

Four guns of No 4 Section under 2/Lt. JEFFREYS

① Your section is in Reserve at the front of f O x
   H Q at U13a 70.95

② You must be prepared for either of 3 eventualities
   (a) Advance to such a position that you can assist
       in covering overhead fire.
   (b) Advance to CHEESE SUPPORT TRENCH to
       reinforce line
   (c) Advance through these guns to either
       the 1st or 2nd objectives.

③ You will report to Bde H.Q. and have a runner
   detailed to remain there for any orders.

④ You have with you a trained signaller.
   He will be in direct communication by Phone
   with Company H.Q.

⑤ Keep a reserve of men at your H Q and
   only use 1 N.C.O, the gun numbers and one
   runner per team if ordered to advance.

⑥ If ordered to advance do so by following route
   to Road in U.13.a & along it to U.13.b.0.4 where duck
   walk track crosses it. Follow track across to grounds
   of CHATEAU in U.13.b.9.8 & thence to Coy H Q where
   further orders will be given you.

⑦ Attd is map showing your positions boundaries,
   1st, 2nd objectives etc.

⑧ Zero time is 8 a.m. 19/7/17.

⑨ The S.O.S. signal is a rocket bursting
   into 4 blue lights.

Note ① Take usual Trench supplies of all kinds
   with you
   ② QUARRY in U13a will supply all your
   requirements for R.E. material
                                    J. H. Gardner W.
                              Comdg. No. 175 Machine Gun Coy.

Army Form C. 2118.

WAR DIARY
or
INTELLIGENCE SUMMARY.
(Erase heading not required.)

MG Gardner hut
175th Machine Gun Company
Vol VII

Place	Date	Hour	Summary of Events and Information	Remarks and references to Appendices
O.35.d.	27/7/17	9 a.m.	Divisional Tactical Exercise. For 175th Brigade the exercise was a trench to trench with three objectives. 12 machine guns went over, four to second objective, 8 to first objective, following immediately after the waves of infantry that took the objectives. 4 guns remained on our original front line. Special attention was paid to communications in forward areas, and to organisation. Weather hot. 2 O.R. to M.G. base for course.	J.J. Mack.
O.35.d.	28/7/17		Company training. Tactical scheme. Baths in afternoon. Divisional Race meeting held at FOUR WINDS farm held in afternoon. Weather good. 1.O.R. to Hospital.	J.J. Mack.
O.35.d.	29/7/17		Weather very bad during morning. Voluntary Church Parades. 2 O.R. rejoined from M.G. base school. 1 Off. (2nd Jeffreys) and 1 O.R. returned from course.	J.J. Mack.
O.35.d.	30/7/17		Company training. "Training in Barrage work". C.O's conference at Brigade H.Q. on work in Tactical exercises. Weather fair.	J.J. Mack.
O.35.d.	31/7/17		Company training. Range work with German gun. Weather fair. 1.O.R. returned to duty from gas course. 1.O.R. from hospital. 1.O.A. reported for duty from A.H.T.D.	J.J. Mack.
O.35.d.	1/8/17		Company training. Weather very wet. Divisional T. Exercise postponed. ½ company left at 6 p.m. 1.O.R. rejoined company from leave to U.K. for field firing range, and bivouached on night of 1st 2nd. 1.O.A. to Hospital	J.J. Mack.
O.35.d.	2/8/17		½ company field firing. Remainder company training. Weather very wet. 1.O.R. proceeded on leave to U.K.	J.J. Mack.

Map. Ref. 1/40,000 57 C.

Army Form C. 2118.

WAR DIARY
or
INTELLIGENCE SUMMARY.
(Erase heading not required.)

195th Machine Gun Company.

SHEET 2
VOL. 6.

Place	Date	Hour	Summary of Events and Information	Remarks and references to Appendices
O.35.d.	3/8/17		Company Training. In the afternoon the Divisional T.E. of 27/7/17 was carried out again with only officers present, and their staffs, e.g. runners, signallers. The exercise was a test in communication and the action to be taken when the attack was held up from various trifling causes. A directing staff consisting of the generals in the division informed the attacking troops when these situations arose. 1 O.R. from hospital. 2 O.R. to hospital. Weather dull.	J.J. Mack.
O.35.d.	4/8/17		Company Training. The company was paid out in the afternoon. Weather fair. 1 O.R. to hospital. 2.Lt. W.M. LETHBRIDGE evacuated to U.K. on 24/7/17. (Transport Officer). 1 O.R. rejoined from A.S.C. depot HAVRE.	J.J. Mack.
O.35.d.	5/8/17		Church Parade. A cricket match was played in the evening, first XI versus, and was very successful considering the ground. Weather fine. 1 O.R. to hospital. 3 O.R. to III Army Rest Camp.	J.J. Mack.
O.35.d.	6/8/17		Divisional Tactical Exercise. Company marched to ROEQUIGNY. Company moved from there in the direction of BARASTRE and an then warfare attack was launched from there in the direction of ROEQUIGNY. Division attacked on a two brigade front. 176th Brigade on a third battalion front, with one battalion in reserve at BARASTRÉ. The objective was roughly a line between ROSQUIGNY and LE TRANSLOY. The 178th Brigade the left brigade. The attack was successful but was carried out very much more quickly than had been the case at actual fighting. In the evening a lecture was given to Officers and N.C.Os on the new 'mustard' type of gas, as used at YPRES in July this year, by Div. Gas Officer. 2 O.R. to hospital. 1 O.R. from hospital. 1 O.R. to Divisional gas school 10 R.T. depôt speaking in diff. phase before HAWKE.	J.J. Mack
O.35.d	7/8/17		Company training as usual. Lieut. H.W. DUFFIELD from 206 M.G. Coy joined & assumed Command of the Company. Authority A.G. A.B.1Q. wire 2 O.R.s to HankIV Tupo do rejoined at O.W.S.W. from refresher returned wagon and then 1 O.R. gas school. Forms C.2118/13. to repairs. wagons. dull. By Flores that Style.	D.J.C

WAR DIARY or INTELLIGENCE SUMMARY

Army Form C. 2118.

M.K.Duffield Capt.
175 Machine Gun Company

SHEET 3
VOL 6

Place	Date	Hour	Summary of Events and Information	Remarks and references to Appendices
O.35.d	8/8/17	—	Company training. Camp fatigues. Reparations made for field firing next day. This was stopped on account of heavy torrential rain around actions of Capstan. Lieut DUFFIELD orderly Co. Bde to around actions of Capstan. Weather very wet. T.O.R returned from hospital.	J.F.S.
O.35.d	9/8/17	—	Company training. Field firing put off in letter. Weather. Postponed by Brigade School to at 42 GOVERNMENT FARM. Arranged owning the nuisance of gas flies treated from D.R. Caus. Trucks of hospitals scared & no after training.	J.K.G.
O.35.d	10/8/17	—	Company training. Barrage work in accordance with printed instructions from D.H.Q. H.Q. School at CANIERS carried out. Major BASDEN the acting Sec'd ponied D.H.Q. Co. called to observe barrage, is having with future movements & informed that in our hostility the Company was strictly to avoid thoroughly known by all ranks. Co. was chiefly for barrage fire which he said would absolutely no ammo, & it hardens the need for ammunition fillings for finishing barrage, otherwise the said it would send us various fillings for finishing barrage otherwise the weather dull & cloudy. I.C.R. (Transport Sgt) left on Leave to U.K.	J.K.G.
O.35.d	11/8/17	—	Company on Divisional Tactical Exercise, in trenches between STELLY-SAILLISEL to LE TRANSLOY. Spread over being the Bronze passing through awaiting which has already gained in defences. In the afternoon the 178 Inf. Bde played the Corps at their H.Q. Cricket The 175 M.G. Company was represented by 2/Lt. K.G.JEFFERYS who made 42 not out. Result of match. Corps 13 innings 100 declared. 178 Bde. 14 innings 67 & 2nd innings 79. Bathurn punctua further play. Football 177 Inf.Bde v Chalenya 178 Inf Bgn. This company represented by Co. 2/Lt.HOBSON. The match which was a good one resulted however in the defeat of 178 Bde. by 10-0. Weather fair. Cloudy.	J.K.G.

Rep. France. Sheet 57 d ÷ 40000

Army Form C. 2118.

WAR DIARY
or
INTELLIGENCE SUMMARY.
(Erase heading not required.)

N Fougières Cor
175 Machine Gun Company

SHEET 4
VOL 6

Place	Date	Hour	Summary of Events and Information	Remarks and references to Appendices
O.35.d	12/8/17	—	Church Parade. Washed out by heavy rain. Camp fatigues & afternoon Gun Store promoted & RE's started by the Company on its own. We also being uncertain IOR from Hospital (OR from Duty) Sgt Crown. Going fully footbridge relieved by DAPHNE Pauling & nothing by Coy Enthusiastic Pauling's firing at best two strands thus DAPPS	NFG
O.35.d	13/8/17	—	Company Training Barrage drill. I Gun & 2 Spare Gins to M.Gy Chiffey. Cleaning and Repairs to DADOS. One I and reconnoit our Barrage visits. CO & M.G. Coys Conference at HQ 2nd M.G. Coy received offers of tea but owing to Fac at 8 pm cannot be furnished fixed. QADD M.C. Commanding 2/5 S.F's Gun a heavy fire & actual Return of Raids showing the various points for Consideration, then of Ammunition, numbers required etc received. 2/Lt 197 M.G. Coy to the Company. IV Corps Authority Corps No 15 A.A.A. 9/5/17 I.O.R Transferred from Base but duty with many Showers of Rain Weather V damp	NFG
O.35.d	14/8/17	—	Company Training. Barrage Drill and Packsaddling drill. Preparations for Field Firing the following day. I Gun sent to DADOS to be overhauled and to be sent daily till all guns overhauled. A football match was played in the evening against the D.A.C. and lost by 3-1. The finish was spoilt by heavy rain. L/S J.H. GARDENER left to proceed on leave to U.K. 2.O.R. to Hospital. All No 15 in the Coy made unpaid P/O/Cpl. if not already holding the rank. Reinforcements 3.O.R from Base (N.E.O's).	J.J. Mash
O.35.d	15/8/17	—	The Company moved off at 9.30am for Field Firing. Firing took place in the afternoon; the weather was vagaordly, and dull with heavy showers at intervals of about an hour. Indirect fire was carried out at ranges of 2700x and upwards with very good effect considering the weather. The Coy arrived back in camp about 10 P.M. The Brigade Band gave an excellent selection in our IOR from Base to U.K. camp in the evening	J.J. Mash
O.35.d	16/8/17	—	Company Training. Bombing. Rifle shooting. 1st day of Divisional Boxing competition. Lectures of Field Firing. Weather. Wind & Showers	J.J. Mash

A 5834. Wt. W.4973/M687 750,000 8/16 D. D. & L. Ltd. Forms/C.2118/13.

WAR DIARY or INTELLIGENCE SUMMARY.

Army Form C. 2118.

175th Machine Gun Company

Instructions regarding War Diaries and Intelligence Summaries are contained in F.S. Regs., Part II. and the Staff Manual respectively. Title pages will be prepared in manuscript.

SHEET 5

Place	Date	Hour	Summary of Events and Information	Remarks and references to Appendices
O 35 d.	19/8/17		Coy. training. Physical Training etc. Preparations for Night Attack Rehearsal on night 19/7/18. 2nd. Day of Divisional Boxing. 175 M.G. Coy. wins in two classes @ Stevens FEATHERWEIGHT L/Cpl. Spanton MIDDLEWEIGHTS. The CRUMPS gave a performance in the Quarry in the evening to an enthusiastic audience. Weather fine.	J. Mack.
O 35 d.	16/8/17		Zero hour for night attack was 1 A.M. The guns of this company were divided into three batteries of four guns for barrage fire. The remaining four guns were in reserve. Two batteries were engaged putting up a barrage over the whole front of the infantry attack, (1200x) three hundred yards in front of the artillery barrage and lifting in conformance to it. The third battery was concentrating fire on certain tactical points behind the enemy's front system. 177 Bde. Race Meeting in afternoon.	J.J. Mack. 2 Lt. F[?]WFND on leave to U.K. 2 Lt. ELFICK M.S. and 2.O.R. returned from [?]
O 35 d.	19/8/17		Church Parades. Recreational Training. This Coy. have marked and completed a football ground. In an unter-auction cricket match No 1 beat No 4 A Rugby match was played with Welsh teams proving very popular. 3 O.R. to Third Army Rest Camp and 3 O.R. returned to duty from thus.	J.J. Mack.
O 35 d.	20/8/17		Company Training. A Lecture to officers was given at BARNSTAF on Aeroplane Photographs. Capt. Mumford, the lecturer, intelligence Off. 59th Div. explained very clearly how one could make the best use of these. A Rugby match was again played in the evening.	J.J. Mack.
O 35 d.	21/8/17		Company training. Officers out on reconnaissance for Field Firing. Rugby match v. 7/5 Sherwood Foresters won by 12 pts to 5 pts.	J.J. Mack.

Mt. Ref. 57.C. 40,000

Army Form C. 2118.

WAR DIARY
or
INTELLIGENCE SUMMARY.
(Erase heading not required.)

M.T. Officer Capt.
175th Machine Gun Company

Sheet 6
VOL VI

Place	Date	Hour	Summary of Events and Information	Remarks and references to Appendices
O 35 d	22/8/17	6.00 am	Company moved off for field firing. Digging order; all pack mules and 4 limbers. Took up position as for barrage in at N.W. of VILLERS-PLOS. Advanced over the top with pack animals to RIONCOURT. Advanced again to BEAULEY COURT pulling pony cart. Set up line batteries at S gun good line, practising line for creeping barrage, finishing with firing on allotted targets and S.O.S. The Divisional Commander was extremely pleased with the performance. Reached camp again 6.15 p.m. Fine; Hot. H. NABISIEN [?] EU UK.	Place B
O 35 d	23/8/17	5.0 am	Onwards. Day spent in preparations for a move. Cricket in afternoon — Officers v Other Ranks. Fine, dull, overcast. High Wind. 3 O.R. admitted Hospital.	Place B
O 35 d LOCK	24/8/17	7.25 am	Transport moved off under Brigade Arrangements. Parade starting point DROMORE JUNCTION at 11.25 a.m. and proceeded via SAILLY - COMBLES - GUILLEMONT - MAMETZ - ALBERT to AVELUY, arriving 2.30 p.m.	Place B
AVELUY CABSTAND HUTS W 16 c 6.8		8.0 am	Company moved off and entrained in motor buses at ROCQUINY - LE MESNIL Rd. Motor bus accommodation for half Brigade. Remaining half marched via DROMORE JUNCTION to LE SARS. Coy LE SARS takes longest. Company marched from LE SARS to AVELUY arriving 11.30 p.m. CABSTAND HUTS are the best camps we have yet come to. Ample accommodation available to all ranks, plenty of elbow room. Pals ready for harm lunch, good horse lines, cookhouses, latrines etc. Water not as handy as usual but within a mile distance. Under bivouacs sparsely in habited and under cultivation ALBERT slightly but within a mile distance. Surrounding villages practically undamaged. Fine, High Wind. Sgt. FLOWERDEN from base UK. Bath – 2/7.	Place B
AVELUY	25/8/17	9.30 am	C.O.'s inspection. Balls overhauled; cleaning up after march. Afternoon – recreational training. Fine Cool. High Wind. Steward Forsake at cricket, and also played with action football.	Place B
AVELUY	26/8/17	6.6.30 p.m.	Church Parade, all denominations. Bathing in lake on road ALBERT – AVELUY. Fine, Hot, high wind. 1 O.R. admitted to Hospital.	Place B

Map Reference 57c 1/40,000 + Contoured sheet ALBERT 1/40,000

M.T. Officer Capt.
Comdg. No. 175 Machine Gun Coy.

A5834 Wt. W4973/M687 750,000 8/16 D. D. & L. Ltd. Forms/C.2118/13.

WAR DIARY
or
INTELLIGENCE SUMMARY.
(Erase heading not required.)

Army Form C. 2118.

SHEET 7
VOL VI.

175 Machine Gun Company

Place	Date	Hour	Summary of Events and Information	Remarks and references to Appendices
AVELUY	27.8.17		Company Training. Route March in the Morning. Bathing Parade after Bain in Bois Behind Railway Embkt. TARRET CO5. Men to be taken as a case of drowning has occurred the previous day. Weather Fine God high wind much heavy rain. Lt. J.H. GARDNER 2/Lt returned to Coy from leave to UK 1 O.R. Rifle Reilly from Hospital. 2 O.R.S. Evac'd sick to C.C.S.	JAF
AVELUY	28.8.17		Company Training. Route March. Bathing. Weather. Still very Bad. 2/Lt J.R. WATSON 10R to SURGHUTTA (Bde) on a weeks party to mud arras reported to RTO ALBERT Station at 7:30 am.	JAF
AVELUY	29.8.17		Company Training in forenoon. After noon Coy (S) Suite ready to move as per movement orders received 12p. 1738 2nd Bgde. A.I's No.8 Rec'd 22.8.17 No.46 " 22.8.17 No.47 " 28.8.17 No.48 " 28.8.17 Occurrences 24.8.17 Rec'd 25.8.17 " 27.8.17 " 28.8.17 and also 59th Divisional A.I's No.7 " No.8 " No.9 8.17 and also. AARTO ALBERT Rec'd 28.8.17 This move ordered 8 an error at H.Q. was cancelled at about 10 pm. Weather still being uncertain and	JAF
AVELUY	30.8.17	10.30 PM 10.25 12.0 Midnight	Company & Transport paraded ready to move on to pass starting point at 10.60. Company marched the road to BEAUCOURT for Entraining Company arrived at BEAUCOURT & Commenced Entraining Weather still pretty unfavoured. Moon light helped examinably. 1 O.R. to R.H.Q. Small Arms School. GAMIERS 2 OR's OR TO OCS. Mapp Ry. Combined sheet ALBERT 10000	JMC

HRD Wyllie Capt
OC Combined Sheet

Army Form C. 2118.

WAR DIARY
or
INTELLIGENCE SUMMARY.

(Erase heading not required.)

175 Machine Gun Company

SHEET 8
VOL VI

Place	Date	Hour	Summary of Events and Information	Remarks and references to Appendices
1.12.a 4.7	31.8.17	1.30 am / 3.0 am / 7.0 pm	By this hour all entraining of animals & loading of limbers was completed. Train left BEAUCOURT & travelled via AMIENS, DOULENS, ST POL, MARLES LES MINES, BILLERS HAZEBROUCK to GODEWAERVELDE which was reached at 1.35 p.m. Company transport detrained & moved off at 3.10 p.m. Marched via STEENVOORDE and WINNEZEELE to road junction in C.30.d. then south to point which was reached at 7.0 pm. The march was fairly stiff as the men were 1.12.d.4.7 on a after the journey. Had not slept & were carrying their packs. There resulted some 20 or so falling out on route of these quite half were genuine cases. The 4 section after tea was visited in turn billeting in farm buildings by 1.12.d.4.7. Men in barn O.R. in living room of farm. Fifteen men of the transport & CSM's stores in C.30.d.3.6. Weather much improved. Field was acutely by either side so night passed without the usual at not much service actually by either side so night passed quietly. Securely & sound of guns at the distance some 2 miles from front line.	JAF
I.12.d 47	1.9.17		Company settling into billets. QMS Stone & transport were moved down to the Company HQ. kinsed park in Hoare field & Head lines behind C. fifteen forms billets in farm billets out of & held and at night toutes being dropped on surrounding villages. Weather unchanged. Some EA activity.	JAF
I.12.d 47	2.9.17		Church Parade. C.of E. Voluntary service N. conformist in Transport lines of Company work 2 to 2/8. S.F.3. Some service & usually by enemy at night. Weather unimproved.	JAF
I.12.d 47	3.9.17		Company training. Salvage Guns Reaming. The Chief feature of work performed during the fortnight was leaving. The afternoon was everyone on the farm, making repairs washing etc the various men of company genuine everyone on the farm, making repairs washing etc the firewater E.A. dropping bombs as usual at night but now near the fields. Weather very fine. E.A. dropping bombs as usual at night but now near the fields. It J.T. MACLELLAN returned from leave to O.K. 2 O.R.s to Hos. Paal. 1 O.R. proceded on leave to O.K. 1 O.R. returning to duty from Auto Aircraft Course. NCo. This course was instituted but the N.C.O. Sect was kept busy on salvage work.	JAF

MAP ref. Belgium & France. Sheet 27. Edition 2
40000

Army Form C. 2118.

WAR DIARY
or
INTELLIGENCE SUMMARY.
(Erase heading not required.)

Sheet 9.
Vol VI

175 Machine Gun Company

Place	Date	Hour	Summary of Events and Information	Remarks and references to Appendices
I 12 d 47	4.9.17	—	Company Training. Route March. Respirator Training after dinner. Weather very fine. Sgt No 4 Section got foot on the forward way. Owing to Leeds. 10 Weak being to company D.O.R. Musketry School. 2/Lt E.J. Friend reported for duty from leave to U.K. 10.R to be executed to CCS. Issues returns as following 9 EA.	JHF.
I 12 d 47	5.9.17	—	Company Training. Barrage drill. Precautions Training in the afternoon. ADMS Inspection of animals. Quite satisfactory. 1 OR admitted for treatment 3 OR returned from IV Corps rest camp VALERY-SUR-SOMME. Sgt Pitman returned to duty from hospital. Weather very fine. Str POP. 4 OR to 4 CCS 48 YPRES. 1 OR to 4 OR 100.	JHF.
I 12 d 47	6.9.17	40 am	Heavy bombardment this South of YPRES salient. Afterwards reported the our attack on HAIDU COTT. SOMME & HILL 35 which it was said included capture of GALLIPOLI FARM which lies beyond these N of HILL 35. A fairly heavy thunderstorm was following in the morning.	JHF.
		10 am	Company training was continuing in the morning when Co 2/Lt we see the P.S.H. & Sgt. I see Sgt a Inspecting offr. left to go to Divisional HQ in WINNEZEELE to proceed thence by motor bus to NINE ELMS Camp, N of POPERINGHE to run a Sand model of the XX Corps front. The mode was on a fairly large scale in relief, with trenches filled over roads railways &c. We should arrived there & see names twenty punched astride in treating the great portion of STROUP point. It was obvious that the original Salient had been very much flattened out by the recent offensive and it was clear on our line near an follows. WINNIPEG, HINDU COTT, SOMME, GALLIPOLI (perhaps) on west line of HILL 35 (nothing positive) IBERNIAN BEER HOUSE, our line of BORRY FARM, a BP. WORK. The front was forward of the stream running in the valley S of ST JULIEN RIDGE, on the North and by the ZONNEBEKE Road, reducing in the Centre the Spur containing H14 &35, 4 37. The ground was still flat in a very bad state & fairly wet already. Thunder again in the late afternoon. Summer weather was quite past but wet very heavy beyond rainfall. Small numbers drawn our own transport, were again in use around POPERINGHE. No much E.A. activity. 2/Lt T Maclellan left Company for orders via POPERINGHE to base to enter for Medical Examination by Boards at M.G. Base Camp for their future on obtaining for service in front line System. Pte Chas Jacobs, A.B. for vanish. (was asked not) reported for duty. This was also Sgt PITMAN above had been away on the way & kept him away that & returning him back to duty, were forming equally among this last rightful act of Corps due food as many them. 2 Cpl attached for duty aircraft corner. Transf. (Signal Hartoole about FREZENBERG,) Luke Guard WINNEZEELE & returned Winnezef, MSA. into Belgium afflue SUL 27/8/2/4 cons.	JHF Coff.

WAR DIARY or INTELLIGENCE SUMMARY

Army Form C. 2118.

175 MACHINE GUN COMPANY.

SHEET 10 VOL VII.

Place	Date	Hour	Summary of Events and Information	Remarks and references to Appendices
I.12.d.4.7	7.9.17	—	Company training. Barrage drill and doubtful S.A.A. remounted from belts. Good stuff filled in exchange. Afternoon bathing parade at J.11.G.33. Inspection of transport & A.O.V.S. & D.S.L.O. Brigade Band Contests. Small music in the evening from 6 to 8 p.m. Weather as clear but dull. Used much in early morning. Dusewell sunny. Very hot.	OKG
I.12.d.4.7	8.9.17	—	Company training. Barrage drill & characters. 10.R. G.C. C/8. Weather warm & fine. Morning & Evening mists low visibility.	JKG
I.12.d.4.7	9.9.17	—	Church Parade. Weather unchanged. 2 O.R. (Ptes) to Recuperation at Auxerath Course. 21 Zywcum.	JKG
I.12.d.4.7	10.9.17	—	Company training. Barrage drill. bit filling etc. Becoming above for practice etc.	JKG
I.12.d.4.7	11.9.17	—	Company training weakling Barrage & bit filling drive. Weather very fine. Company band out. Bathing. 2 O.R. returned to duty from Rest Camp. 1 O.R. to Hospital. Known E.A. tooth ache. Nephritis.	JKG
I.12.d.4.7	12.9.17	—	Gas anti-gas training. 10R to S.A. Course. 20 O.R.s returned from M.G. Course. Commandants lecture in P.B. Grampound Contest in Transport field under tife the & limb. Altems turned to secure the best being the Contribution 15th Brigade in Vides. Beans inumbation. Weather & fine.	OKG
I.12.d.4.7	13.9.17	—	Company training. Barrage drill & Gas drill. Company unit at Gas with Cylinders. 35 new Grands & Companies. Before returns to 4 O.R.s. 3 O.R.s to Hospital. Weather v. fine & milder.	JKG
I.12.d.4.7	14.9.17	—	Company training. Park drive. Dry. 27 Officers match as a Bogy Area to Brigade Cup V R.G.A. H.Q. L.T.M. Battery. Park Estd. End Park 100 games. 1 O.R. to Vet. Course at Oaklands. 1 O.R. Evacuated and & Coys Area. 1 O.R. to Hospital. Weather been fine misty morning. Some E.A. activity.	JKG
I.12.d.4.7	15.9.17	—	Company Route March. Park Chemicals taken out on march. 1 O.R. to U.R. or Course. Weather fine.	JKG
I.12.d.4.7	16.9.17	—	Church Parade. Preparation made by Coules Contraction. Qu. Sgt with the then Returning at Conference of Bogie Q.Mtr 11:30. Closing Back ant Quats gaining. Gunfire quest with O: Boles their days out 17 Q.R. (2) Future Operations on the YPRES Front. 1 O.R. Ltd from M G Course 2 O.R. Hospital. 10R Evacuated wt. TOE's. Weather fine.	JKG
I.12.d.4.7	17.9.17	—	Company fatting parade in morning. N°5 3 & 4 Sec. took part in a Fg.d. Fund Day. Being attached temporarily to 24 & 48 S/B. They were employed in going over the top with stretcher & gum weather from Reason. 1 O.R.to E.S. 1 O.R. to Hospital from 24 N.M.T.A.	JKG

Map Ref. BELGIUM & FRANCE Sheet 27. Pts 2 1/40,000

Army Form C. 2118.

WAR DIARY
or
INTELLIGENCE SUMMARY.
(Erase heading not required.)

175 MACHINE GUN COMPANY

SHEET II
VOL VIII

Place	Date	Hour	Summary of Events and Information	Remarks and references to Appendices
I.12.d.4.7	18.9.17	—	Company training. Tactical Exercise near Billet with Offr & N.C.Os in attendance from 10 am to 1 pm. Senior Courses in Barrage fire from selected battery positions, also the taking up of gun positions for anticipating the lanes of an attack of E Company was paid out at 5.0 pm. Rum rats were issued under supervision of an officer today. Weather very fine & warm.	J.A.G.
I.12.d.4.7	19.9.17	—	Major BARDEN lectured to Officers & N.C.Os in the morning on Barrage work, illustrating his remarks by diagrams on our unexposed Black Board. He afterwards had a practice demonstration. Cut points in the work of the Officers after it. Meanwhile the Company uses the P/B road for route march via NORTHEOUT - WIRAHOUT - CASSA road. On unshaven telephones morning at 8.30 that the Company was to be ready to move next morning early. Details orders for the above (B.O. N.2.60) were not issued by 9.45 pm. Officers & Company 8.8.Os were round at 11.30 am to & 6.0 am. The order to march late, and the midnight. Company lent to UK. Weather very fine and hot. No EA activity at night observation. L.13.d.34. 2/Lt Adkins Sent to UK.	J.A.G.
L.13.d 34	20.9.17	6.15am	Company L.1 Billet at I.12.d.4.7. The take was in starting was caused by ours in Bivouacs in Somme area by the Culinary Department & resulted in the Company leaving late at the starting point and during the transport beginning to attack the road & the Company it took some time running in the Company itself through ABEELE. The Company is in DOUDZEELE, WINNEZEELE, STEENVOORDE etc. was waiting until our anxiety & some trouble falling out on the march was in ODDEZEELE, WINNEZEELE, STEENVOORDE etc. The Company is Dickebusch is only the L.S.H. seen after a few kilos before the part of the line as other officers who have previously had been working south. The day had been abord o' hot say had to obtain & room we did not take place. Next day the late outside of a Midday halt. I.m.d. 47 when the Company was in little billet's hut when Buchanan & Buchanan shown the last of these of a Park. Out before here the food taken in the farm we have getting men going with the gun march & accommodation. The horses & the wants few - Clean fully & warm morning.	J.A.G.
L.13.d 3.4.	21.9.17	2.15am	Orders reached us by S.S. General from Camp all officers. This was given in the case of 2/Lt BURNS this morning on his marching up of Camp. He most of the men were in Camp but there were & 4 Kilos from Dickem about the screening officers in which the Company was known, they were various Companies about the screening and after a few loads dropped. L.O.R. Same E.P.S. Jr/64. 1 O.R. (HP/MARSHALL) to UK for communion. 9 O.Rs were allotted the Company to convoying party. 1 & 2 Pack from 26.18. E34. 5.F. & 3 from H.O. & Ten & running strongly at 9.32 am would not find (....) moved & casualties arriving Thursday. The first is in Communication to a French Company in connection with watering, we stated and during the 24 hours march. The first was allowed to many local Companies passed through. The new method in this area has been too much improved. Company played was Gun 60 Sap foot 100 meters to the rear. Officer NE 4 See list HQ in rear. Moved out 10.22.9.17 to connect with cancelled Sheet 27 & 2	J.A.G.

Ref Major Belgium & France Sheet 28 N.W.S: 6.A.
Belgium 1/40,000
20,000

WAR DIARY
or
INTELLIGENCE SUMMARY.
(Erase heading not required.)

Army Form C. 2118.

175 MACHINE GUN COMPANY.

SHEET 12 VOL VIII

Place	Date	Hour	Summary of Events and Information	Remarks and references to Appendices
L.18.d.3.4	22/9/17	—	A certain amount of Company training was done but must work consisted in getting ready to move next day. Orders from Brigade were received at 9.15 pm. This was B.O. N°51 giving instructions to move to 18 Camp in G.6.d.4.4. in BRAND HOEK area also Bde administrative instruction N°1C giving particulars. Later on 4/Bde having one of 69th Div in ?? of change of 592 Bde position N°25 Emplacement this not also 69. Bde instructions then giving medical arrangements. Weather fine but rather showery. Evening night chilly. Sent EA actively. 2 ORs to ?? Hospital	24C.
G.6.d.4.4	23/9/17	3.0 P.M.	Company Transport left Camp in L.18.3.4. & marched via POPERINGHE — BRANDHOEK N°2 area. Quite a difficult experience awaiting good stops. Arrived 7.30 pm. Women huts for all. Good weather. Officers and mens sheds on arriving. Separate Officers & Petrol store made for an early start the next morning. Bivouac section to ?? shown had ?? ?? the same night. Weather fine. No ?? preparations. 10 R admitted to Hospital.	24F
G.6.d.4.4	24/9/17	—	Section paraded early & set off at 7.30 am. N°1 Section under 2/Lt HORSON went to DM90 for Barrage work. N°2 Section under 2/Lt FRIEND sent 3 Guns to 2/5 S.F.s. 1 Gun to 2/17 B. S.F.s. N°3 Section under 2/Lt JEFFREYS sent 3 Guns to 2/8 B.S.F.s at 10.am & the 2/7 B.S.F.s N°4 Section under 2/Lt GARDINER) all Guns to (?) 2/Lt ELDER N°3 S.G. & 2/Lt TALINTYRE N°4 Sec. Transport & carriers - HQ, personnel & all ranks Co. E.S.H went up the line at 8.0 am at B.2.d. HQ at WEILTJE. G.8.a. Roads at B.3.0 am. Main Road Moved assumed by Brunnent booked up and moved to B.de Transport G.6.a. Roads. G.8. S.28 D. main Road Moved remainder on and there. Having no room after a train bombardment at ready to ?? up for Brigade, Brunnent still poorly attended. They also a V being bombarded. Suddenly they might be ?? a ?? but E.A. actively cleaning up. Hugh movement. up the line cleaning up. Keep ducky. 10.B paraded to U.K. 10R ?? B.F.C.S.	1.MF1
H.2.E.62	25.9.17	—	WARRINGTON CAMP Company left at Camp at 3.0 pm. ready but was kept ?? by Ana BRUNDROD. halted was up from ?? Bde. Transport Camp. Gun & food guards but having done the attention for EM at night. No news from the line. Brigade await announced at Poelcapelle ?? Occupied line by the Company. Much making no mention of ??. Gottliners ?? from ?? L Dam. Or return to ?? to duty. Much OA work actively & barrage.	1.JR1.
H.2.E.52	26.9.17	—	This was Zero day for the attack by the 592 Division on our front. Between broughly from the HANEBEEK Stream on the left to the STEENBEEK on the right. N°2 Section ?? ?? opelts settling down. has returned ?? behind throughout the Barrage very great agreed actively in the Barrage where and much to do for cases and tired was ?? ?? ?? ?? N°2 Bde already good. they were busy small in showing all comments known carefully in the morning ?? ?? feels tired. ??? ?? ?? ?? ??? ?? ?? ?? ?? ?? ?? from our ports ?? ?? ?? at ?? ?? slight shelling of contact with A.V. shells Heavy bombardments all day ?? in the ?? 1.OR to Hospital. 1.OR killed to Eliks from Vet. Hospital at ??	1.JR5.

Maps Refs { Belgium & France Sheet 27 Fd. 2. 40.000
                                    28 N.W. & 56A. 2.700
(French & Belgium & France Sheet GRAVENSTAFEL & Belgium & France Sheet 28 7d.3
French Half GRAVENSTAFEL & Belgium & France Sheet 28 7d.3 2000
#3600

Major R.f ??

WAR DIARY or INTELLIGENCE SUMMARY.

Army Form C. 2118.

M94/M/363

175 MACHINE GUN COMPANY Vol IX

Rev Elken 2nd day of O.C.

Sheet I Vol IX

Place	Date	Hour	Summary of Events and Information	Remarks and references to Appendices
H2 c 5.2 and DE LETTE (Railway cutting 5th)	27.9.17 to 29.9.17 (inclusive)	—	Orders Received at 11.0am by O.C. Coy stated at WARMINSTON CAMP pre-selecting 1st LT J.N. GARDNER 2nd LT FLEMING 1st LT 10 Coy Runner to report to Brig Red Hd at WHEETSE dug out. This party left at 7.30pm and on the on arrival a message was received by Adj. travel Guides at JANET Farm. Driver to go to the Guns & an Advance MG Coy to relieve two guns of 2/5 Coy at CLUSTER HOUSES. This was done but enough troops for relief & cover of colours Guides were not available then (Total 5 guns of 175 Coy to the same place CLUSTER HOUSES.)	J.N.G.
			REPORT ON ACTION OF 59th DIVISION ON 26-9-17 & SUBSEQUENT EVENTS TO 29-9-17 (INCLUSIVE)	
			Divisional	
			BOUNDARY on Left. HANEBEEK on South (R.) STEENBEEK R.S on BOUNDARY from GALLIPOLI FARM in an almost straight line to OTTO FARM. The Division attacked on a District Front, 177 Inf Bgd on Right on the right of 178 Inf Bgd on the Left with 175 Inf Bgd (58th Div) on the L of 178 Bgd, the 3rd Division attached on the R of the 59th. The 59th Div relieved the 55th Div which had attacked on 20.9.17 & obtained all their objectives. The 178 Bgd Stachel from a Line Running from SCHULER FARM in the North to GALLIPOLI in the South and were given the line Running through 'TORONTO' 'OTTO FARM'. There was a chorus into the Front parts R.S.T. & o area which were after capture to be consolidated in support of the Battles Responsible. There Battles were 2/6 S.F. on the Right Scorpion R wa. } First Wave. _____ } Second Wave. _____ } 2/7 ____ } 2/5 _____ } Left Right	
			The artillery barrage advanced from 150 yds in front of Jumping off place to the Pine Line, 1st objective at Rate of 100 yds in 4 minutes. To the Red Line (2nd Objective) at Rate of 100 yds in 6 minutes, & after the Red Line to the Blue Line at a rate of 100 x in 8 minutes. It paused at Same Line from +18 to +38 Rest +56 +105 Paused +145 +185 yellow +205	
			Smoke was to be used also, and a barrage of 40 Machine Guns was to be put down on hostile strong points such as FORRED FARM, TORONTO FARM, OTTO FARM, SP LIGHT of from the road made from the Artillery Barrage came down on HANEBEEK VALLEY & Subsequently Right of to BIRDEN'S FARM GUENCHEN RAVENSTAFEL LINES. Barrage blowing points were ahead & then made Such as MARTHA HOUSE Road POTSOI OTTO FARM HERENHOLBE. Machine Guns were also to be put down on BL CHAMBERLAIN ROAD. Three 2 barrage points also to the Farm Battery position on the S.O.S. + Barrage attacks also fired at a Ten hour from additional B Guns.	
			One Section 175 Tanks was ordered but did nothing much owing to the attacked state of the ground still being Visible for this. Most of them were put out of action almost immediately some before they arrived up to go. L.T.M. Batteries were ordered to ENGAGE GALLERIES Troops between them & the Battery.	

A.334. Wt. W4973/M687 750,000 8/16 D.D. & L. Ltd. Forms/C.2118/13.

WAR DIARY or INTELLIGENCE SUMMARY.

Army Form C. 2118.

175. Machine Gun Company

R.W. Elkins 2/Lt for O.C. 6/10/17

Place	Date	Hour	Summary of Events and Information	Remarks and references to Appendices
DELETE witherup Elvert al—	27.9.17 to 29.9.17		1. Guns were distributed as follows on the 24/9/17 — A. N°1 Section 4 Guns under 2/Lt HOBSON & O.M.G.O. for Barrage work. B. N°2 Guns N°s 5, 6 & 8 to 2/5 S.F. under 2/Lt FRIEND. N°s 5 & 6 were to cooperate as should soon N°2 B was to occupy Strong Point N°4 as soon as made at Thebes on Road at D.14.d.3.4. N°2 Section bett 9 to 2/6 S.F. under 2/Lt WATSON. Guns N°s 9 & 12 f/u at the disposal of O.C. 182 for consolidation. Gun 10 & 11 to occupy Strong point N°3 in OEDIPUS at D.14.d.2.9. as soon as made under 2/Lt CARROTHERS. C. N°4 Section Guns N°s 13 & 14 under 2/Lt JEFFERYS f/u at disposal of 2/8 S.F. O.C. to consolidation. K°13 gun in the Strong point N°5 at RIVERSIDE as soon as made. D. N°4 Section Gun N°7 of N°2 Section f/w at disposal of O.C. 2/Lt S.F. to consolidation. Gun N°16 to f/w with Gun N°7 of N°2 Section. — Zero hour was inevitably 24.9.17.	$J#4$
		7/3	Guns moved up by 9 am. & joining their respective pens immediately on the 24.9.17. Replies was no appt. "3" On the same night Guns were received by O.C. Coy. from 9.0.0. 178 Inf. Bgde. & Bellevue 174 Company from holding the line for the night Sp 24.4.9.17 day & 25th.	
		4/5 6	Size guns were thrown Ballistic from Ralphs & sent into the line. All guns resumed their respective pens on the night of the 26.9.17. in accurately positions. The attack was launched at 5.50 am. on Zero day 26.9.17 The subsequent history of the respective guns is as follows —
			N°1 Section. Barrage Guns under 2/Lt HOBSON took up Battery position N-W of HINDU COTT at D.13.a.1.6. before Zero hour & opened fire at Zero, in cooperation with artillery. They did good work in efforts to Barrage & Catalogue shelling throughout the day & Every Galleon. At 4.30 pm the shelling westward became a barrage for, and the guns were relieved. That an having with given to shelter & the Combe Commander. It was for this reason impossible. Before the work their guns during the night but they were pulled back next morning by the D.H.G.O. and carried to CRPS RESERVE TRENCHES for a leaf. The position shown in the machine & getting their guns & gun stores all ready to counter guns attack. Entries & the O.C. Coy. so satisfied hire was and their shelling above defences to E.A. which resulted in the heavy shelling above defences to
			N° 2 SECTION under 2/Lt FRIEND Guns N°5 Sgt COCKBURN Objective overpower OTTO FARM. This gun & a the Road junction W.G. OTTO FARM at D.15.d.0.10. On Zero night owing to the wet drawns of Infantry beast it was couplet to fall back to front line about 240r W.O. OTTO FARM the ballred g/ 175 M.G. Coy on night of 28.9.17.

WAR DIARY or INTELLIGENCE SUMMARY.
Army Form C. 2118.

SHEET 3
Vol. IX

Signed: R. W. Etkin
2/Lt. a/a h.q.
175 Machine Gun Coy B.E.F.

Place	Date	Hour	Summary of Events and Information	Remarks and references to Appendices
DELETE written up ahead of —	27.9.17 to 29.9.17		**6 (Cont'd)** **SECTION No. 2** (Cont'd) **GUN No. 6** under CPL BROWN. Chychien occupied Spur Trench about D.14.a.8.1. Chychien was reached and gun remained there till relieved on night of the 29th. **GUN No. 7** under CPL SEAGAN. At 2.2/LT S.F. Chychien occupied Pill Box at D.14.a.5.4. He reached this but with a badly damaged tripod. Later gun was hit by shrapnel and put out of action. Remainder of team joined No. 8 gun team under Sgt. DENTON-COX. **GUN No. 8** under Sgt. DENTON-COX. Ordered to occupy strong point No. 4. It arrived there but as no strong point was found there, took up position about D.14.a.2.4. and remained there till the night of the 29th. **No. 3 SECTION** under 2/LT WATSON. Guns Nos. 10 & 11 under 2/LT CARROTHERS were detailed for strong point No. 3. This was reached and occupied. But 2/LT CARROTHERS was here wounded, during withdrawal in the evening by the garrison. This strong point was later reorganised and the guns remained until taken out on the night of 27th. **GUN No. 9** CPL SPARKES. Chychien occupied Metres S.E. of DEEPTRENCH. This gun team arrived at MARTHA HOUSE – L/CPL SPARKES being wounded En Route by shrubs. However, taken on by L/CPL STARR and remained in position until the night of the 29th when withdrawn. **GUN No. 12** L/CPL ROBINSON, N. Chychien occupied was FOKKER FARM, Metres south of Road. This gun reached Metres at D.14.a.4.0. and remained there until relieved on night of 27th. **No. 4 SECTION** under 2/LT JEFFERYS. **GUN No. 13** under Sgt RYDEARD & GUN No. 14 under H/Cpl TILLEY. Chychien occupied then Chychien and remained till relieved on night of 29th. TORONTO FARM. These guns reached then Chychien and remained till relieved. **GUN No. 15** under Sgt SPENCER was detailed for strong point No. 5. This was reached and the position taken up at Metres first W. of RIVERSIDE. Sgt SPENCER was wounded on arrival and later both gun & teams were drawn up. Survivors of the team reported to 2/Lt RYDEARD at TORONTO FARM.	J.H.R.

WAR DIARY
or
INTELLIGENCE SUMMARY

Army Form C. 2118.

175 Machine Gun Company

Vol. IX Sheet 4

Place	Date	Hour	Summary of Events and Information	Remarks and references to Appendices
DELETE	27.9.17 to 29.9.17		**Report on Action 26/9/17 Conf d Sub B Coys No 4 Section**	
			Carried Reinf TRENCH at D.14.a.57. The team arrived then with a badly damaged tripod. So the gun was mounted on a corpse. Cpl BAILLIE was killed en route. Flown up by a cloud hit, and the survivors reported to TORONTO FARM on the 27th.	
		Gun No 16	N°Co. Cpl BAILLIE was att to 2/7 S.F. the objective.	
			Guns were relieved by O.E. Coys from 96 & 178 Inf Bgd. & take over on the night flank guns of the M.G. Coys of the division on the eft. 2nd Barrage guns as ordered. All of 2/4 WATSON's gun team under 2/4 ELLIER's, so brought up. The 4 guns went up at the night of the 27th to CLUSTER HOUSES. 2/4 CARLISLE (17 Coy) was 2 guns of 177 M.G. Coy were also sent for the purpose. They arrived first through the dug out of the 215 Coy at CLUSTER HOUSES. This officer appears to have taken a vague idea of the situation, but 2/4 CARLISLE, the officer att to WATSON & ELLIER arriving later, had to swing into position from other to take over that (being a Lewis team) Beauregard down from HOOLES RIDGE, just in front. They Reformed the team at that point. They remained there till relieved on night of 29th.	
			The whole Company was relieved on the night of 29/30 by the 2nd IV 2. M.G. Coy & relieved to VLAMERTINGHE.	
			GENERAL NOTES ON THE ACTION	
			By attaching guns to Battne O supply of Ration water & SAA (Small Arms Ammunition) Ransom team was assured, but this was found that reports for H.Q. Other information necessary for the H.Q. Communication were often held up, with the result that it was late enroute very difficult to maintain.	
			The attack was successful all the objectives being taken, the enemy had no less being OTTO FARM, from which the infantry retired, then leaving the gun team in the position in the air. They arrived a stone fealed.	
			CASUALTIES	
			M.G.S. 1 offices (2/Lt CARROTHERS) wounded. 8 O.R's killed, 25 O.R's wounded (One of these Remained at duty) & 1 missing. Of the Carriers att 9. 7 were wounded & 1 missing.	

WAR DIARY
or
INTELLIGENCE SUMMARY

Army Form C. 2118.

SHEET 5
VOL IX

R.W. Elkin
Lt. 9/24.F. OC
178 Machine Gun Company

Place	Date	Hour	Summary of Events and Information	Remarks and references to Appendices
DELETE battled up abt at the Pics a	27-9-17 to 29-9-17		Of the guns 3 were blown up by shell fire & was brought back to Refund & tripods were badly smashed. 8 left also a number of Belt boxes, Pull 344, Spare parts & small saluts etc. A certain amount of gear was sent to 177 & 174 Companies and distributed was afterwards recovered. The supply of S.A.A. Stores etc. was carried out successfully inspite of drawbacks & difficulties owing to roads & shell fire, and the (2nd) condition of the country. The Company was fortunate in loosing no mules or horses, but up the line, 1 O.R. by E.A. though several were previously lost very heavily. There was a complete absence of information brought down from Bn. at HQ of WIELTSE after 8 relieved Regt. HQ was moved to POND FARM. The supply guns of tripods had spare parts etc. was good. 175 was a all company being award due for the It containing in the Division. On relief the Company with Hd Qtrs. were brought out returning in lorries to WARRINGTON CAMP W. of VLAMERTINGHE and remained there about between 3-5 am The Condition of the men after the extreme heavy shell fire to which he had been exposed for 5 days was naturally a very trying one. but at the same time they were in good spirits were very pleased with the way things had planned out. All ranks had close extremely well and intense confidence was had in the M.G. fire especially that of the barrage frosts which was very effective. The artillery barrage was also 1 Effective & caused much losses to enemy. The number of prisoners taken in this offensive was about 2100 & wounded about 300 were taken by the Division. Two days rations were sent in for immediate Reserves. The following were sent in for immediate Rewards. 2/Lt J.A. HOBSON, Sgts C.F. WHITTLE, F. DENTON-COX & Pte G.W. SMITH. all Officers had food cooks 2/Lts WATSON & JEFFERYS were also noted I Div for keeping it both of the retirement of 176 D.S.O.E Reorganising the line	D.A.G

A5834 Wt. W4973/M687 750,000 8/16 D.D. & L. Ltd Forms/C.2118/13

Army Form C. 2118.

WAR DIARY
or
INTELLIGENCE SUMMARY.
(Erase heading not required.)

SHEET 6
Vol IX

Rw Atkin
24.10.17 for O.C.
178 Machine Gun Coy

Place	Date	Hour	Summary of Events and Information	Remarks and references to Appendices
DELETE with up to that at —	27.9.17 to 29.9.17	—	The following orders for the attack were received:—	
			59th Div. A.I. No 9. d. 22.9.17. Medical arrangements	
			178 I.B.A.I. No 10. d. 22.9.17. Supply & dump arrangements	
			59th D.A.I. No 6. d. 22.9.17. Employment of M.G's in offensive	
			No 10 d. 22.9.17. Police arrangements for stragglers	JAG.
			178 I.B.O.O. No 52. d. 23.9.17. 1st March table	
			178 I.B.A.I. No 11. d. 23.9.17. Details of tracks, provisions etc	
			59th D.A.I. Addendum d. 23.9.17. To A.I. No 9. above	
			178 I.B.A.I. No 52 Addendum d. 23.9.17 Details of strong points to made	
			178 I.B.O. No 6739. d. 25.9.17 Re Relief	
			178 I.B.O. No 53. d. 28.9.17 Re Relief with march table to VLAMINTINGHE	
			178 I.B.O. No 54 d. 28.9.17. To B.O.54	
			178 I.B.O. Addendum d. 29.9.17. Re Stn Buff in 2 spans	
			178 I.B.A.I. No 13 d. 28.9.17 Re Relief & march table to WATOU (cancelled late)	
			178 I.B.A.I. No 14. d. 29.9.17 Re move to BOMY area	
			178 I.B.W.O. No 55 d. 30.9.17 Re move fm VLAMINTINGHE to STEENBECQUE West Train Creek	
			59th D.O. No ? d. 30.9.17 Re 59th D.O. Train Table above	
			178 I.B.A.I. No 15 d. 4.10.17 Re move to BOMY area & bus table	
			178 I.B.A.I. No 16 d. 4.10.17 Re move to BOMY area	
			178 I.B.O. No 56 d. 4.10.17 + addenda N°s 1 & 2 to above	
			Maps up to above are Trench Map. GRAVENSTAFEL. 10000 Ed.1.	
			Belgian France. Sheet 28. Ed. 3. 40000	
			Belgium Sheet 28. N.W. 5d. 6.a 20000	
			(HAZEBROUCK) 5A. Edition 2. 100000	
			Period 27.9.17 — 29.9.17 (inclu)	

WAR DIARY or INTELLIGENCE SUMMARY

Army Form C. 2118.

SHEET 7
VOL IX

175 Machine Gun Company

Place	Date	Hour	Summary of Events and Information	Remarks and references to Appendices
DELETTE worked up while at —	27.9.17 to 29.9.17	—	During this period the following was reported. Transport lines constant bombing by E.A. at night. Some damage done & a good number of animals of other units knocked out. Blankets issued to men of Company. 1 O.R. leave to U.K. N.C.O. course GAMIERS. 1 O.R. R.T.R. leave from M.G. Course GAMIERS.	J.A.F.
WARRINGTON CAMP H.20.c.2.	30.9.17	3-5 am	Company returned from Line. Remainder of day spent in Bathing & filling Respirators. Mass and dress parade on following day. Men greatly in need of sleep.	J.A.F.
Bulls Road Camp, BOESEGHEM 4.F.20.	1.10.17	9.30 pm	Company arrived in this camp. The transport left the camp at H.2.E.5.2 at 7.10 am and moved by road via POPERINGHE, STEENVOORDE, HAZEBROUCK arriving 3.0 pm. Rest of Company packed up & left camp at 12 back on lorries to BRAMIR's & 2 B.S. at VLAMERTINGHE Station. Train left at 2.35 pm arriving STEENBECQUE at 7.15 pm. Whilst in Ypres and around off at 8.0. and asking off two other ranks still sick. 1 O.R. to Hospital with Trench fever and Gut. Party Good settled.	J.A.F.
BOESEGHEM	2.10.17	—	Company resting, cleaning up etc. and arranging Respirators. 1 O.R. & up to Camp Sick. 2 O.Rs severe sick. 1 O.R. from 4.70 R.E. Coy returned to Refine duty after course at Nurses. Bathy. Company paid out in afternoon. Weather good. Some rain.	J.A.F.
BOESEGHEM	3.10.17	—	Some Company training done. Inspection by O.C. Division on third N. St. Church in BOESEGHEM at 3.30 pm. B.E.s drove up & came from Mons. M.G. Coy. Congratulated on recent cleaning & smart appearance. Several ROKER then said a few words about the recent attack High praising the D.S.G. refusing stones they had has now made a name for themselves and must live up to this to reach as much honour. At 6.15 pm went to shown an ARMY BAND which was visiting and in the billets. We then went away & back again. 2 O.R. severely sick in billets.	J.A.F.
BOESEGHEM	4.10.17	—	Company training in morning. Orders returned in evening for move to the Body Training area Company went to culture on Recce & Roads N.T.S. A & B STR S.E. of THEROUANNE. Orders were sent out about securing. These W. to take care about on receipt of first orders sent out by B.U.B. of 6.15 pm. Regt HQ & HQ4.F.2 to first line by Official (10 minutes distance) at 7.10 pm. The rest of Coy & Q. & Bill to march horsed & A, B, C, STR others moving at 7.30 pm furnishing car, 8.2/3.5 men to leave Coy Grounds arriving on to DELETTE Hill. A rest after about 10 p.m. Rifles closely were loaded at 10.45 & 12 mid-night & were fed refitted as circumstances permitted. 2 O.Rs remitted hospital.	J.A.F.
DELETTE	5.10.17	12.30pm	Company having moved as above and to be arrived in village. Village rest and ——— in Transport, which however and Road carried 24 (3.25 am arriving and were billeted down. Different parts of village all about and the Company had started at 7.30 am & reached H.Q. and on 7.30 am & very tired. Good conditions unable for billet and men were tried to performance tasks, journey arriving for 7.10 am. Map Ref. Belgium HAZEBROUCK 5A Ed 2.160.000.	J.A.F.

A.5834 Wt. W.4973/M687 750,000 8/16 D. D. & L. Ltd. Forms/C.2118/13.

WAR DIARY *or* **INTELLIGENCE SUMMARY**

Army Form C. 2118.

Sheet 8

Vol. IX

175 Machine Gun Company

Signed: Rawlkins? 2/Lieut. p. O.C.

Place	Date	Hour	Summary of Events and Information	Remarks and references to Appendices
DELETTE	5/10/17	—	Company training in morning, interfered with by heavy rain in morning. Rebels sent Off. Prov at WANDONNE CHATEAU about 3½ miles distant. 2/5 B.Fs & 1/70 R.E. in the village. Weather unsettled.	O.A.P.
DELETTE	7/10/17	—	Church Parade. 1.O.R. 101 p.m. U.R. Sim. I.O.R. Pte PERRY THOMAS 2/14 fm Hospital & 5.30 pm PERRY THOMAS GUYER reported for duty with 175 M.G. Coy from M.G. Base at 5.30 pm posted to No. 2 Section. No action being necessary.	O.A.P.
DELETTE	8/10/17	—	Weather so bad that no training was possible. 1.O.R. held to-day 2/14 M.JELFICK been to U.K.	O.A.P.
DELETTE	9/10/17	—	Weather still very bad. No orders received to proceed forward. Known on following day that Woodhine BO-67 & ALS 17 Reed	O.A.P.
SACHIN or room No 6, N.W. of SACHIN	10/10/17	5-10pm	Company transport arrived having left DELETTE at 11.0 am. They marched via ERNY ST JULIEN, SUNEN, FLECHIN, FEBVIN- PALFART, FIEFS, SAINS-LES-PERNES. Company marched very well. The distance was about 18 miles. Company billets somewhat scattered. Latter Coords owning to various found this wet with rain. Advance party was 2/Lt JEFFERYS & 2 Sgt. Left behind was a Sgt. BOB to remain in charge of stores which were to be brought up the 13th to the marshal area. In other Coys brought up to day. Hammocks reported at midday. BO 59 rec'd more men they need. Weather was so hot for the most part and through some rain fell at midday troops for the hilly	O.A.P.
SACHIN or Room	11/10/17	—	As above. Company did not get under arms. Read the English orderly but this newsagent reported them to they march to the Chateau of this same. While awaiting others they. The Officer was instructed to bring This ? to the nearest Station to the Chaplain of the Medical ?attention of ? Head ? Sunise was discharged as as if the was a ground-or below. Being for a ground near bolongings to this Charyman holes above came through ? Contain to SAMs billets. So SAMPAM wo before this was a day a few alterations made in the distributions around CANE if any, Kosping had a practising to the airport Report BO N.P. 59 A. M. 7: 14 Reveille at 2.15 am for those not at daily ? 8.50 at 3.00 am Wacky this Bar Reed.	O.A.P.
Coys H.Q. to the W. of Road from G.W. to GOUY	12/10/17	4.10pm	Company arrived having left SACHIN at 8.45am & was fighting at Packs on Coys Route around GOUY-SERVINS. Roods taken were huy hiller roads & LERDES MARDUL VIA PERNES, CAMBLAIN-CHATEAU DIVIO-VNE? Taxest Read to BRUSH-AR-BOIS & ESTREE-CAUTHIE to GOUY SERVINS. Ning was oldhampter in wood Coys was was with the BDE. area Shelter. The weather was fine, but to say they only from ? water. Very bad was Communicated. a mile gos or ? before ? being fed. The night was outreast & had be men were that all was walking. An invoice ? 2/4 FRIEND & Shatting Sgt. got ? to whom Coy in our Camp but food & later found us very had contribution see here. Winds the sit ? won't ? G. 2 & G. 61 = All was Read at 7.30 pm to more most day.	O.A.P.
CARENCY Coys. H.Q. on W. of CARENCY- SOUCHEZ Road NO 3 as JEFFERYS Branch to O.K.	13/10/17	1.15 pm	Company & Transport arrived at CARENCY having left at 11.30 am. Men in huts a few in huts marked to a Chalet. Otps. Km. of Carey Camp way ready for us the training & twenty billmouth afternoon from just a Packboard and ? would by night the look Shorts long with them arrived. Village approach particularly knowable again authorised the ? pice to still in sech man fright the along Sections are Marked in LENS RAVON SECTION, CAMBRIDES 177 MG Coy in same camp 260 a little further East 174 MG. Brin Haverfield in main Bath SA No. 2 relief MG Coy 2/Lt K S JEFFERYS Branch to O.K.	O.A.P.

Map refs/ HAZEBROUCK 5A SH 2 (Belgium) 1:40,000 / LENS II. SH 2 (France) 1:40,000

WAR DIARY or **INTELLIGENCE SUMMARY**

Army Form C. 2118.

SHEET 9 VOL IX

175 Machine Gun Company

Place	Date	Hour	Summary of Events and Information	Remarks and references to Appendices
CARENCY	14.10.17	—	Company cleaning up and getting ready to go into the line in about a weeks time.	RacAtkin
CARENCY	15.10.17	—	Company cleaning & refitting. Work commenced on camp improvements, approved to shelter, road & wash point. Standings for Limbers. 141 OR transferred to 174 M.G. Coy. 2/Lt GARDNER proceeded U.K. on special leave U.K.A.	RacAtkin
CARENCY	16.10.17	—	At work on camp improvements. Company halted in morning. Peak Company 5.30 pm. C.S.M. on leave U.K. 1 O.R. returned from leave. Grand 11 am.	RacAtkin
CARENCY	17.10.17	—	Camp improvements. 6 O.R. to annexes. 2 O.R. to hospital.	RacAtkin
CARENCY	18.10.17	—	Camp improvements.	RacAtkin
CARENCY	19.10.17	—	Final preparation for going into line. 2 O.R. & M.G. Base Carriers. 2 O.R. in annexes.	RacAtkin
CARENCY	Sunday 20.10.17	—	Church parade 10.15 a.m. 1 O.R. returned from hospital. 2/Lt MacLELLAN absent off strength on posting to 165 M.G. Coy.	RacAtkin
CARENCY	21.10.17	—	Camp improvements. Ordered to move transport lines, which proved to be an error.	
CARENCY	22.10.17	4.30 p	Moved Transport lines and Q.M. Stores to new camp at X.17.c.69. Found good standing, well under cover, limit not water standings. Accommodation for men not as good. Owner Hut for O.M. Slain. 2nd Lieut from Base U.K.	RacAtkin
		8.0 p	Relieved 177 M.G. Coy in at sector (AVION sector) Health man early 212. Fair, morning.	
			Company in line Disposition:-	

COMPANY H.Q.	No. 1 Section 2/Lt HODSON	No. 2 Section 2/Lt FRIEND	No. 4 Section 2/Lt TALLENTYRE	No. J Section 2/Lt WATSON
Advanced T.1.d.3.9	Sec HQ. M.36.c.55.20	Sec HQ T.1.d.3.9	Sec HQ T.2.6.20.85	Sec HQ T.2.6.20.85
Ration Dump T.1.d.8.9	Gun 1 N.25.c.75.10 ONTARIO	Gun 5 N.31.d.3.1	Gun 9 T.2.6.20.70	Gun 13 T.3.a.45.00
Rear X.16.c.9.5	2 N.31.a.65.90 GROUP	6 N.31.a.4.2 ABSENT	10 T.2.6.55.55 BEAVER	14 T.3.a.2.2 APIBLE
Transport X.17.c.6.7	3 N.31.d.3.9	7 T.1.c.25.55 GROUP	11 T.2.a.35.30 GROUP	15 T.2.d.4.6 GROUP
	4 M.36.a.39.75	8 S.6.b.55.55	12 T.2.a.5.2	16 T.2.d.7.6
	Dump N.31.a.3.3	Dump T.1.d.8.9	Dump T.1.d.8.9	Dump T.2.d.2.9

| | | 2.30 p | 2/Lt ELIPPER proceeded to line to take over No. 3 Section. Maxim gun maintained on important targets during night. Rained intermittently all day. | |

MAP REFERENCE 1/10,000 Sheets 36c SW3 and 36 b

J Gd Atkin Lt Col for O.C. 175 Machine Gun Company

Army Form C. 2118.

WAR DIARY
or
INTELLIGENCE SUMMARY.
(Erase heading not required.)

175th Machine Gun Company

SHEET 10   VOL. IX

Instructions regarding War Diaries and Intelligence Summaries are contained in F.S. Regs., Part II. and the Staff Manual respectively. Title pages will be prepared in manuscript.

Place	Date	Hour	Summary of Events and Information	Remarks and references to Appendices
CARENCY	24.10.17	4 p.m.	Moved to area of camp, made details etc., 5 X 17 c 6.7 on urgent order from Bde. Found no accommodation except by arrangement with C.B. of 6 neighbouring camp vacated by so, was not taken over by anybody. Men were finished in rain, and accommodation had to be extemporised under three tarpaulins. The distance seemed about 1000 yds. Sent up ration to WB section 8 CYRIL TRENCH and LENS ARRAS road as VICTORIA ROAD was being heavily bombarded with 5.9 cm.	(Rab)
X 17 c 6.7		11 p.m	Company in line informing teacher and emplacements during day. Much work is necessary as the junction CM chiefly in disused tastes, and improvements unless carefully camouflaged would expose the guns to aerial observation in daylight. There are chiefly tracks which every must cross in approaching LENS. Ground road during night in great length. 4 O.R. from Corps Drivers d. Gas School. 2/Lt. WATSON came again to draw HQ. G. pressed a beam U.K. Weather fine, cold ceased during night, rain."	(Rab)
CARENCY X 17 c 6.7	25.10.17	11 p.m.	Heavy intermittent Shew fire maintained by M.G. up to zero hour (1 p.m.), rate increased to S.O.S. speed during heating of Gas Projectors on Gun target slow fire allow fire maintained for rest of night. 22,000 rds. fired in all. 2/Lt. WATSON proceeded leave UK. Rained heavily all day. Spirit lantern used up with gun tools, oil, etc.	(Rab)
CARENCY	26.10.17		Heavy rain during day. Sealed off to observers at night with intermittent bright moonlight. Usual harassing fire maintained during night. 1 OR. posted to 32 M.G. Coy. 1 OR. to hospital.	

MAP REFERENCE 1/20,000 36c S.W. and 1/10,000 36c.

R. Elkin
2nd Lt. 9/4
for O.C. 175 M.G. Coy.

WAR DIARY or INTELLIGENCE SUMMARY

Army Form C. 2118.

175th Machine Gun Company

SHEET 1 VOL X

Place	Date	Hour	Summary of Events and Information	Remarks and references to Appendices
CARENCY	27-10-17		7 turn. draft Clothes and camp improvements. Weather showery. Reconnoitred Bde. Works camp but found no accommodation. Began to harness new limbers. 1 plane seen in enemy lines. Harnessing for during night on Targets N21a 85.55, c 97.44 55., v 8.7 27.69.15, v 8.2. 27d 35.75 v 78.33 & 38. 24b 21.6 - 13,500 rds. Enemy artillery active in canal battery N.H.Q. Sec. called with 16.30 a.m. 11.30 p.m. 16 rds at LA COULOTTE - 15 of these blind. Fine, cold.	Paid
CARENCY	28-10-17 SUNDAY		Entrained & moved to Bde. Works Camp (Transport & R.A.) No arrangement had been made for accommodation. Paraded unless any one this is detailed to look over Pers. (unbr) (Bde) at 1 p.m. Tents, camouflage and 40,000 rds S.A.A. with ration. 1 O.R. to hospital. 5 O.R. to arrive A.A. firing 2 O.R. armed H.A. firing. 2 2nd Lt. Jefferys retired for the Gun U.K. Harassing fire during night 10,750 rds. on targets N21d, 27 D v C, 33 & v 34r. Artillery & aerial activity normal.	Paid
CARENCY	29-10-17	4.30 p.m.	Moved 4 lorries to Bde. Camp in accordance with D.A.I. III. Two small rooms allotted for details etc. Therefore returned with men. Q.M. Stores details and orderly room & repair quarters in M.4. rest camp across the road. Weather fine. An artillery ammunition machine torpedoed behind the Drocourt Bethn. trench, damaged. Weather fine, very cold. 9mm 2nd Lt TAYLENTYRE proceeded to artillery course. Artillery & aerial activity normal. 1 O.R. to hospital. NYDN. Harassing fire 13,000 rds on wood back and TH B55.85. 1800 rds fired on targets covering.	Red
CARENCY	30-10-17		Obtained material from Div. R.E. dump LENS SIDING, to construct a building for 32 O.R. at transport lines Collected material for cook house at same place. Went up ration in evening very cold, secured all information, lines for convoy day might firing by all sections. 11,000 rds. 1 O.R. proceeded U.K. leave. S.M. returned from leave U.K.	Paid
CARENCY	31-10-17		Proceeded to erect cook house at Transport Lines. Detach cleaning limbers. Commenced work on new hut for transport personnel. Throwing Fine, 12 goo rds. 1 O.R. hospital accidentally injured. Fine & cold.	Red
CARENCY	1-11-17		Carrying on with new hut & hut for 32 transport personnel. Erected 16 beds latrines & urinal in new camp. Maj Genl ROMER G.O.C. Division inspected horse lines. 5 Bde and accommodation. Artillery active fine Mag.4 engaged targets at N33482, N21a 7555. N21C, N33b3UB. 19670 rds. 10.30 p.m. F.A. engaged during day but 107/pay firing 9350 rds Gun Aeroplanes seen active, Our plane was seen to crash in enemy lines.	Red
CARENCY	2-11-17	6 p.m.	Quilting new hutment. Drew material from R.E. dump for Limber, door & windows. Gardiscred apr pay on payslips. During discharge at 6 Q.M.S. (at rear) on N.33b, v.N.27a, afterwards wording to target on N.21 v N.27. 19,100 rounds. O Artillery active as usual. E battery very quiet 2 dfs by an anti-aircraft. Mist & rain, cold. Lest when correct for on alternative emplacements changing + camouflage.	Red
CARENCY	3-10-17	6 a.m. 10 p.m.	Continued construction of new camp. Aerial activity nil. Artillery enemy quiet. Enemy normal. 3 guns TALENTYRE for Artillery Course. Enemy discharged gas shells at Chap Cabin. Effect were purely local and no casualties resulted. Heard heavy rapid fire on N 21, V.37, N 34c. Round fired 21,000 to hospital. Very warm February. Cold. Improvement in communications camping 2- O.R. ex casualties, return. 3- O.R. from R.A. Course. 1. O.R. returned from U.K. leave. Map Reference 1/20,000 36 c S.W.	Red

Army Form C. 2118.

WAR DIARY
or
INTELLIGENCE SUMMARY.

(Erase heading not required.)

MG cover sheet
174th Machine Gun Company

Sheet 2
Vol. X

Instructions regarding War Diaries and Intelligence Summaries are contained in F.S. Regs., Part II. and the Staff Manual respectively. Title pages will be prepared in manuscript.

Place	Date	Hour	Summary of Events and Information	Remarks and references to Appendices
CARENCY	4.10.17		Drew and sent off 21,000 rds. S.A.A. went to new camp nr Lorbern. Muddy, fine, cold. Little or no artillery or aerial activity on either side owing to exhaustion by four visibility. Manoeuvring for at night by M.G. on hedge leading to LENS in N.21.c.x.d. and N.27.a.d. Note. Down information received from prisoner it is known that Mine Kecks are used by enemy at night to examine surfaces. Rounds fired 21,000	Ref
CARENCY	5.10.17		Continued work on new camp not Lorbern. Muddy, fine, cold. Camp and country drying up well. C.O. came down from line & proceeded to CAMIERS, advanced course. Sent up 160,000 rds. S.A.A. ret. returns. Artillery and aerial activity again below normal owing to the prevailing fog, alternative emplacements & camouflage. Fired 18,000 rds during night W on selected length pst in Lorbern.— Recorded in counter-belt enemy accident to CAMIERS Shrapnel ttl. 25,000 rounds pst.	Ref
CARENCY	6.10.17	2.30	Proceeded nr hut at Rest 28 transport Personnel. Muddy, fine. Artillery and aerial activity again. C.O. and 2 O.R. proceeded to CAMIERS for course. 176th R) Bde relieved 178th Inf. Bde on right sector. Less machine gun companies. Manoeuvring night post by enemy opp trenches. 14,000 rds. Rets. rounds pst. for 150 rds. (Capt. H.M. DUFFIELD and 1 O.R. to course CAMIERS. 1 O.R. (sergeant) to CAMIERS. 1 O.R. transferred from 174 M.G. Coy.)	Ref
CARENCY	7.10.17	9 pm	Allotted 7 G.S. Wagons & draw line bags for Lorbern standing. Marched Q.M. Stores & rooms — Transport lines vacated by transport personnel on completion of new huts. Heavy rain. 2/Lt WATSON returned from leave U.K. Company relieved by 174 M.G. Coy. 9a came to Rest Bn (distance brought forward not in Lorbern. Rain during the morning delayed progress of relieving company. In enemy the detachment, yet offensive very slight, Company returned to M.G. and camp. CARENCY X/16.2.3. On their arrival buses remained in station grounds at Jn GARDNER reached to duty for Camp U.K. Orders received to reassemble immediately Red & Blue lines and approaches in Division of SOLES, and so for Rest in Hill 70 work — seen to reinforce the line in the event of an enemy attack on that Hill, and as a normal for example detached Coast reconnaissance led recorded routes & activity & tracks lines and concentration of troops. A foreman composed the and started the objective to be HILL 70. No one activity reported in the Hill Bn. day	Ref
CARENCY	8.10.17		Company on rest. Cleaning up. L/Cpl GARDNER reconnoitered RED LINES are what Divisional Front with DM.S.O. 2 Officers reconnoitered RED & BLUE lines and approaches in LIEVIN sector, and 4 Officers reconnoitered RED LINE in right sector. Rain. There was a good deal of aerial activity in the early part of the day. 4 enemy E.A. were were when 2 cars our planes. Lots on fire from shot of one E.O. latter on the ground it charge and destroyed it. 6 Artillery regarded a positive barrage exceptionally right acts. I.O.R. to hospital. Fine, cold, showery. Map Reference 50,000 36 c S.W.	Ref
	11 mn			

A5834 Wt.W4973/M687 750,000 8/16 D.D.&L.Ltd. Forms/C.2118/13.

Instructions regarding War Diaries and Intelligence Summaries are contained in F.S. Regs., Part II. and the Staff Manual respectively. Title pages will be prepared in manuscript.

Army Form C. 2118.

WAR DIARY
or
INTELLIGENCE SUMMARY.
(Erase heading not required.)

J.W.G. Carr - Lieut.
173rd Machine Gun Company

Sheet 3 Vol X

Place	Date	Hour	Summary of Events and Information	Remarks and references to Appendices
CARENCY	9-11-17	8 a.m.	Company falling in to see. Musketry lectures under Section Officers, cleaning and refitting.	Ref 3
		9 a.m.	Lt. GARDINER reconnoitred PARTRIDGE TRENCH and other parts of DAWSON track for M.G. sites in RED LINE defence scheme. A certain number of advantageous emplacements are available for M.Gs. in this line. Heavy rain mixed with bright intervals.	
CARENCY	10-11-17	4.10 p.m.	Drew 10,000 S.A.A. ammunition. Drew motored and paraded limber landing. Section Officers went up to RED LINE night recce. Improved manned and camouflaged M.G. positions installed. 7,000 rounds S.A.A. at each position. Very fine early, later heavy rain. 1 O.R. to hospital.	Ref 6
CARENCY	11-11-17		Company making Church Parades 11 o.c.a - at 6.30 p.m. Cos 1/2.1.c & CHATEAU DE LA HAYE to attend High Mass. General Salve, Brigadier following a Leale for, the number of CO's to Corps Gas School Coupigny ta course. 1 O.R. to hospital. Fine, occasional showers. 2nd Lt. WATSON and 1 O.R.	Ref 5
CARENCY	12-11-17		Company training 2 p.m. Ceremonial parade at CHATEAU DE LA HAYE. G.O.C. Division presented ribbon of decoration won in the battle of YPRES 25th Sept 1917. Military Medal. Sgt WHITTLE & Denton Cox - Military Medal. 3rd Lieut. VA 140 ASSON - Military Cross. 200 M.F. range; 300 M.F. Cy at Range Practice. Fine, bright, warm.	Ref 5
			2-11 reconnoitred MARQUEFFLES FARM M.G. range.	
CARENCY	13-11-17	8.0 a.m.	Company proceeded to MARQUEFFLES FARM for range practice. Fired six practices with good result, including barrage. Competing barrage and box barrage fire. Returned 5:30 p.m. Stack pickup and cleaning limbers and filling belts. Preparatory to move. Fine, windy. 2 O.R. returned to duty from Hospital.	Ref 5
DUISANS	14-11-17	8.45 a.m.	Company arrived at MG from CARENCY and proceeded SOUCHEZ - MAROEUIL - ETRUN - DUISANS, 10½ Kilometres. Company in CAMP E LOUVRE; transport lines DUISANS. Motor lorry attached for G.M. Stores to Dimbeck. Fine. Brigade at ETRUN.	Ref 6
DUISANS	15-11-17		Company training. Cleaned limbers, overhauled gun stores, and filled belts after range firing on 13/4. Fine, cold. 1 O.R. proceeded U.K. - Leave	Ref 2
DUISANS	16-11-17		Complete instruction by Co. by addition of personnel, guns and gun stores. 2 O.R. to Bde. bombers signalling course. 1 O.R. to Grantham to instructor's course. Recreational Training. Fine, cold.	Ref 3
DUISANS	17-11-17		Company having Recreational trips-off. Fine, cold. 1 O.R. from leave U.K. 2/Lt WATSON from Gas Course and 1 Oth rank. 1/3 O.R. from course. 1 O.R. to A.A. firing course.	Ref 3
DUISANS SUNDAY	18-11-17		Church parade and inspection of camp. Fine, cold. Inspection & transport personnel @ Transport 3 O.G. Coy.	Ref 5

Map Reference Lens 11, 44,170 — 36c & 51c

Army Form C. 2118.

M. Gunner Unit
173 = Machine Gun Company

WAR DIARY
or
INTELLIGENCE SUMMARY.
(Erase heading not required.)

SHEET 4
VOL X

Instructions regarding War Diaries and Intelligence Summaries are contained in F.S. Regs., Part II. and the Staff Manual respectively. Title pages will be prepared in manuscript.

Place	Date	Hour	Summary of Events and Information	Remarks and references to Appendices
BUSANS	19/11/17		Company packing limbers and preparing to move off. DRO's conduction research to machine of warfare. Photo of HAVRINCOURT and CAMBRAI centre received. Moved off 4.30 p.m. and proceeded via WAGNON LIEU - BROMONT - BLAIREVILLE - HENDECOURT. Camp to times checking, but otherwise a successful night march. Arrived 8.30 p.m. Lorry of Q.M. Stores failed to report. 2 O.R. from signalling course	Recd
HENDECOURT	20/11/17		Company training. C.O.'s conference. Officers and N.C.O.'s. Open fighting, pursuing a loader the even unknown grand map reconnaissance of ground round CAMBRAI. Learnt that a successful attack had been completed with HAVRINCOURT - HINDENBURG LINE carried, 5000 prisoners taken and everything going on well. Paid Company 2 O.R. from course. 9.30 11 FRIEND Special leave U.K. Rain.	Recd
HENDECOURT	21/11/17	8.30 p.m.	A day of conflicting orders. March later for march out and embussing to two different destinations received. Rain. Formed dump of officers kits, blankets, packs, and surplus Q.M. and gun stores at N°2 camp BLAIREVILLE. Proceed starting of M.T. of HENDICOURT (cross roads) and proceeded via ADINFER - AYETTE. Bde. column with transport.	Recd
GOMIECOURT	22/11/17	1.0 a.m. 10.0 a.m.	Arrived GOMIECOURT. Camp of canvas and huts C.O. with Bde party reconnoitring area of recent advance at HAVRINCOURT and FLESQUIERES. Lethal area. Captured at MARCOING, MASNIERES, NOYELLES, CANTAING + FONTAINE-NOTRE-DAME. 8000 prisoners + 21 guns. Company under short notice to move. Fine. Cold.	Recd
GOMIECOURT	23/11/17	1.20 p.m. 1.37 p.m.	Transport moved off with 2° Echelon of Bde Transport via BAPAUME - ROCQUIGNY. Company marched S.A. x roads N.W. of church at GOMIECOURT. Entrained 2.57 p.m. ACHIET LE GRAND. Detrained at FINS and arrived billets in EQUANCOURT 5.45 p.m. Transport arrived 8.30 p.m. Fine. Cold.	Recd
EQUANCOURT	24/11/17		Company training C.O. with 2 officers reconnoitred ground behind MARCOING - MASNIERES line. Henry gun fire on left flank of advance. Salvable map above BOURLON wood which had formed a recent salient. Captured. Cold. Strong W. wind. Rain during night.	Recd
EQUANCOURT	25/11/17		Church parade. Paid Company. CAPT. MCINSPEN B/Major) took over command of Company on arrival from U.K. CAPT. H.W. DUFFIELD relinquishes command and proceeds U.K. on course at CAMIERS. Fine, Cold, High W. wind.	Recd

WAR DIARY or INTELLIGENCE SUMMARY

Army Form C. 2118.

175 M.G. Coy.

Sheet 1 VOL XI

Place	Date	Hour	Summary of Events and Information	Remarks and references to Appendices
EQUANCOURT	26/11/17		Company Training. Coy under short notice to move. Cold fine. Situation doubtful	P.a.B
EQUANCOURT	27/11/17		Company Training. 2.Lt. HOBSON & JEFFERIES reconnoitred night flank of CAMBRAI salient. Cold fine.	P.a.B
EQUANCOURT	28/11/17		Company Training. Prepared to move to Reserve line FLESQUIERES – RIBECOURT. 2.Lt. HOBSON reconnoitred progress & route and toward BOURLON & FONTAINE. CO to conference at Bde. Coy conference later. Situation obscure.	P.a.B
EQUANCOURT / TRESCAULT	29/11/17	5a.m.	Adv. party sent to take over M.G. camp near TRESCAULT from 96s. Coy. Coy moved off at 1.15 p.m. as a fighting unit to FINS GOUZEAUCOURT. Settled in to new camp about 6.0 p.m. Bgr. HQ just dug out at RIENCOURT. Coy spread over children in 6 Bristol gaul live. Roads in a very filthy state. Transport stayed with Coy.	P.a.B
TRESCAULT	30/11/17	11.a.m.	Improved shelters and mounted A.A. & A.T. guns. Bristles schan in BOURLONS Wood finit. Situation quiet but obscure. Resent that Barry Difle is being fought in BOURLON WOOD. Red attacked with numbers - coy preparing to follow at once. Attacks against GONNELIEU & LA VACQUERIE, Gonnelieu & ridge and capturing GOUZEAUCOURT. Our division practically lost and all communication broken. Thousands prisoners, guns destroyed by gunners and abandoned. Section 14 2 moved to portion SE of RIBECOURT in HIGHLAND RIDGE. 3 & 4 to FLESQUIERES. Guards Division who had just been relieved counter attacked at once from EQUANCOURT, supported by cavalry. Counter attack successful machine guns few flanks assisting for large mural. of enemy thrown back as original line with shelter of GONNELIEU & LA VACQUERIE. 470 F.R.E. Coy were one of the first units in both areas to form a defensive line and start to repel the attack. 5 Enemy planes raided SE of our HQ by dawn in TRESCAULT. NW & NE of FLESQUIERES, and 2 Coy in HIGHLAND RIDGE. Transport led to 1 Coy in portion TRESCAULT. Counter attack. CO w/ Bde. RIBECOURT. Surface obscure. QM at EQUANCOURT.	P.a.B
RIBECOURT	1/12/17		Artillery exchange – regained at dawn. Germans attacked E. of GOUZEAUCOURT and repulsed. R & m 4-Q shelled in evening. Ras Hqs and Transport (now limbering) moved to Q G central approx. HAVRINCOURT WOOD. Further further salt action. Fine Cold.	P.a.B
RIBECOURT	2/12/17		Orders received for 1 & 2 sections to release 200 Coy in sectors of FLESQUIERES at daybreak & reconnaissance. Were hit by shell in vicinity CO. 2.Lts HOBSON & WATSON proceeded to reconnoitre. Were hit by a shell in RIBECOURT. R.I.h-Q 2nd Lt. HOBSON instantly & severely CO. Capt. INGRAM, and 2.Lt. WATSON. 2 Lt. Letter died of wounds shortly afterwards. Lt. GAFFORER took charge, and the relief of 200 Co. was effected by midnight. Fine Q.m.	P.a.B

Army Form C. 2118.

M Mason M
F Mason M
175th Machine Gun Company

Sheet 2
Vol XI

WAR DIARY
or
INTELLIGENCE SUMMARY.
(Erase heading not required.)

Instructions regarding War Diaries and Intelligence Summaries are contained in F.S. Regs., Part II. and the Staff Manual respectively. Title pages will be prepared in manuscript.

Place	Date	Hour	Summary of Events and Information	Remarks and references to Appendices
FLESQUIERES	3/12/17		Coy H.Q. at L.19 a.1.1. Reard H.Q. at TRESCAULT. Day generally quiet. Some bombardment in direction of BOURLON WOOD. 2 O.R. FRIEND & 1 O.R. from line Coy. U.K. Shelled enemy. British aeroplane passengers wolad	(RcJ)
FLESQUIERES	4/12/17		Preparing position in and around FLESQUIERES. Learnt that we should be relieved on night 5/6/12 by 200 M.G. Coy. Worked all night & 5th constructing a series of new posts around N. side of FLESQUIERES and in stack of cottages, all in orders to support the line coy. during day. Relief will take place from ABERLON WOOD - MARCOING line during night. Learnt 2/Lt S.F. on outpost-line along the road GRAINCOURT - FLESQUIERES. Relieved without difficulty. Fine Cold.	(RcJ)
FLESQUIERES	5/12/17	6 p.m	Enemy constantly bombarded CAMBRAI & MARCOING and attacked out between what had been considered by us a Relief by 200 M.G. Coy. not heavy. Coy. has seen towards enemy barraging N. of BOURLON WOOD. 3 O.R. slight & 1 O.R. MISSING.	(RcJ)
		4 p.m	77 Coy. arrived also holding position near FLESQUIERES.	
TRESCAULT	6/12/17		Coy H.Q. TRESCAULT. 1 Section attached Coys in N.A. roads near BA.Llours. 2 & 3 got British front line in its HINDENBURG LINE. Some near front lines up. Day quiet. Learned that M.G. not working had opened up left flank later on. 1 O.R. from enemy CARRIERS. Enemy advancing across open from le FLESQUIERES. Drew bivies to bill lodges to 200 cy.	(RcJ)
TRESCAULT	7/12/17		Improving billets and trenches in TRESCAULT. Bn. booked briefly at 3.0 p.m.	(RcJ)
TRESCAULT	8/12/17	4.30 p.m	Company Transport Carts arrived at 4.0 p.m. at the time that Boys came to relieve 177 M.G Coy. Coy. Q.M. recovered position returned indented. Packed limbers. Moved off from TRESCAULT about 9 p.m. and returned under great difficulties, owing to & darkness and bad condition of tracks. Lt C.E GRADWELL & Lt P.FERRIS refunded to duty. 1 O.R. Loint U.K.	(RcJ)
FLESQUIERES	9/12/17		Outpost line well dug and trenches, and dumies holding a line in front of FLESQUIRES. Enough to outputs already set up has practically returned to original hand on the walls of enemy at 1077 in wide different from post of line. Coy. Arrived as under 1, 2 & 4 Sections in line. 3 section in reserve. 2 Coy H.Q. 200 Cy. Soldiers Post huts.	(RcJ)

H.Q. Lt. GARDNER 2nd Lt GREENING	1 SECTION Lt. C.E GRADWELL 2nd Lt. VALENTINE	2 SECTION 2nd Lt. FRIEND	3 SECTION Lt. MOELNIK	4 SECTION Lt. P. FERRIS 2nd Lt. HAWKER
K 29 d 05.20	SEC. H.Q. L.19 a 2.3	SEC. H.Q. L.19 a 2.3	SEC. H.Q. K 29 d 05.20	SEC. HQ K 18 c 15.56
DUMP AT K 24 b 6.8	No. 5 gun K 24 b 9.1	No. 1 gun K 12 b 7.3	No. 1 gun K 29 d 26.20	No. 9 GUN K 24 a 3.6
TRANSPORT & PACKS TRAIN	6 gun K 24 b 6.8	2 gun L.13 c 10.05	2 gun K 29 d 07.20	10 gun K 24 a 00.65
Co. 14 c	7 gun K 24 b 1517	3 gun L.19 a 35.45	3 gun K 29 d 06.20	11 gun K 18 c 05.57
2/Lt. SILVER	8 gun K 24 a 25.43	4 gun K 24 b 9.3	4 gun K 29 d 09.20	12 gun K 18 b 15.70

* Isolated and attached K 200 Coy. 2 O.R. killed, 4 other ranks wounded. 1 shell fire at dondona, and at Rosefort Lane. 34.7 x 8 guns used for night firing. Rear front broken and trenches very muddy.

MAP REFERENCE
MARCOING 1/10,000
57 c   1/20,000

WAR DIARY or INTELLIGENCE SUMMARY
(Erase heading not required.)

Army Form C. 2118.

Aylwin M.G. 175th Machine Gun Company

SHEET 3 VOL VI

Place	Date	Hour	Summary of Events and Information	Remarks and references to Appendices
FLESQUIERES	10/10/17	9.30 a.m	Company in this Neighbourhood of GOUZEAUCOURT during 15 previous days. 9 enemy planes flew over front line. Flew low and slowly from my lines from MARCOING and towards HAVRINCOURT WOOD. AA. guns did not engage. All they were able in way back and out of range. The relative position of the day was observed activity on enemy front. 5 Balloons went up and filmed flew over FLESQUIERES & GRAND RAVINE all day. At 4.0 P.M. 3 to 6 our fighting planes engaged a large number and a C/H1 six machine flew away in front of FLESQUIERES. Heavy M.G. & rifle fire was observed. Many shells burst red as shown for T.R. burnings in down. Two planes crashed. T.R. 24c.d and burst into flames. Two pilots both wounded picked up on ground and were taken prisoners. Enemy's own artillery normal. A Sec. HQ apparently knocked out during day. Harassing fire by 24k.9. & 2 guns, following targets throughout night — 13,000 rds. Sunken Rd. K.2.9.c. White & valley in L.7a. and square L.7a. South of K.12.6. Constructed howitzer gun. Note. H.Q. to be mounted by transport for No 4 Section. Transport had been mounted and installed for 1 mile. 1 or 2 lorries still short. L. Half a Sec. has been advanced to 175th M.G. Coy.	RueB
FLESQUIERES	11/10/17	5-P.M. 7.30 P.M.	A quiet day. Wireless low. Aerial activity nil. Improving positions and trenches. Coy Commander and reserve Officers busy reconnoitring HINDENBURG SUPPORT & FRONT LINE & OLD British FRONT LINE, with a view to installed along defence scheme for village of FLESQUIERES. Gun activity full down, a shrapnel barrage on DARWIN VALLEY in reply to S.O.S. (K.28.a. & K.24.b.) L.19.a. 2 or light 1 fm higher. Harassing fire during night. 16,500 rds fired on targets.	RueE
FLESQUIERES	12/10/17		Very fine bright day again mounted by E aerial activity. Bombing, photography and reconnaissance accurately. Four aeroplanes with little or no opposition on our part. 9 E observation balloon up back of our artillery which in marched in GRAND RAVINE. 1 D Balloon put up by us at about 8 a.m. and brought down by E.A. 2/10.30. Put up another one late and down off enemy attempt to bring it down by A.A. fire. Enemy shelled on valleys in GRAND RAVINE with E.A. shell. Also an oil and front line of Brown on right. Our artillery normal. At 11.0 a.m. a dump was seen to go up S.W. of GRANCOURT 400 yds a fire SSE of BOURLON WOOD. 3,00 rds fired on E.A. during day. 1 man to crack in Two Tree was a result of our fire. 2 or Sm direct. On a result of continued shelling. A Sec. HQ moved to K.23.b.29. 9va 11 & 12 guns silenced guns of 17a Cap. at K.17.d.2.2 and K.17.d.3.2. Some harassing fire on enemy moving at K.12.6. during day by machine gun of 2 Section. 300 rds. Night firing 12,000 rds on K.12.6, L.7a., L.7c., L.7d. roads and for crack wire 5 LLL h.s and front.	RueB

MAP REFERENCE MARCOING 57C 57C 200 76.200

WAR DIARY or INTELLIGENCE SUMMARY

Army Form C. 2118.

Autumn/Light
175th Machine Gun Company

SHEET 4
VOL XI

Place	Date	Hour	Summary of Events and Information	Remarks and references to Appendices
FLESQUIERES	13-12-17	8.0 a.m.	Practice barrage fired by our artillery. Damp with mist. Low visibility. Situation normal & quiet. Naval bomb improvements, and change of position No 2 from L19a.05.20 to L19a.25.82, & 9v10 to K23c.95.65. 11.v.12 manoeuvred 9 v 10 & 9 v 10 November 11 v 12. Concealed defenders:— **Coy H.Q.** Lt A. Hale Lt W. Gardner 2nd Lt Mar Enkin — K29d.05.20 Coy Dump — K24b.65.20 Transport — 2nd Lt Guyer — Q1w *IN RESERVE 	No 1 SECTION	LT.CB. GADWELL 2/L TALINTYRE No 2 SECTION	SEC H.Q L19 a 2.3	2/L FRIEND L19 a 2.3	SEC H.Q K29d.05.20	No 3 SECTION ANTI-AIRCRAFT	L.T.P. FURNISS No 4 SECTION SEC H.Q K29d.01.80	L.T.SK. JEFFERY K23 b 2.9 | Very quiet. Enemy quiet. Retaliated & own practice barrage by shelling FLESQUIERES from 9.30 a.m. to 10.10 a.m. The period is now been a concentrated shoot on GRAINCOURT. Harassing fire during night. Rds fired 16,500 on targets in K12.b, L7b, L16, L17b, L8a, and NW corner of ORIVAL WOOD.	Place A
FLESQUIERES	14-12-17	11.0 p.m.	Cold, damp. Aerial activity not satisfying below normal. 1 EM.g. afforded control in L12.d. Patrol down to enemy barrage (shelling) on G foot line in front of BEETROOT FACTORY. 2/L Stafford worked an enemy post. 4 casualties. No Forward action. Oil can by 11.25 pm enemy station unoccupied. Harassing fire in Gun N.E. of ORIVAL WOOD and targets as L1.d, L7b, L8a. 25,000 rds.	Place B
FLESQUIERES	15-12-17		Very fine January day but some aerial activity otherwise quiet day with nothing to report. Usual night firing carried out on about same targets as previous day. Casualties N.E. 1 O.R. from O.R. 2 O.R. Except my 10 R. from Hopkins	747
FLESQUIERES	16-12-17		Quite day nothing to report. Working parties. Orders for the relay of the Company were received. By the relief 177 Coy & to go to base to O.P. camp at TRESCAULT with view to employment being so as to contain allied continuing where necessary the old A.A. tire with a view to securing of Head-d-Red. Night firing as normal. Night rather dark but still on ground & day being maintained. Casualties — Nil.	747
MG.GAMP TRESCAULT	17-12-17	8.30 p	Companies in FLESQUIERES support conference. Relieved without incident by 177 Coy who took over 179 in Grand Ravin Relay Cinnplin. All ranks in new camp quitted by 11.30 pm. Night firing over as before from having carried passed by not one of our C/m. Coy was unable to hand over Lewis Guns (6 D) Relief made by 3/4 on ground. 177 Coy were unable to effectively change their Lewis for the 24 hours, they who handed over to 175 when returning. Sick. 1 O.R. to hospital.	747

Map ref. MARCOING 1/2000
20-000

WAR DIARY or INTELLIGENCE SUMMARY

Army Form C. 2118.

(Erase heading not required.)

Instructions regarding War Diaries and Intelligence Summaries are contained in F.S. Regs., Part II. and the Staff Manual respectively. Title pages will be prepared in manuscript.

SHEET 5
VOL XI

Army Form C. 2118.

17.5 Machine Gun Company

Place	Date	Hour	Summary of Events and Information	Remarks and references to Appendices
TRESEAULT M.G. Camp	18.12.17		Company billeted in dugouts & shelters in Camp, also in A.F. huts nearby. H.Q. at TRESEAULT. Shelling & B. Coy Transport in HAVRINCOURT WOOD 09.h.70. B Coy relieved TPOETS this march and moved to O.B.F hut K.32.c as owing to 47th Div on left coming under orders of 36th Div. H.Q. The camp was out of Brigade Area. New huts was allocated 22½ feet long & 7.6 sharp pl. arrangements were made. Remainder was granted. Said was ready and after some trouble traps at TRESEAULT & our own huts were built. 12h/12h & drones & Timbers 12 remain in Camp at TRESEAULT to wait for arrivals. Enough selection Bay said Guns GRAND RAVINE (Wind field) sent on his return. 5.95 w 2.5. During having their 3 to 7 pm selecting for our batteries. Some E.A. shells a little touching. Very heard MG Wind feed NY Wind hard fuse.	J.A.F.
O.B.F hut K.32.c	19.12.17	10 am	Company (less Transport & Advance Party (Army)) reached new location. There was at one commenced on unpacking & erecting shelters, making huts, also clearing OTP Room, also living Room, etc. Also the huts shelter a Cook house were constructed. The men really so a working to keeping shelters. All the dugout there dark. Others had out room in a dug out & delivery to keeping shelters. All the dugout in the parts of time there was quite a little. Before & Ambulance at P.T. As above Company 19th the evening at reporting some going there shelters of GRAND RAVINE at HAVRINCOURT VILLAGE during the day. A few amount of E.A. shelling. This was however much better than our A.P. on the hill & the firing was noticed during Ob. Observed. South Coy having been built first nearly hit. fely been firm. E.A. shelled out trench on which Coy was working during. The shellers slightly dashing out. Batteries of observer were in course of constructions when ordered to relieve by 513 M.G. Coy. Result falls at night.	M.G.
O.B.F hut K.32.c	20.12.17	2.30 am	Orders Received. Eaily in the morning, orders who carried out. Preparation postponed was received but to late again to attain as deported. Time was having late. All arrangements were complete. Before time and Company stood by waiting for relieving Company to arrive.	J.A.F.
			Our guns & crews went to TRANSPORT lines at 2.30 & orders by 513 at 3 am	
		3.0 pm	No.5 M.G. arm limber took over Pack Over Traulen & Horses to draw the Relief Supplies. & 3.30 when 513 Coy move off 56 to Transport lines. Here there are limits again. A were brought a rearender off horse parked. O Company left at 6. 45 pm. Transport arrived at training camp at 6.30 pm.	
	5.45 pm		Remd Rec. Road thro' HAMELTZ, NEUVILLE, YPRES + BUS to BARASTRE M.G. Camp. K.2.d. Pocket Suffering Road: Sp. much weather cold & dust in truck. The journey was completed without incident in spite of the snow was behind nebir down in trenches. Company was turn served in 6 times hut, a hut & hut. Transport arrived at. the weather was very bad all day, had frost or Ice (for permanent Army, Reservation further than 20 yrs untrue yard. The day was healthy being just Ice. Shelling occasionally visited for a Division. Reinforcements from base, 1 MSO. 9. OR0.	

Major cmdg MARCOING FORCE
17/c
2000

A5834 Wt. W4973/M687 750,000 8/16 D.D.&L. Ltd. Forms/C.2118/13.

WAR DIARY
or
INTELLIGENCE SUMMARY.

Army Form C. 2118.

April 1917 —
115 Machine Gun Company

SHEET 6
VOL XI

Place	Date	Hour	Summary of Events and Information	Remarks and references to Appendices
BARASTRE A 16 a 82	21/12/17	—	Company at rest. Orders for next move to Achieu received giving march tables to BEAULENCOURT. Next day also instructions to hand surplus stores into the Brigade salvage dump for final distribution in HOVIN area. All surplus stores today with two men left in charge at EQUANCOURT. Men brought to Stamps dump. This included all the officers valises so that officers got a welcome change after 24 days without a change of clothing. G.O.C. Bgde. inspected camp in afternoon. We walk being extra muddy almost impossible through good orderly condition of the horses forage head fuel attn N. wind. 10R to Hospital. 10R fm Hospital.	9 A 8
BOUSAT ATTILZY BEAULENCOURT N 18 a 72	22.12.17	1.35 pm 3.30 pm	Company packed up Struck camp so as to leave starting point at 1.3 pm 01 5a 36 in Q.R. March Column. Coy. was second Coy. by (114 M.G. Coy. absorbed) after its Coy. Arriving absorbed two 3/6 oF 15 Coys supplies stores 2/C crews each men (left BARASTRE for LE BOURY at 10AM) Company marched via VILLERS AU FLOS to Coy pay. Coy arrived in new camp (all Nissen huts) play was made at H.Q. Weather keep dry but fine half fast. Snow still in places, huts being used. Some E.A. at night dropping bombs.	9 A 9
BEAULENCOURT	23.12.17		SUNDAY = No Church Parades. Coy. Resting + cleaning up. This was in an O.R. himself had arrival refits Enemy thing have furze very bad Day very fine Cut intensely cold wind. M.E. Some EA bombarded night steamy sheet. Two officer funnels were taken from HQ area to BAPAUME but returned in same condition 10 R since took 10R since to BES.	9 A 9
BEAULENCOURT	24.12.17	7 am	Transport bus + fighting Limber (Containing 6 guns 6 tripods + other necessary stores) to the cart troubles sent out camp bivouaced under BSTO via BAPAUME + BIHUCOURT + TORIET LE GRAND + ACHIET LE PETIT Gun teams to new area field of camp arriving at HQ HABARCQ by 4 pm sound some huts tour per a/settle etc. V arrival train to road work to horse ambulance (all surrounded to French huts). Coy as appointed three was done away with @ HABARCQ by ground superbien. During the night many E.A. were about dropping bombs. Coy was caught in Light Army kitchen where it was till 7am. R. Caney missing + horses bombed gunnery luring 2 horses was heard buffy our guns. Location on across Wingham. Night was heavy and windy. Saw half dieu in afternoon + evening lost wet temperature kept low at the calm stamping to 5 W used night. Conjecture of sentry Grass to Hospital 10R.	9 A 5
HONEHEAUX B 25 c 50	25/12/17	5.30 am 8.15 am	CHRISTMAS DAY: Spent by the Company in hard work. Mucking & Spring by a Fire Every Coy. Churches team Reveille. 7 am. Coy. marched out of camp at BEAUENCOURT to BAPAUME RY Station to entrain for party between camp arriving on their dept. 2/11 ELFFE to help Coy. entrain at Ry. Stn. Kits + Stores were put in trucks + men entrained on train. March from 57e 40000 Lens 11 e. 70000 8 e. 51 e. 70000	9 A 9

WAR DIARY
or
INTELLIGENCE SUMMARY.

Army Form C. 2118.

Alfred Muhi
175 Machine Gun Company

SHEET 7.
VOL XI

Place	Date	Hour	Summary of Events and Information	Remarks and references to Appendices
MONCHEAUX B.25 C.50	25.12.17	10.10 am	(cont.d) The Coy entrained via ARRAS & ST POL to PETIT HOUVIN which was reached at 4.0 pm. Unloading was rather difficult owing to darkness & lack of platforms, but was finished at 6.30 pm. The Company led by Lieut. DIX arrived in the safe marching to BONEVILLE RIVER. March Discipline throughout was good, there being very little straggling, although their boots were in about an 1½" contour line composed of Brussels Rations & mud as well as their own bright new hob-nails. No ill will (taken up on 118 Lt.T.M. Battery HQ) much speaking took place from BONEVILLE, there being hardly any lying down which was easy for the Cheering Groups very quiet after the difficult road restful hand today. The price that in S.A. rare ??? ang HENETZE GRAND. At BAPTONE and the as mentioned at one 3 places was immediately brought down at FINS. The front ?? through being carried in the scrap heap in the lorry was that according a Baris at gift that was ?? to PLESQUIS to take the Baggage down by ORW & NOOD. Then arrived the ?? was reported for Stopped loading up on the day to 5.0 wish	JAF
MONCHEAUX B.25 @ 50	26.12.17		Spent Coy cleaning up equipment. Settled in press very wet weather showing any slushy 2nd wind. Preparation made for holding Christmas dinner on 27th inst. Rumour current from Brig. 1 of R (??)	JAF

Map Refer LENS. 11 1/20,000
Sheet 51 C(Pts) 1/40,000

Army Form C. 2118.

WAR DIARY
or
INTELLIGENCE SUMMARY.
(Erase heading not required.)

Army Form C. 2118.

175 Machine Gun Company.

Vol. 12

Sheet 1

Place	Date	Hour	Summary of Events and Information	Remarks and references to Appendices
MONCHEAUX B25 c50	27/12/17	—	This day was observed as Christmas day by the whole Company. Parade was sounded at 1.30 pm & consisted of Roll Call. Whole Battalion assembled & then dismissed. Christmas pudding (mince), & there were also beer, cigarettes & nuts & pieces for tea. The meals seemed to be appreciated by all & everything went off without incident. The men thoroughly enjoyed themselves when it was booked & prepared most of the just so food & it would otherwise have been. Some very fine shooting & singing took place but there were bright spells. Both worked at divine and service conducted at 10 am in spite of rest of hustle fine for both sections.	(App)
MONCHEAUX B25 c50	28/12/17		Company continued clearing up & reorganising. Spms Snow Lowry Good. Free Kerr & Scott Culverty. 1 OR (a/sgt) to Bruax in UK. 2 ORs read to Hospital. 3 ORs (Corpls) to 5.4.S army cyclist Res.	(App)
MONCHEAUX B25 c50	29/12/17		Company were on Fatigue Parade are moving at HOUVIN where we left water & clean clothes (much needed) were supplied. The Coy: 2nd Lieutenant missed their run there, but this time was 19 at the type & was a conference of COs at BSSe HQ at 12.30pm to discuss a scheme for tomorrow. Had day of 3/12/17 usual authentic & first wood coughs Cavalry keep finding amongst for running some great captures happened. Reinforcement of two G/POR backs also split not all last. Mens N being tried were 1 OR returns to duty from leave to base. 1 OR to Hospital.	(App)
MONCHEAUX C25 c50	30/12/17		Church Parade at Houvin before which a Communion service was held. After service the Cards of Commendation to those of B'gs. who had been remembered for their gallant behaviour. Gen. Coy was 33 583 89 Pre SMITH G.W. for gallant conduct during the Reinforcement at YPRES on SEPT 26th. & subsequent days. The scheme was fired but the whole event continued. Bleuvrie at YPRES returning to duty the Hospital.	(App)
MONCHEAUX B25 c50	31/12/17		Last day of 1917. Company having completed its programme. Programme. The Bearer, TA & other flemenburg wire CO 2/Lt. 9 sergeants & 30 runners were out & carried out below Scheme under TOE direction in the quick walking of old Boche break through on a circular front & & advance to BOE supposed to have been rushed. Advanced up in attacking team. The artillery & Cavalry Counter attack by a B.G.C. Supposed to have been launched. Coy was split up into 8 Barrage guns under 2nd Lieut one per Battalion Ballabey, when one attacked the evening returning & a Communion took carried out about the end. The rifle was "Pull z try 5, 8 Stop. The barrage guns had to carry loaded fires on a front (vacate 2000 yds) & on shoulder outside up to 3000 one & fire. Conclusions who fell known them on finding Pvms that the was on tips for nil as an exercise of the 1st Communion. This was 2 RFLMEB was forming all day it was moderate, but washing. Church Service at 10am & a pm. Camp Imurand Guard. The synaltius to rum were keenly had a 9 about 11.0 pm advance Sergeant Gratting to Pay guns were removed from 1714 FUS. Cap abd 5.30pm the Company 2 lumar left for BOUVAL to relieve & Signed to Arcin. Coy paid out at 2.30 pm	(App)

END OF YEAR 1917

MGT Nº 51 E/20000

WAR DIARY or INTELLIGENCE SUMMARY

Army Form C. 2118.

175 Coubeny Machine Gun Corps

SHEET 2 VOL 12

Place	Date	Hour	Summary of Events and Information	Remarks and references to Appendices
MONCHEAUX B25 c 50	1/1/18	12.3 am	New Years Eve. 1.O.R Rgr. wishing Company good luck & good success in year 1918. Both transmitted message was received from g.o.c Division. Company training as per programme in Musketry work. Nothing extraordinary. Being first day but being cold still wind still in the N. some bright spells. Nothing apparent so along front (South West). Raining doubtless told him! Great Boulevard life at peace apparently.	1/1/2
MONCHEAUX B25 c 50	2/1/18		Company training. Nothing further. Fairfoot weather set in. Much warmer. Bright Parade about 10 P.M. 1 O.R to Hospital for toothache.	1/1/2
MONCHEAUX B25 c 50	3/1/18		Company had Baths & Change Clothing during the course of the morning. After Resuming during Rose's Wing put up. Being the Giving of day from stars during moving rather more clear. sky had first feeling of night, colder during, Gunnery & Ordnance for cleaning arms put in to area. 1 O.R to hospital 1 O.R to Rest.Camp. 12 O.Rs for duties.	1/1/2
MONCHEAUX B25 c 50	4/1/18		Company training. Conference at 9.30 H.R. Coys Commanders. Lieutenant Plaza in West 15 S.E. in Course of 6 miles miles to test speed at which one could m. across country. 1st completed in 63 minutes. After spending the course given by three scrubbed & stooped at day Coy Targets. Bare Corps B, C, D sections. Carried parade given. Coy 10s. 0's acquaints. Bay Coy & target of service 1 O.R returning for the Hospital.	2/1/7
MONCHEAUX B25 c 50	5/1/18		Company training. Nothing to report. 1/4 of the day (Saturday) at 3.7 ¼/18 Zone. ordinates Hampson's 11/1 Bey. The Bourns much in the above in motoring. Picking up the advance is no information on warning. Stop, the deparking 36 hours after the arrival Brookwood took to work Brigade Boy. are at been half but in evening Kerb history of Sgt. 9 O.Rs to MT Mg coy. 3 O.Rs to Hospital.	2/1/7
MONCHEAUX B25 c 50	6/1/18		Sunday Church Parade C O. E. & R.C. Cons. Nouun Pacifie S.R. at Teeb fan. in Church 9.05 am: afterwards Regimental Parade Resuming from 10 am till 12.30 pm. Signed man SARS ESCROIS & REMIER Addey in applying a request from the Cribean (general) life drawing of off on the B/n. When where Regtl; have put offered und the attack. The beginning of the ground showed how inadequate was the apparatus, and had he seen to together. See the ground when accumulate. During week in to Room on nation. Any hay his act wars each feels off held was charged to cash. to Hospital case being abroad. Kind of: 2nd it. R.A. Peakins, 1 OR proceeded to UK on 6 days branching train. Will Return aboard. Lease on 10 Zehn Gerald. Chipjern in Nomeoy Roaded to Letterson. They are frown how branching to Western hand back dress drop in wind with 1st LG. [?]	2/1/7
MONCHEAUX B25 c 50	7/1/18	-	Company Training. Nothing to report. Weather Changed completely and a Sharp thaw setting. Old Cornet from about 7.30 PM. to 8 am til Sunday been water to blow water much foot to house throw bombed out which will. Low Bombings. Lookout after midnight signs appeared of a foreign change wound in raining appeared instantly. 1 OR Keyword by from 7.0.R. hospital. to M.T.I.S. Coy burying. 10 sup. A/40/07/30. Map refs SHEET 51 C. Ponsoo Frame.	2/1/7

A 5834 Wt. W4973/M687 750,000 8/16 D. D. & L. Ltd. Forms/C.2118/13

WAR DIARY or INTELLIGENCE SUMMARY

Army Form C. 2118.

(Erase heading not required.)

Aylwyth hill
17th MACHINE GUN COMPANY

SHEET 3
For 1.12

Place	Date	Hour	Summary of Events and Information	Remarks and references to Appendices
MONCHEAUX B25C50	8.1.18		Snow fell heavily from about 8.45 am & continued till about 10.30 am. Snow lay on the ground. The Coy were out patrolling and training and 2 Pl were day firing for the date issue. Weather hard frost followed by snow. I.O.R. for Hosp.	24.9
MONCHEAUX B25C50	9.1.18		Day fine at start. Coys at Run lost place of a equipment men on Cadburys Butts & shacked & checked in the 2/2 & 7/5 S. Marching Coys old then to the M.G.G.n. Coy was a european on main duty Machine. Shooting at a practising Coy cured Fullers. Maj the Coy Lieut Houvin, MAGNICOURT, Coy ENTERPRIS to the MONTHEAUX Percentage of hits fining better on the sat action was taken. Coy ENTERPRIS MONTS ENTERPRIS percentage work on the Present with 5 to have a hit & 6 have been for man to Once a certain percent. Run was in compulsory though working hard being trained in places at the mens below. Once Training so that after the eye's fix'd be until men were called troops & all mens men they separated count Company for the 6 men was superior, 60 minutes which was added to the to complete Emolument and to keep a fall of snow 4 inches. Snow was at 11 mm as made TMB on 8.1.18 on a 14.3. 17.5 M.F.C. did a good turn out a 11.4.1. 4 ORs were out at Junk 7 of men being shut out by grounds Ong Left aid, table of brown freed at in 8:30 manch Coy a half about 1.0 pm Coupled foined heavily. This Condeners for about 6 pm - thenceforth weather Coy of topic Colman. Then I had write this rest in about 8. This Contained all mught. 5-13 wound going strong	24.9
MONCHEAUX B25C50	10.1.18		Day continues the thaw & hulks on previous night. Company training in the morning. Coys relieved Enterprise also Range practice on shot Range Post 1 Relief Affordd Officers Lost as Strand had gone 2 Rifle B.M.O. Govs N. Goo'vin the 12 practising MG Coys musselsdierine on part of MG Coy to the men. I the very part Coy tried to be Repeat practice foot ball cliniffind 4 2/1 S/s landed in difficult and Southam had been drawing lectures on TMB by 7 Hd men was finished & Rifles for the husband on Even in Morning she much improvers equipment. No details up to about 9 hours had yet to knusten Coye were in the Morning leaving the Coys the Stood up. 2 or OR's were at the Redoubt. There Pacific going with Reposaugumps of Corps Security Coys who meant being against 8 0 gun at Brigade of Offer from a Batt. of first Troops under a Colonel. Officers were on the log forced to be offered signs Although they may have been Corporals above and at first signs of shaking up Covid be attached turned & that dry covered under as a gruel at skirm	24.9
MONCHEAUX B25C50	11.1.18		Company Training Continued to By All Run Patrolling. The Coy Cay Sams logged O'R's are as well in Confirmation at at this under purchased the support proved out that Such effective differentiations were lengths in binding. Many training of inland transport & successful were here in leading Room in the evening here the Continued all day. Much off the snow from roads still dead. IOR leave to U.K. 10R to hospital	24.9
MONCHEAUX B25C50	12.1.18		Company had tasks in Bowling during the morning afternoon Trashing officer torpoint Weather bitter Colder. Frost set in about 10 pm. Major Johnson reported for ducks from Base Apps 1 gun sent to DADOs for repairs being inspired by returning. These were all second line Colour orders on 4/1/18 Artificer Remand reported that teaching A Sgt & ag was Dont & Rifle for all will have gun to the Company gun could not be repaired sec 15th 3 men from duplicate	24.9

MAP. REFS. FRANCE SHEET 51C

WAR DIARY or INTELLIGENCE SUMMARY

Army Form C. 2118.

175 MACHINE GUN COMPANY

SHEET 4
VOL 12

Place	Date	Hour	Summary of Events and Information	Remarks and references to Appendices
MONCHEAUX B25 C 50	13.1.18	—	Church Parade in the morning. Nothing of interest to report. Weather very fair. Enemy firing. 1 O.R. to Hospital.	JHP
MONCHEAUX B25 C 50	14.1.18	—	Company Training continued. Enemy Guns working on the Cavalry Stand. Ran uncertain of our fire. Enemy was paid back for short Carlen. Same firing night. Coy paid out. 1 officer rejoining strength. 1 O.R. from leave to U.K. 1 O.R. from leave to U.K. came.	JHP
MONCHEAUX B25 C 50	15.1.18	—	At 7.30 a.m. started off to the C.S. road where at 9 a.m. we finished at 3.0 pm. Company arrived on our respective guns in case of 15 Coy the Saturday morning Enemy taken was re-calibrated... The weather was very bad all day Enemy at the wind to heavy rain all day. Rain that on roads got been blown into pieces also keeping the fields sodden. The Inner contour was soaked through & rendered as far as as the other contour covering to map storm contour were soaked & wet. The suggestion of all fire all morning. 5 O.R.S to Hospital as suffering from light. 1 O.R. III. and Composed 2/Lt. H.S. JEFFERYS started & proceeded to Lechaux. S. O.R.S to Coll. Capture & bathe 5 and in the move of 2 mile Coule. Given home 6 were now in hospital.	JHP
MONCHEAUX B25 C 50	16.1.18	—	Company training in morning. In afternoon 9 O.R.S to Coule. Amount of Training done. Then was interrupted by heavy showers. Our Artillery fleeted ant. Moved home and the Enemy fought fast set in & O.R.S. Leave to UK on leave. 1 OR. WAS: OUR. PICK. 3 O.R.S. to Hospital. 2 O.R. to Sick.	JHP
MONCHEAUX B25 C 50	17.1.18	—	Rain very wet all day. Company training was quiet unsettled. Report from B. fact about Belters firing were outbursts in the trenches. Nothing to report. 3 O.R.S. (NYK) joined for duty from base. 2/Lt. R.G. JEFFERY'S to Hospital. N.B. Stationary.	JHP
MONCHEAUX B26 C 50	18.1.18	—	Roy The Coy's and daily in torrage of Contd. Transport lines Rifle & Bayonet Exerciser. Gas came Rifle to U.K. 1 O.R. proceeded on leave to U.K. 1 O.R. to Hospital.	JHP
MONCHEAUX 41.5 C 50	19.1.18	—	Company training Bayonet. Exercise Scheme for 16 Coy. Was Dowling Soc by L/Cpl Cpl O.G.M. acting on O.R. Coy Central inspection 2 Respirators. In the afternoon. Officers were lectured by Lt.-Col. Cox. Sudden parade. Weather fine. Very wet. Had in Camp. 3 O.R.S. to Hospital & 1 rejoin unit.	JHP
MONCHEAUX 41.5 C 50	20.1.18	—	Parade to 1 Section by Section Comdr Company drill at 12.15 . . . The 2/Lt. H.C. WOOGENE W TTIF PLUNKE- S. O.R. was DENTON, to work in . . . for Company (suitable duties) chung in Eveniest CAPTEL & E. WOODEN Capt. 2/Lt. H. rejoined. Coy. At the Aux Parade the Morning. . . . the wound church Service was held. Weather dull 1 O.R. to Duty	JHP
MONCHEAUX B25 C 50	21.1.18	—	Company training Damage drill & lecture on the Range. Nothing further to report. Weather dull & wet.	JHP
MONCHEAUX B25 C 50	22.1.18	—	Company Training in Coy competition on the Range. Wind section Coy No's 3 section to ordered back to Memph affected Marching ability & will in Battery 2/Lt TRIPPITTS 4 1 O.R. present in the Comp. went to U.K... Capt. 6.0. ordered for to be informed that ruling & Autumn Sound to felt the sounds prepared by the rest of Winches of himself decoyed the Preserver. Then to face a Muir. Recruit training to Brigade fell. Six 3 Platoon Scout Officers and driving stiff to L/Cpl to duties in the ... C.O. to the 2/4.5 L. Day Tree. Crte. Base doing rifle to training gives full Evidence and Gave permission to give approved spec. They charge to duties to form the 150. K. He having full explanation giving Col. Col. comments greatly affect the Support and called that the matter after. His recordd in the temp. Office for the Correctn of trans. Company in advance of 1/4 scale Second contest was for the Correctn of troops. Map Rifle France Sheet 51 C 1/20,000	JHP

WAR DIARY or INTELLIGENCE SUMMARY

Army Form C. 2118.

175 MACHINE GUN COMPANY

Place	Date	Hour	Summary of Events and Information	Remarks and references to Appendices
MONCHEAUX B25 C50	23.1.18	—	Company training continued. Bullets unclaimed. Weather cold. Nothing of interest to report.	
MONCHEAUX B26 C60	24.1.18	—	Company training & preparation for G.O.C's inspection on the 25th. Tactical Scheme report sent in. Tactical Scheme in connection with attack on Lille. On the march to expected meeting of enemy C.O. sent the M.G. Coy. to be placed near the head of the Column. He was to take whatever action he considered best. Leaving a rear guard in the infantry on the road, and to gain more ground whenever possible to his Section Commander. After position & working out hypothesis, conclusions formed. W.T. 8.30 a.m. & arrived about 4 p.m. to join details. Section Chiefs. Made a very brief report off a long length of action. L.O.R's returned from Base reported from 177 Coy. to join unit for duty, 2nd off a good guide for Leave. 30 O.R's sick in billets. Needle Army gas mask carried. Night in the Enemy?	
MONCHEAUX B25 C50	25.1.18	—	Morning spent in finishing cleaning up & getting ready for G.O.C's inspection at 2.15 p.m. Co. inspection which Company by Sections during the morning. Company paraded at 2.20 p.m. & were inspected outside the town "Machine" at 2.20 p.m. Papers were had on field B25 S32 on N. side of MONCHEAUX - MONCHEAUX - MONTIGNY-EN-OSTREVENT Rd. Transport was drawn up on the road facing S. to Column of route. Company were in marching order. General Romer (BGC Staff) wounded ? of 2.30 gave the Transport a quick run over by sections, then asked questions as to loose animals & equipment. The arms office & others officers were also inspected. The Company was drawn up in mass, nut-a-thing when at T. P.O.R's, Capt? Lewis etc. (from further trees) was dismissed. The Service took then parade, inspected Company was drawn Letter in T-O.R's mess. Captain Company was dismissed. The Service Church Parade after being then some small details. Sergt. oasB Ryte am. animals mortuary act but within his Parade but observed was being well polished with the turn out to Mm whits after parade. His face was not the best to him were ashes but all the test turned out spotless & work very well during that I enquired hoping to remain that it was of the past he had seen in the Division. Entering his H.Q. in a letter? a caution was issued that today's tuberculous was giving out was due in the people getting home about 6.30 when an inquiry to investigate? Coy. 2nd Lt Russ arrived today. They Ruby for Duty. Dues on unwilling to fustily and was for fears all afternoon & Evening. 1. O.R. Scan W.L.(at.2 trans). 1. O.R. being in Hospital.	
MONCHEAUX B25 C50	26.1.18	—	Company training continued. Football Friendly V 470 bayRE last 3-1. At 6.0 pm the 7/5 Coy. Comets gave a very successful concert in the Helega Sabot Room. The costumes were quite good and two very attractive young ladies helped out the programme with great success. Bays rang fine but Edsor Trevany wet with in failing ash? all night. Nothing of interest during 1. O.R. taken to Indian above to remain his rejoins a Signalling Course at CONSTANCE. Le worried to take the until above Sept.	
MONCHEAUX B25 C50	27.1.18	—	Church Parade as per B.T.O. orders. Day mostly at first but bright afterwards. Kaiser's birthday. 1. O.R. returned to duty from Leave to UK. He had been unavoidably return to those due to as course of GRANTHAM & so was detained. again unavoidably on his arrival as per orders it had been impossible to stop his drawing leave.	

Map Refs. France Sheet 51

178 Infantry Bde.

Extract from a letter addressed to the Divisional Commander by Lieut. General Sir J. Aylmer Haldane, K.C.B., D.S.O. Commanding VI Corps.

"Will you please convey to all ranks of your Division my admiration and thanks for the very gallant stand they made against overwhelming numbers of the enemy supported by a tremendous artillery.

The Division nobly did their duty on the right of VI Corps, and from all accounts that have reached me have inflicted heavy loss upon the enemy. I grieve for the heavy casualties among your gallant officers, NCOs and men, but the 59th Division have the satisfaction of knowing that they did their duty in as trying circumstances as can possibly happen in war."

[Stamp: No. 175 MACHINE GUN COY. ORDERLY ROOM 2 MAR 1918 MACHINE GUN CORPS]

AG/4/2371

To H.Q. 59 Div
from O.C. 175th M.G. Coy.

Herewith War Diary for this Unit during period 21/1/18 to 20/2/18 inclusive.

C H Gadow Capt & Adjt
for O. Comdg. No. 175 Machine Gun Coy.

WAR DIARY or INTELLIGENCE SUMMARY

Army Form C. 2118.

175 Machine Gun Company

Place	Date	Hour	Summary of Events and Information	Remarks and references to Appendices
MONCHEAUX 62.S.C.60	28/1/18	—	Company still at rest in some billets and continued training. Weather fine & growing clear. Nothing of importance to report. 1 O.R. from hospital to duty. 1 O.R. to Base U.K.	2/A.9
MONCHEAUX	29/1/18	—	Company training Nos 1 & 4 sections were on the 500° Range in the afternoon. 2/Lt & Co. Lt. Pierre as O.C. Range. The day was fine & clear. Gun firing practice was done. Zero party returned at 10 p.m. Lt Davies returned to Company at 6.30 p.m on return of training party. Bath improvement continued. 2 ORs (Clafferman & Bennett) to Hospital 1 O.R. on 14 days leave U.K. Wattle getting worse & fog at night. Nothing else worth reporting 16.15 p.m well under to Socam are lightly he was done. Hope to Base ser. Patf. R.J.	2A9
MONCHEAUX	30/1/18	—	The programme for the two days' work was the same as that of the 29th. 2/Lt E Brine was getting better. 2/Lt Sharp was unfit. Heavy Rain morning & evening. Pushing again continued. Weather returned on 29/1/18. 1 O.R. on 14 day leave U.K. 2/4 E Brine sick. 2/4 Section title began leave estimates leg 1 week on W.O. authority. 2/LtK C Jefferys continued to base hospital 29/1/18 re sick hospital. Hope on recommendation. Name of Villain permitted on orders as adjunct to village. Co.R. three days' Furlough 14/5/18/20. In 3 hoildings in G.R.O.	2/A.9
MONCHEAUX	31/1/18	—	Whole Company was extra range all effect. Presence to range in 144° for firing by an attack and those who fail to bring out previous 5 days. While firing practical drill did famous diser was down. Dampness & fog which partly was fairly wild, attacked Unoccupied the Coy & might have Executed since that 1 O.R. transferred from 3/2 F.A. to 137 F.A. 2 ORs evacuated to M&B eels. 2 ORs R.M.D to duty from hospital	2/A9
MONCHEAUX	1/2/18	—	Company Training & Bath baths in the morning. In the afternoon 2,3 & 2 had hoping in Chewing Competition for a competition to had been on pinion fatigue by same care of imperious baths. In the transport been in position for battalion against Co. A attacks Godhra moved village Rueling in morning and left O. Lt. lt. In the Company would probably move on Feb 9th. This was part Conferred by Major O order No89. Firing that Finnseus were more over, & 97 troops into Compa troops into the buffet from Sister in charge of the B475 Division. Daytime brig ext. & rain had while part of buffer mid all day. 4 O.R two weeks leave. 1 O.R (Brune) to duty fm hospital	2/A.9
MONCHEAUX	2/2/18	—	Company route march 9-11 a.m. followed by Rd inspection. Rifle board grades behind No1 S.C. Billet from 2.30-3.30 pm. must all company being present. Bad same grad selection. Officers having used day. Lat. Sharp one up at front going face to thaw albeight transition Rate on wind at first. Trouble fair. Person to South 1 O.R. to Hospital, 4 2 ORs returns to duty from Hospital	2/A.9
MONCHEAUX	3/2/18	—	Church parade & same to Chrisan fm 8 o'ck the day Coy: also talked in the afternoon. 2 O.Rs to OR, 3 ORs fm leave for 1 OR 10R to Hospital. Weather veering fine & like showing. Nothing to Report	2A9
MONCHEAUX	4/2/18	—	Company training including gun or Lewis & Range training & M.G. Enfield arm competition. Shook of getting Wet for in position Target for Corps Gunnev cutter on Tuesday 5.2.18. Company was bad out on two day. Weather warm. Fine & settled in. Tower of carne in the sp. of cause & fm hospital	2/A9

Map Refs. France Sheet 51.E. 1/40000

WAR DIARY or INTELLIGENCE SUMMARY

Army Form C. 2118.

SHEET 2.
VOL 13

175 Machine Gun Company

Place	Date	Hour	Summary of Events and Information	Remarks and references to Appendices
MONCHEAUX	5.2.18	—	Inspection of 175 MG Bn by General Halland KCB, CSO, on ground near 2/7 S.15 on GOUY-ENTERNOIS Rd. Was drawn up in Hero at Close Column distance. The unit being on extreme left flank. After inspection a Hollow square was formed, where the general made a few remarks about the inspection and the war in general. He said he was much pleased with the appearance of all ranks of the units on parade and the way they behaved on parade. He said that he noticed a rifle Regt there (?) and hoped that they would not the steam main good use of them after when in the line. He mentioned that the troubles in that part (Russia), the R.F.A. were having, would refer troubles suffered from frostbite, & referred all ranks to another bad experience they had. He said that it was not Russia expected, where the Enemy was usually preparing to a leave attack on our front with rolls. But that in any case the troops which it forced ring from the E front were not comparable with those on this front. In the Encore area — the eventful general — with songs, hours & songs. Was sung in the village chose to Encore hours. The Mayor & many children long closs present. No. 58529 Cpl NICHOLSON, J. appeared in Divisional orders as having been awarded the CROIX DE GUERRE & H.M. King of the Belgians. For conspicuous gallantry devotion to duty during the offensives on Sept. 25-29, 1917. E of YPRES. No. B.S.89 & Rau table for move on 8th and 1st Red. RE Company cancelled.	(N.A.P.) G20.00 90. AP. 35 (N.A.P.)
MONCHEAUX	6.2.18	3.6 Pm – 0.11 a.m.	Ordinary routine. Nothing unusual. Rugby football match at BONNEVILLE V 37 N M.F.A. B.O 90 & A1 seed observing Day. Pay for fine in way & Enemy. But clear signs of change of weather approaching. Enemy will (?) to-morrow will probably turn wetter as breaking my. In Coy to do duty than again wrestling the Division & officers of 175 Brigade gave first class Concerts tonight in Billet which was to be cite to 175 Bde B.O. 37 P.M. Now, in the line E & CROISSALES, I of 88 Battery 0. 2.O.Rs loaned to	(N.A.P.)
MONCHEAUX	7.2.18		Preparations to move on the 8th all hutted packs & cases closing Mo. weather being wet. 2.O.Rs still leave for the 8a Gunnery Course. MO.Rs Scients. B.O. 9/1-92 giving much take on 4th 6 10 inst. relating over instruction reed. All orders respecting more composites Capt. A. Holt Commanding 2.O.Rs licenced to be a full lodged with returned body. 2.O.Rs.	(N.A.P.) 05.a.c. 0.0.90 A.P. 34

Maps used: Sheet 51E Good.

Army Form C. 2118.

Sheet 3
Vol 13

WAR DIARY
or
INTELLIGENCE SUMMARY
(Erase heading not required.)

175 Coy. Machine Gun Corps

Place	Date	Hour	Summary of Events and Information	Remarks and references to Appendices
BARLY	8.2.18	2.45 PM	Crossing & transport arrived from MONCHEAUX Coy HQ at 17 RUE SOMBRIN P14 & 81 Meat SIE HQ at BOARD HOUVIN SETREE - WAMIN Left at 4.50 am & 17th gave time for midday meal. Passing the starting point Cros. Coy Passed 9.45am. Left at 4.50am D with ORDERS RULLE COURT at 1.16 PM. Men marched well Coy. waco'd under Capt. (LH GARDNER Roads N.W of D with ORDERS RULLE COURT at 1.16 PM. Men marched well Coy. waco'd under Capt. (LH GARDNER O/C Capt. A. HOT Coy Boney unit 2/Lt ERAING & 7 ORS to take one the line. Bue a cril George JAMES (lieutenant) in command 15 S.W Buy) was not put into the starting point 200 words. He entered men 200m the straking past parquait & Bretpanals of the Coy. The Coy. is sected 3 lines of his orders timed (Reserve put again taken. & entered the transport arrived at BARLY then used in huts O/Cs in trilats, & animals were 500 m on good stables. The Men Coy Kent for O/Stour alt advance. HOUCHENOUX he uses is was water tapic was, to 610 so were BARLY but after 5 PM and NCO on orderly stone on the men were exempt. Coy, but was sent to the and and the the the and be was toiling healthy was also it as could duly Rame Bgde HR at HOUVIN. MONEY let out on kench at 1m. The Coy Conveyed the Citing hearts was also The Coy, and the both Coy, but was sent Returnce either. The Major adianced Coupond to the tellsquallir puint, went filled Supp ferme Coy Show CAN ate Re Returnce either. The Major adianced Coupond to the tellsquallir puint, went filled Supp ferme All Coulds at BARLY were paid some supp to as 5 Abr 2LT TALINTYRE allegehend to Recent for Suco served only Saal tatoon to day	NfR
NORTHUMBERLAND CAMP MERCATEL	9.2.18	4.0 PM	Company arrived fm BARLY marching via GOUY EN ARTOIS, VISSEUX MONCHIET, BEAUMETZ LES LOGES (starting point), BELLECOURT, RIVIERE, BRETENCOURT, BLAIREVILLE, VICHEUX, TO MERCATEL. Men marched well but rs at past to camp was very hot going. Coy's wog battalion. Coy was seen setting in a trench would up see after arrival 600 their Day few. Wind East Bride half Coy. Just before soaking HUMMUIZ at GOD NO MANS LAND 2min Kelsed rejoicth Coy fast after camp was reached. Transport pushed with Bye beyond YORK Camp 2 miles distant. Dust might No EA	J.A.F. S.00.93
NORTHUMBERLAND CAMP	10.2.18		Church parade in morning. Cleaning up, Recht of day returns. F.H. inspection 2pm No an frud life kid Co. 2/Lt JACKIN & 7ORS obtained fm Men on which they there fuomate To 6 ORMS. Reconnotes new TP line in STOYENVILLE Shakin Pile good but regularly bound at night. The funct seemo the quiet for short duration can be observed. The camp support fm Cinic Brecewise Cafotron en in evening. Su Offr to T.O & Recommutu buid. H.Q & Affredreckins in the morning Major marked EH Kearing WD wind WD EA at unght	J.A.F.
NORTHUMBERLAND CAMP	11.2.18		Day spent in proparing wiring into the line on the 12 hod inst CAPTN Gibson G 4our & WE SHAW & ORS devours de Licorge T.O. wiring up time on weekend 2/LT Rm' talintyre reported for duty fm leave with 2/LT N G JEFFERYS Evacuated 2/LT N.G. JEFFERYS evacuated Day fain wind West Showing Guiet Mab Refo Meat SIE 400m Lens 11.4.51.6 40,700	J.A.F.

A5834 Wt. W4973/M687 750,000 8/16 D. D. & L. Ltd. Forms/C.2118/13.

WAR DIARY or INTELLIGENCE SUMMARY

Army Form C. 2118.

SHEET 4
VOL 13

A.P.M. Lett
175 Company Machine Gun Corps

Place	Date	Hour	Summary of Events and Information	Remarks and references to Appendices
ST LEGER B.4 & 25	12.2.18	—	The Company moved off by sections starting at 8.30 am to relieve the 244 Company in the left sector of the BULLECOURT sector. The relief was completed by 5.5 pm and all officers & positions taken over. Company HQ etc. all guns. No. 1 Company in the line on the 88th Front and 4 guns & 200 rounds S.A.A. for local purposes to this company and the B.Pd. Front near ECOUSTE. All guns laid on S.O.S. lines and have also battle lines. This forward battery being provided with Special forced containing A.P. S.A.A. for dealing with hostile tanks should they come other H.Q. Defence Scheme is under Corps arrangements, a Battery position on being built in Champagne emplacements for Batteries found on So.5. & So.6. & S.8 guns are distributed in depth. R.S.A front at about 1750 yds by 2 guns in front of one M.G. in support. On the Bogle front the high ground is to the enemy lines and barrage lines are run down on B/K 3.9 on height 177 firing into the Enemy lines. The feature are the hollows struck General Raids have taken place. The Enemy positions appear to be doubtful in places, as his front line faits vague & are on the head of the slopes rather than a definite front line system.	JAR

Transport moved to BOYNE CAMP MOYENVILLE
Officers up Line. 2/Lt EDKINS with N° 1, 2/Lt FRIEND N° 2 Sec. 2/Lt GRADWELL N° 3 Sec. Lt FERRE N° 4 we
O.C. 2/I.C. & 2/Lt ELRICK at Co. HQ. at Transport lines. 2/Lt GUYER (T.O.) 2/Lt TALLENTYRE & 2/Lt RAMSAY
I.o.R. to duty few hospital. 10 R. Oth. Ranks (Sigs) attd. to HQ. at own Regiment.
Company distributed in the Sector as per table below.

No 1 SEC	MAP REF	CORPS N°	Present N°	No 2 SEC	MAP REF	CORPS N°	Present N°	No 3 SEC	MAP REF	CORPS N°	Present N°
GUN N° 1	U13d 7038	50	40/1	N° 1	U20a 3222	46	46	N° 1	U25d.8503	34A	37A
— 2	U13d.8850	51	46/2	N° 2	U20a 3228	47	47	N° 2	U25d 5630	35A	38A
— 3	U20a.0084	48	39	N° 3	U20b 1550	44	44	N° 3	U19c.2508	36A	39A1
— 4	U20a.0060	49	39A	N° 4	U20b 1550	45	45	N° 4	U19c.8022	37A	29A
SEC HQ	U20 Q.0060	—	—	SEC HQ	U20a.3222	—	—	SEC HQ	U21a.3545	—	—

COMPANY H.Q. ST LEGER B.4 & 25 (Rum Q.) | TRANSPORT LINES & QM Stores MOYENVILLE A.40 (Continued on next Page)

Map Refs. LENS II 1/10000 / 1/20000
Sheet 51B 1/10000 / 1/10000
Sheet 57B
BULLECOURT Trench Map 51B SW 9 1/10000
Id. 6A

WAR DIARY
or
INTELLIGENCE SUMMARY.
(Erase heading not required.)

Instructions regarding War Diaries and Intelligence Summaries are contained in F. S. Regs., Part II. and the Staff Manual respectively. Title pages will be prepared in manuscript.

SHEET 5
VOL 13

Alfred Hill Capt

175 Coy. Machine Gun Corps.

Place	Date	Hour	Summary of Events and Information	Remarks and references to Appendices
ST LEGER. B 4 b 25	12.2.18 (contd)		Gun positions taken over in Sector (Continued) as per following table	

Nº4 Sec	Map Ref	Corps Nº	Present Nº	E Battery	Map Ref	Corps Nº	Present Nº
Nº 1 gun	U21 C2810	42	34	Nº 1 gun	C2b 2892	30A	E1
Nº 2 —	U21 C 8111	43	35	Nº 2 —	C2b 1580	31A	E2
Nº 3 —	U 26 c3345	36A1	36A1	Nº 3 —	U26 C7218	32A	E3
Nº 4 —	U 26 C1968	36A2	36A2	Nº 4 —	U26 C6820	33A	E4
Sec HQ	U 20 a 3222	—	—	Sec HQ	U26 C 8020	—	—

'E' Battery was supplied by a Section from 200 M.G. Coy. Rationed & administered by their H.Q. but for tactical purposes under command and orders of OC 175. M.G. Coy. 214 M.G. Coy. is in divisional Reserve

to the 59th Div. 121 Coy. Div. Reserve to 3rd Div. on left & 102 & 200 (Coy. remainder of) Man rear Corps positions in the Sector in case of attack. Sector when taken over was being quiet. Artillery only normal & little to be seen or heard of the Enemy. Visibility poor. All map refs, ranges, and R.E's taken over were carefully checked & corrected where found to be at fault.

ST LEGER B 4 b 25	13.2.18		C.O & 2/Lt Elfick (who with 2/Lt & 16 ORs over at HR) went round all gun positions & saw that everything was in order. They left at 10 am & returned about 6.30 pm. Day very wet. Drizzle No visibility. Everything found in good order. A considerable amount of work is in hand. A Battery position with mined dugout for 4 guns & teams is being made in W. bank of Sunken Road at T24 d7075 which will give when complete a very fine field of fire all along the ridge and on western slope of hill in front. Another couple of mined Emplacements (2 guns each) is also under construction in Ry Embankment fm U26 C to C2 b. giving fire down the valley. For these Emplacements which are being cut by the Tunnelling RE Coy. Labour is being supplied from all Sections. Ration dump for the Company is at Nº 3 Sec HQ (see above) whence they are carried Nº1 & 2 across Country to STRAY support, & for Nº & 4 Sec 200 Coy along RAILWAY RESERVE & for Nº4 HR & 2 guns up PELICAN Trench. The Intelligence sent in by Section HQ for the 1st 24 hours showed No Casualties & no activity of any kind on either side. 4 men & went deaf were transferred to 200 Coy on Authority 59 Div. A.91/68/149 d 8.2.18. Gun positions improved & camouflaged. Men given all necessary orders. Range cards. R.E's & 80's battle lines closed & all as & Cleaned & checked.	JH9
ST LEGER B 4 b 25	14.2.18		C.O went all round guns again. Work etc Continues. Weather wet still. S.W wind fresh at times. Intelligence Summary. Hostile activity Artillery shelled U21 Cuthral and valley in U26 C at 12.30 pm. also N of BULLECOURT. Some gas shells reported over Trench Mortars active on U70. Various Coloured lights green & orange put up by Enemy during the night. Our artillery was normal, our Heavies replying to Enemy Shelling. Casualties NIL. Visibility very poor. 2/Lt GUYER Off to Vet Course at ABBEVILLE. 1 OR to M.G. School CAMIERS 2 ORs for Hospital. 1 OR fur Leave to UK. 1 Man of 200 Coy. E Battery wounded by one of our shells (prematured) fired from Battery position behind in ECOUSTE.	JH9
ST LEGER B 4 b 25	15.2.18		C.O & 2/Lt went Round line starting 10.30 am returning at 5.15 pm. Guns, positions & sentries all found direct. Hostile Artillery was quiet during the day but between 7.30 & 8.30pm & from 10.30 to 11.15 pm he shelled certain parts of the sector pretty heavily. He was particularly attentive to ECOUSTE & Railway Reserve but obtained no direct hits on gun positions though he blew up the dug out of one team of 200 Coy without however wounding its 3 occupants. At 11.15 pm the Enemy discharged about 100 gas projectors which fell in front of our lines at E 5.695. gas reported to smell of Chlorine & Mustard. Cloud gas formed at NOREUIL and rolled up valley to VAULX. Casualties unknown. Weather damp & foggy. Visibility poor. Nothing further to report. 2 ORs Leave to UK. Died B.O.94.	JH9

A5834. Wt. W4973/M687 750,000 8/16 D. D. & L. Ltd. Forms/C.2118/13. Map Ref. BULLECOURT TR Map 51BSW 4 Ed 5A $\frac{1}{10000}$ 51B & 57C $\frac{1}{40000}$ & HENDECOURT Special Sheet Ed 7H $\frac{1}{20000}$

WAR DIARY or INTELLIGENCE SUMMARY

Army Form C. 2118.

Sheet 6
Vol 13

175 Coy Machine Gun Corps

Place	Date	Hour	Summary of Events and Information	Remarks and references to Appendices
ST LEGER B.4.b.25	16.2.18	—	CO visited lines all day with Lt Col BASDEN DMGO. Wind west. Rising Barom. OC in line reported normal activity on both flanks. Visibility poor overall. Slight evening S.E. wind. Our own obs station 20 m from area was taken & swung by an aban. Battery RE's watch. getting colder & clearing for frost. Clear sky. 2 ORs (McKenzie U.K.) & O.R.S. (three previously with this Coy) from BASE Depot as reinforcements. Up RO 12.00 am. OC staffs above BORs att(d) SF R13 Transport tt-19 Echo. 35 Planes reported overhead during day down 19 aircraft hit JAA then	JAP
ST LEGER B.4.b.25	17.2.18	—	CO up line. CO & OC Coy arriving at R13 HQ found Coys newest Battery Positions. Had 2 see this was Poor. Gunners Obers resumed rate at night. Evening 10.30-11 p.m. & Boys up to Ridge of Trench. This Coy has 4 Relief 175 Coy in Centre Sector. Ammunition made. At 2/Lt EDKINS MGRE tells night firing on road in Europe line. See ops reports — Artillery took shelter, normal E.O. Balloon up all day. Balloon deflated CROISILLES EAST. Nothing of interest to report. Weather very fine. Very cold had frost. Visibility very good. Wind blew a much this wood but mostly from the SSE. OC & me Coy. MO informed. See LEGER (Parade)/Candidate for Commission from the SEE of the Corvette. MH to Brasten Island & Trenches line	JAP
ST LEGER B.4.b.25	18.2.18	—	OC & 200 Coy arrived early, totally over relieved on following day. During the relief being stopped at PROSULLES FYL after dusk the relief carried to make up to cases when this unit took over line from 2nd Coy. Ammunition buses hit aircraft accordingly. The camps & transport lines of this two units are like orchards. See ops reports — Quiet during the night but Enemy Artillery Aerial Activity normal EA bombed various back areas during the day. Aerial observation fairly active with EA very high. There was much activity until 7 am BOYELLES territory & MOYENVILLE occurring to 3 occasions. Heavy active. Up to & at U23 D8 m M.19.5 & rid 22.80 Rds from U19 ch59 95 on Bruno Roads, MOYENVILLE-HENDECOURT road from at V15 A8130. Fm 6.30 pm to 4.40 am. Weather continued very fine but light an day. Very windy Coy NO (E) up to & as day very high turned back our scene tune Lines to attend Field Conference at 6.0 p.m. 2/Lt ELFORD also went down line with him continuing the line of inspection. 2/Lt Trollope A/TO normal at Coy HR for discipline Note own Coy's Orderkeeping took over lines of aid arranged for aid. 12 N.S. 2's of 2 OR sent up to arct for as L.O.R.	17S.M.P.700 0.0. 17S-7 JAP
ST LEGER B.4.b.25	19.2.18	19.30 pm	2/Bn Cas Ammn & Stoke Over H.Q. to Queant 9.30 pm. All ammunition a few position to Queen H. Sector was sent Completed. O.16 the weather at 9.30. The incoming dd our Company A. Sector in CROISILLE, while owing to incidents occurred up the light meaning up part remainder of this station to stand to ammunition (to) after dusk. No 2 & 3 Section followed at 1 am. M Lords Queant of the released (rd & M) Medium over No 27 — One section of 17S Coy sent up to Bullecourt Tramp 51651 w 8 ust-1700 HENDECOURT Spec 615 & 570 S16 & 57C Medium 40100	JAP

WAR DIARY or INTELLIGENCE SUMMARY

Army Form C. 2118.

SHEET 7
VOL 13

175 COY. MACHINE GUN CORPS

(signed) A. M. Wall

Place	Date	Hour	Summary of Events and Information	Remarks and references to Appendices
ST LEGER B.21.B.2.6	19.2.18	—	To Ration Dump where stores were packed on four Coy, limbers and men proceeded to Coy H.Q. The last Reliefs returning (N.C.) reported at 8.45 p.m. stating that they had been relieved at 6.30 p.m. & were with B.P.W. Coy relief (N.C.) about 12 a.m. Packed and Carts at DURRO CAMP HQRY B.21.A.65. Coy 12.6 B.P. arrived and has had its third Relief from 7th & 6th Batt. East Yorks Regt from 2/6 B.P.S.F. This Company had already held Post pace and the night was very quiet where slight relief ground for part but fairly thick in places. Column 1.0.R. returned from their School School. Transport came at 13.45 & 6.5. Quiet night. No Casualties.	JAG
DURROW CAMP HQRY B.21.A.65	20.2.18	—	No. 3 Sec. in the line as before. Rest of Coy. at DURRO Camp. Transport as before. Coy spent all day cleaning up stores and packing limbers. Unloading & sorting out in afterw. Weather fine. Chd champ from Field Cashier at BEHAGNIES & Coy had out after tea. Coy alto traferm came on duties Q & Cad S.M. Wend. Night otherwise ? Quiet. No firing Raids. 4 O.Rs. transferred to Coy from 2/6 S.F. & ORs do pm. 7th Bn. S.F. & 3 O.Rs. pm 2/5 S.F. Cited a defic't killing out relative on M.G. Corps Strength & received these men as being kept on the List of ? Estabt. strength men forming that ex-R.M.N.R. (Hg.H.). Who is posted to the Divisional B.M.G.Offr. returns surely D.H. & Brass tacks Temporarily Attd. to this unit. All others will so sept. ? returned to ? ? Arms and approach of Battalion "A","B" ? "C" which while the Coy. was their Groups ar manned in case of Emergency Brown total effect seen got out. The previous Coy ie 2/4/4 which is 23rd Divisional reserve left. Batt. H.Q. Arlo are a practice alarm, as Batts there have ready in position (2 am) in 1 hour 7 minute after attack of alarm. 8	JAG
DURROW Camp HQRY B.21.A.65	21.2.18	—	Continuing as above. Packing limbers completed rear sufficient limbers cleaned. Avoiding all day. Stores as the position nears over Coy. Lines. Coy 2/4 R.T.R. went up in relief for No 3 Sec. Ofo came out Relief over No.3 See also in relief on the ? Wards near fine C.O. Wend Gunning S.W. Some Artillery actively Ready or after noon. Quiet. Heard a.coustly. Chief gun over. 4 O.Rs pm 7th Bn. S.F. & 8 O.Rs pm 2/8 S.F. & 3 O.Rs pm 2/5 S.F. Posted to M.G.C. this unit Under authorit'y A.G.R. L/16.47/83.2 & A.2.18 S.O.C. 17 Lnd Batt. 18/1 & D/18/218 Those in addition to 8 O.Rs Ally already transferring 17 5 15	JAG
DURROW Camp HQRY B.21.A.65	22.2.18	—	Company and transport remain on 21st st. Coy training. Pactising ? Auto continues Co. reconnaissance A B & C Battery positions Weather Cold wind S.W. 10.R. Returned to duty from hospital. 10.R. from U.K. Leave 10 R for (56) ? 7/6 Bn. S.F. posted to Bringside 106 ? OR's for infantry units to M.G.C. as per authority quoted in 21st and Entry 10 R (s6.) to 2/8 S.F. 13.2 S.F. as it Clark 73 Aud R.A.M.U. Author'y P.17 Sec. L P.A.C.I. 8 E.U.A. Regis hat for ?? 2m Psh R? ? Enabing GRO Isabuse A.162 & 218.2.2/218 Quiet	175 16.8 Coy G.O 28 / JAG
DURROW Camp HQRY B.21.A.65	23.2.16	—	As above. Nothing unusual to report. Coy. O.C. No. 2B Academy went relief of No.3 Sec. By No.2 Section Patterned. No 2 Sec returned at 4 gms B. 2.0.0. M.G Coy. with "E" Battalion positions whose in term ? with offr ? No 2 Sec. 175 Coy relief Complete 5.5 pm. No 2 Sec to re-occupy Patterned Sevens of H.Q.Y. about 11.0 pm. 0/2 Carrot the annoueled Lt. Col. ? and Butt. Garden hes 2/c called in Enemy to See Lieut A.R.Q Wright Who is attd. 0ths Coy till the Bn. H.Q. is formed. Weather Cold below Wind. S.W. A.aurothy broke out Gas Alarm near Jent 3.30am our 3 Batty? Guns retuned Gun fire No casualties. 10R R? Returning Course 10.R. to Base & Machine Cond 2 O.Rs. to U.K. 14 days leave. Hapa'pe (Bulldozer? TR. pageant 51 B. Sec. 2 E 5 A K/m000 s and check S 7 6 S. 7 6 Sundow to HENDECOURT ? ? 7 A. ?	JAG

Army Form C. 2118.

WAR DIARY or INTELLIGENCE SUMMARY.
(Erase heading not required.)

175 Coy MACHINE GUN CORPS

SHEET 8 VOL 13

Instructions regarding War Diaries and Intelligence Summaries are contained in F.S. Regs., Part II. and the Staff Manual respectively. Title pages will be prepared in manuscript.

Place	Date	Hour	Summary of Events and Information	Remarks and references to Appendices
DURRAN Camp B.21.d.65	24/2/18	—	Company and Transport as before. Church Parade in morning. Bathing for Company. No. 2 Section in the afternoon. C.O. & Capt Garden left at 10.30 to go up to Line. Coy relieving on 27th (with) agoing round the Contn. Section. Day cold and dull. Slight rain work day to Omnions. VII Artillerie chain. Brig. Div. on our right relieved Truery at 2.30 am on 25/2/18. A bombing for trains Lens as reported. Otherwise Everything fairly quiet. No bombing.	J.M.G
DURRAN CAMP B.21.d.65	25/2/18	—	As above. Company training classes for newly transferred Infantry continued. C.O. went to HR 177 M.G. Coy & met Lt BASDEN and discuss arrangements about the formation of the M.G. Battalion. Heavy rain fell most of the day. Guns of 177 Coy in the Contn. Section were served very heavy bombardment between 9.30 pm & 1 am. All Section of weapons was firing & cleaning Learning Continuous M.G fire. Bosche put up a number of lights including rockets bursting into a number of yellow stars and also many green lights. No firing was seen for this purpose. He at a General attack was to be expected at 5.15 am on the following morning as on Br Rifle Lincoln rgt returned to baggage wagons the night. Demar parts quickly and although being fired will full moon are trusting. Very cold night. Just 2 O.R.s to UK on leave and 2 O.R.s returned to duty from UK Leave.	J.M.G
DURRAN HUTS B.21.d.65	26/2/18	—	Company training. Also officers arrived on the gun work returns (with) went up the line for demonstrating purposes. The Nº 2 Remount Dept (Bn). and fifteen others attended in the afternoon. The Establishment for the M.G. Battalions was examined. Warning returned on H.Q.s Paper were the which will be closer added to a fuller from the Companies as at present constituted. Coys case were a trifle but also all signallers A.S.G. Supernumary. This last is also to supply Bombardier Tailor, Water Cart duty man and also the pertaining training Signallers Those were duly shown in a proper return made to H.Q.E. Capt Tennant of 2 Staffords Regt is Appointed I/c Bn. A.B. No. 2 Section was attended in to PHQ Chequille. Personal of Coys was in energed to 215 all others. Returned to duty from Hospital Cty. O.O. Nº 215 as under MO issued for issue on night of 27/2/18. Weather dull and windy. Cook at times fairly Tresh. D.A. Nº. The Brigade Situation appears the (Lay) anxious of Enemy attack on this front. Webs but thoseg Train Lingl Spint. Not much news of Certainty. It is also known that that an attack as a grand Scale is in preparation. through no definite information has been received. The firing an on-out as often. B.n. Commander on Chief B. forces came in the Contrel during the day.	J.M.G 175 M.G Coy O.C. Nº 29 177 M.G Coy O.O. Nº ?

Map Ref BULLECOURT TR. Map. 51B. S.W. 1/8 SA 1/10.000
France Sheet 51B 9 57C 1/10.000 HENDECOURT Special Sheet Ed 7A 1/20,000

SECRET.

178th INFANTRY BRIGADE ORDER NO.90.

Ref.Map LENS 11.
1/100,000

6th February 1918.

1. In continuation of 178th Infantry Brigade Order No.89, the Brigade Group, plus 200th M.G.Company will march on the 8th February as per Table "A" overleaf.

2. Reports on completion of move, with location of Headquarters, will be sent to Brigade Headquarters by telephone or Special D.R.

3. The 200th M.G.Company will be placed at the disposal of the 3rd Division from 6 p.m. 9th February to relieve a Machine Gun Company of the 34th Division.
The position to be occupied by the 200th M.G.Company will be notified later.
The 200th M.G.Company will be relieved by a Company of 40th Division when the 59th Division goes into the line.

4. Brigade Headquarters will close at HOUVIN at 9.45 a.m. on the 8th February and will re-open at GOUY-en-ARTOIS at the same hour.

5. Administrative instructions will be issued separately.

6. Acknowledge.

J. Shadwin
Captain,
A/Brigade Major,
178th Infantry Brigade.

Issued by D.R.
at 2.15 p.m.

Distribution - Normal
plus 470th Field Coy R.E.
2/2nd W.R.Fd.Amb.
518 Coy.A.S.C.
200th M.G.Coy.
Brigade Supply Officer.
Brigade Transport Officer.

MARCH TABLE "A"

Ref.Map IENS.11 1/100,000.

To accompany 178th Infantry Brigade Order No.90.

Unit.	Starting Point.	Starting Time.	Route.	Destination.	Remarks.
Bde.H.Qs plus 2/8 S.F.Transport.	Road Junction N.E. of D in GRAND RULLECOURT.	a.m. 11.30	GRAND RULLECOURT - SOMBRIN - BARLY - FOSSEUX.	GOUY-EN-ARTOIS.	First line Transport will march immediately in rear of their respective units. 300 yards interval at least will be maintained between the transport of one unit and the head of the next unit.
2/5th S.F.		11.42	GRAND RULLECOURT - SOMBRIN - SAULTY.	BAVINCOURT.	
516 Coy.A.S.C.		p.m. 12.06	GRAND RULLECOURT - SOMBRIN - BARLY - FOSSEUX.	GOUY-EN-ARTOIS.	
2/6th S.F.		12.18	ditto.	ditto.	
7th S.F.		12.32	GRAND RULLECOURT - SOMBRIN - SAULTY.	LAHERLIERE.	
470 Fd.Coy.R.E.		12.46	GRAND RULLECOURT - SOMBRIN -	BARLY.	
178th T.M.B.		1.08	ditto.	ditto.	
175th H.C.C.		1.16	ditto.	ditto.	
2/2nd Fd.Amb.		1.27	ditto.	ditto.	
200th M.G.C.	AVESNES-BARLY Rd Junction N.E.of Y in BARLY.	2.00	BARLY - FOSSEUX.	GOUY-EN-ARTOIS.	

Note. 2/6th S.F. & 7th S.F. will proceed to Starting Point via SARS-LEZ-BOIS - DENIER - LIENCOURT.
200th M.G.Company will proceed to Starting Point via GIVENCHY-LE-NOBLE - AVESNES.

SECRET.

178th INFANTRY BRIGADE ADMINISTRATION INSTRUCTION No. 33.

To be read in conjunction with 178th Infantry
Brigade Order No. 90.

6.2.18.

Ref. Map. LENS 11.

1. BILLETING PARTIES.
   A lorry will be at Brigade Headquarters at 7 a.m. on 8th inst. for the purpose of conveying billeting parties consisting of 1 officer and 4 o.r. per infantry unit, and 2 any ranks from other units in the Brigade Group. The 200 M.G.Company will arrange to transport their own billeting party.
   The lorry will proceed first to BARLY, thence to GOUY-en-ARTOIS - BAVINCOURT - LA HERLIERE.
   Billeting parties will first report at the Town Major's office in each village.

2. SUPPLIES - as per this office message AQ 196 dated 6.2.18.

3. STORES & BAGGAGE.
   (a) Lorries will be detailed as follows :-
   Brigade H.Q.   2.   Each Inf. Unit   3.
   Each M.G.Coy.   1.   Field Coy.R.E.   1.
   2/2 N.M.F.Amb. 1.   516 Coy. A.S.C.   1.
   178 L.T.M.B.   1.
   Guides are to be at Brigade H.Q. at 8 a.m. 8th instant.

   (b) Supply and Baggage Wagons (plus 1 G.S. wagon per Infantry unit) will report to units' H.Q. at 4 p.m. on 7th inst., and will accompany units on the march. Supply wagons must be returned to 516 Company, A.S.C. immediately rations are off-loaded.
   Baggage wagons (plus 1 G.S. wagon per Infantry Bn) will remain with units until completion of the move.

4. Rations for 178 T.M.B. will be transported and delivered by 175 M.G.Coy.

5. A horsed ambulance will follow in rear of each Battalion.

6. Surplus R.E. material in possession of units will be handed over to the incoming unit.
   All surplus S.A.A. and bombs will be returned to the Divisional Grenade Dump.
   "Blob sticks" received in this area will be handed over to incoming units.

7. All billets must be left in a clean and sanitary condition.
   Billeting certificates must be completed, and all claims settled, before leaving. Certificates that there are no outstanding claims against the unit will be obtained.
   Billet Wardens from the 34th Division will report to each unit at 11 a.m. on 7th inst.

8. During the march horses will be watered from the tins carried on the wagons.

9. Reference para 3(a), lorries must be off-loaded and returned to their Park immediately on arrival in the new area.

Issued at 7.30 p.m. by D.R.
Distribution - NORMAL,
   plus copy to 200 M.G.Coy.

Captain,
Staff Captain,
178th Infantry Brigade.

SECRET.

178th INFANTRY BRIGADE ORDER NO.92.

Ref.Maps HINS 1/100,000, and
Sheets 51b.S.W. & 57.c.N.W. 1/20,000.   7th February 1918.

1. The 59th Division (less Artillery) will relieve the 40th Division (less Artillery and Pioneers) in the line on 10th, 11th and 12th February.

2. The 178th Infantry Brigade will relieve the 119th Infantry Brigade on the 10th, 11th and 12th February in accordance with the attached Table of Reliefs.

3. Details of the relief of Field Companies R.E. and Field Ambulances are being arranged respectively between C.R.Es and A.D.M.S. of Divisions.

4. Acknowledge.

                                                Captain,
                                        A/Brigade Major,
                                178th Infantry Brigade.

Issued at 7.30 p.m.
    by D.R.

Distribution - Normal
    plus 470th Field Coy.R.E.
         2/2nd N.M.Fd.Amb.
         176th Inf.Bde.
         177th Inf.Bde.
         119th Inf.Bde.
         516 Coy A.S.C.
         Brigade Supply Officer.
         Brigade Transport Officer.
         T.O. 2/8th Bn S.F.

SECRET.

TABLE OF RELIEFS TO ACCOMPANY 178th INFANTRY BRIGADE ORDER NO.92.

Date.	Unit.	From.	To.	Relieves.	Remarks.
10th Feb.	2/5th S.F.	DURHAM Camp.	MORY NORTH.	12th S.W.Bordrs.	To clear MERCATEL Camps by 11 a.m.. Not to enter ERVILLERS before 10.30 a.m.
do.	2/6th S.F.	ditto.	MORY L'ABBAYE.	11th K.O.R.Lancs.	
11/12 Feb.	2/5th S.F.	MORY NORTH.	Left Sector.	Right Battr. 119th Inf.Bde.	
do.	2/6th S.F.	MORY L'ABBAYE.	ditto.	Left Battn. 119th Inf.Bde.	
do.	7th S.F.	YORK CAMP.	MORY NORTH.	119th Inf.Bde H.Q. and 119th T.M.B.	When vacated by 2/5th S.F.
do.	178th Inf.Bde H.Q. & 178th T.M.B.	MERCATEL.	Left Sector.	119th Inf.Bde H.Q. and 119th T.M.B.	
12/13 Feb.	175th M.G.Coy.	NORTHUMBERLAND CAMP.	Left Sector.	244th M.G.Coy.	
do.	470th Fd.Co.R.E.	MERCATEL.	do.	229 Fd.Coy R.E.	

175 MGC

SECRET.

178th INFANTRY BRIGADE ORDER NO.91.

Ref.Maps LENS,1/100,000.   7th February 1918.
& FRANCE,Sheet 51b,1/40,000.

1. The Brigade Group, plus 200th Machine Gun Company, will march on the 9th February as per March Table "A" overleaf.

2. Reports on completion of move, with location of Headquarters, will be sent to Brigade Headquarters by telephone or Special D.R.

3. The 200th Machine Gun Company will relieve 240th Machine Gun Company at NEUVILLE-VITASSE before 12 noon on the 9th February.

4. Brigade Headquarters will close at 10 a.m. on 9th February at GOUY-EN-ARTOIS, and will re-open at RESERVE CAMP,S.6.a.9.9., at the same hour.

5. Acknowledge.

Captain,
A/Brigade Major,
178th Infantry Brigade.

Issued at 7.30 p.m.
   by D.R.
Distribution- Normal
    plus 470th Fd.Coy.R.E.
        516 Coy A.S.C.
        2/2nd W.R.Fd.Amb.
        200th M.G.Coy.
        Bde Supply Officer.
        Bde Transport Officer.
        T.O.2/8th Bn S.F.
        176th Infantry Bde.
        177th Infantry Bde.

MARCH TABLE "A"

Ref.Maps
LHMS.1/100,000.
& Sheet 51b.1/40,000.

To accompany 1/8th Infantry Brigade Order No.91.

Unit.	Starting Point.	Time.	Route.	Destination.	Remarks.
Bde.H.Q. plus 2/8th.S.F.Transport.	Cross Roads N.W. of first E in RIVIERE.	a.m. 11.30.	BRETENCOURT - BLAIRVILLE - FICHEUX.	RESERVE CAMP S.6.a.9.9.	First line transport will march 200 yds in rear of their respective units. Intervals of 200 yds will be kept between companies. Intervals of at least 300 yds will be kept between the transport of one unit and the head of the next unit. Transport will be parked at M.16.d.
2/6th.Bn.S.F.		11.38	ditto.	DURHAM CAMP S.11.a.	
516 Co.A.S.C.		p.m. 12.06.	ditto.	NORTHUMBERLAND CAMP M.23.c.2.5.	
470 Fd.Co.R.E.		12.14.	ditto.	ditto.	
178th T.M.B.		12.24.	ditto.	DURHAM CAMP.	
175 M.G.Co.		12.28.	ditto	NORTHUMBERLAND CAMP.	
2/5th.Bn.S.F.		12.37.	ditto.	DURHAM CAMP.	
7th.Bn.S.F.		1.05.	ditto.	YORK CAMP.	
2/2nd.N.M.Fd.Amb.	BARLY.	a.m. 11.00.	BAVINCOURT - POMMIER.	BIENVILLERS.	
200 M.G.Co.	GOUY-EN-ARTOIS.		BEAUMETZ - BRETENCOURT - BLAIRVILLE - FICHEUX - MERCATEL.	NEUVILLE VITASSE.	The 200 M.G.Co will leave GOUY-EN-ARTOIS in time to carry out the relief as ordered in para.3.

Note:- The 2/5th & 7th.Bns.S.F. will proceed to starting point via main ARRAS - DOULLENS Road.

178th INFANTRY BRIGADE ADMINISTRATIVE INSTRUCTION No. 34.

To be read in conjunction with 178th Infantry
Brigade Order No. 91.

8.2.18.

Ref maps, LENS 11.
51 B.

1. BILLETING PARTIES.
   A lorry has been detailed for conveying billeting parties, strength as ordered in Administrative Instruction No. 33.
   It will start from Town Major's Office, LABRET, at 7 a.m. on 9th inst. where it will pick up billeting party of the 7th Sherwood Foresters, and will proceed from thence to BAVINCOURT, BARLY and GOUY-en-ARTOIS, picking up billeting parties of the units quartered in those villages, at Town Majors' Offices in each case.
   The Staff Captain will meet the lorry at the Cross Roads at the Western entrance to MERCATEL, in M.29.c. (Sheet 51 B).

2. SUPPLIES - as per this office message AQ.196 dated 6.2.18.

3. STORES AND BAGGAGE.
   Lorries will be detailed as stated in para 3 of Administrative Instruction No. 33, and will report at Town Major's office in each village where units are quartered (LAHERLIERE in the case of 7th Sherwood Foresters), at 8 a.m.
   Lorries must be off-loaded and released immediately on conclusion of the day's journey.
   Supply wagons will march with No. 516 Coy. A.S.C.
   Guides from units will be sent to the cross roads at the Western entrance to MERCATEL, in M.29.c. (51 B) to guide supply wagons to units' Q.M.Stores.

4. A horsed ambulance will follow in rear of each battalion, and will be kept for the night 9/10th with units' transport; being sent on the morning of the 10th to rejoin 2/2nd N.M.Fd.Amb. at BIENVILLERS. O.C. 2/2nd N.M.Fd.Amb. will be responsible that rations are sent for the horses and men of these ambulances:

5. All billets must be left in a clean and sanitary condition. Billeting certificates must be completed, and all claims settled, before leaving. Certificates that there are no outstanding claims against the unit will be obtained.

6. During the march horses will be watered from the tins carried on the wagons.

7. The Brigade Transport Officer will allot the transport lines for the whole of the Brigade Group.

Issued at 7.pm by S.D.R.
Distribution - as for
Admin. Instrn. No. 33.

Captain,
Staff Captain,
178th Infantry Brigade.

178TH INFANTRY BRIGADE ORDER NO.93.

Ref Maps LENS.1/100,000.Sheets 51b.S.W. &   9th February,1918.
57c.N.W.1/20,000. HENDECOURT & BULLECOURT,
51B.S.W.4, 1/10,000.

1. In continuation of 178th Inf.Bde Order No.92.
   2/5th S.F. will relieve 12th Bn.S.W.Bordrs. at MORY NORTH and
   2/6th S.F. will relieve 17th Bn.Welsh (not 11th Bn K.O.R.Lancs as
   stated in Table of Reliefs accompanying 178th Inf.Bde.Order No.92)
   at MORY L'ABBAYE on 10th February.

2. The above Battns.will proceed to their respective destinations by
   march route via BOIRY BECQUERELLE - BOYELLES - ERVILLERS. 2/6th S.F.
   will move off at 10.15 a.m. and 2/5th S.F. at 10.35 a.m.
   Intervals of 200 yards will be kept between companies.

3. 178th T.M.B. will also move to MORY NORTH on 10th inst., and the
   above Table of Reliefs is varied accordingly. They will proceed by
   route mentioned in para 2., and will move off at 10 a.m.

4. On the 11th Feby.the following reliefs will be carried out:-

   (a). 18th Bn Welsh (in Support) will be relieved by 2 Companies of
   2/5th S.F. and H.Qs and 1 Company of 2/6th S.F. 119th T.M.B. will
   be relieved by 178th T.M.B.
   2/5th S.F. will relieve 1 Company in MAN SUPPORT and the Right
   Company in RAILWAY RESERVE. 2/6th S.F. will relieve H.Qs and the
   Left Company in RAILWAY RESERVE. One guide per platoon (Total 8)
   will be sent by 18th Bn Welsh to MORY NORTH and one guide for H.Qs
   and one guide per platoon (Total 5) to MORY L'ABBAYE on 10th inst.
   119th T.M.B. will also send one guide to MORY NORTH on 10th instant.
   These guides will stay night 10/11th with relieving units.
   178th T.M.B. will move off at 9.45 a.m. and proceed via ST.LEGER
   and CROISELLES.
   2/5th S.F. and 2/6th S.F. will move off at 10.15 a.m. in following
   order.- One Company 2/5th S.F., One Company 2/5th S.F., One Company
   2/6th S.F., H.Qs 2/6th S.F. March will be by Platoons at 5 minute
   intervals. Route as above.
   The two companies of 2/5th S.F. will be under the command of O.C.
   2/6th S.F. for tactical purposes until relief (b) is completed by
   O.C.2/5th S.F.

   (b). 2/5th S.F. will relieve 10/11th Bn.H.L.I. in the Right Front
   line System. One guide for H.Qs and one per company (Total 3) will
   be at Bde H.Qs. L'HOMME MORT (B.17.a.8.7) at 5.30 p.m. They will
   proceed at intervals of 10 minutes between companies to Bn.H.Qs.
   where platoon guides will be provided. Reliefs from Bn.H.Q. will
   be via PELICAN AVENUE and BORDER LANE.

   (c). 2/6th S.F. will relieve 21st Bn Middlesex in the Left Front Line
   System. One guide per Company (Total 3) will be at Bde.H.Qs. L'HOMME
   MORT at 6 p.m. They will proceed at intervals of 10 minutes between
   Companies to Bn.H.Qs. where platoon guides will be provided.
   Reliefs from Bn H.Qs will be via LEG LANE.

5. 7th S.F. will move to MORY NORTH on 11th February. They will proceed
   by march route from their camp at 3 p.m. Completion of move will be
   reported to Brigade H.Qs.

6. Aeroplane photos, maps, Defence Schemes, trench and area stores, will
   be handed over on relief and receipts given.

7. Details of work in progress and methods of drawing R.E.Materials will
   be notified by outgoing units to incoming units.

8. Completion of relief will be wired to Bde.H.Qs.by code word "FOX".

9. Bde H.Qs. will close at Reserve Camp (S.6.a.9.9) at 3 p.m. on 11th
   Feb. and reopen at the same hour at L'HOMME MORT (B.17.a.8.7.

SECRET.

ADDENDUM NO.1
to
178th Infantry Brigade Order No.93.

Ref.Maps LENS,1/100,000.Sheets 51b.S.W.
and 57c.N.W.1/20,000. HENDECOURT & BULLECOURT
51b.S.W.4, 1/10,000.   10.2.18.

1. In continuation of 178th Infantry Brigade Order No.92. 175th Machine Gun Company will relieve 244th Machine Gun Company in the line on 12/13th February.

2. All details of relief will be arranged direct between Os.C. concerned, and completion reported in accordance with para.8 of 178th Infantry Brigade Order No.93.

3. Acknowledge.

Issued at 2.15 p.m.
 By D.R.
Distribution -
To all recipients of
 178th Inf.Bde Order 93.

Captain,
A/Brigade Major,
178th Infantry Brigade.

SECRET

175 Machine Gun Company Operation Order No 27.

18.2.18.

Ref: Maps 51b & 57c 1/40000.

1. The 175 M.G. Coy less No 3 Section will be relieved by the 200 M.G. Coy on night 19/20 Feb.

2. No 3 Section 175 M.G. Coy will come under command of O.C. 200 M.G. Coy.

3. All Trench Stores, Intelligence, Special Maps, S.O.S. & Battle lines will be handed over to relieving unit. In addition to above all Tripods, Belt Boxes, & Water Cans will be handed over and Receipts obtained.

4. 2/Lt Tallintyre (Transport Officer) will report to O.C. 200 M.G. Coy at MORY and take over, accomodation, Transport Lines. He will also take over 12 Tripods, 168 Full Belt Boxes & 40 Water Cans.

5. Guides for relieving Sections will report at Ration Dump as follows :- (1 guide per Team).

    No 4 Section   3.30 pm.
    No 2 — . —   4.0 pm
    No 1 — . —   4.30 pm

6. O.C. No 1 Section will hand over to "B" Section 200 M.G. Coy: "Vickers Gun" at present at U.13.d.80.50 and obtain a Receipt for same.

7. The 4 men at present assisting the Tunnelling R.E. will remain attached to No 3 Section.

8. On Relief Sections will dump Gun Kit at No 3 Section H.Q. & will leave 2 men per section to load limbers. They will then report at Coy HQ where guides will meet them & proceed to MORY.

9. C.Q.M.S. will arrange to have Hot Meals ready for Company on arrival in Camp.

10. Receipts stating that Emplacements, Dug Outs, Latrines and accomodation were handed over in clean and Sanitary Condition will be obtained.
    All receipts to be handed in at Coy HQ on Completion of relief.

11. Two limbers will report at No 3 Section H.Q. for gun kit as soon after dusk as possible.

12. Acknowledge.

J.H. Gardner Capt & Adjt
175 Coy. M.G. Corps.

Copies to :-
No 1. 178 Inf. Bde.
— 2. Officer
— 3. War Diary
— 4. O.C. No 1 Sec 175 M.G. Coy
— 5. " 2
— 6. " 3
— 7. " 4
— 8. O.C. 200 M.G. Coy.
— 9. Transport Officer
—10. C.Q.M.S.

Secret.   175 M Coy Operation Order No 28.
                                                        20/3/18
Ref Maps
Bullecourt 1/10.000
57B & 57C 1/40.000

1. 2/Lt Friend and 4 teams No 2 Section will relieve 4 teams 200 M Coy in positions E.1 E.2 E.3 & E.4 at dusk 23/24th. O.C. No 2 Section will apply to O.C. No 3 Section for guides to positions.

2. Tripods, Belt Boxes, Special Maps, S.O.S. and Battle lines &c will be taken over and receipts given. Copy of receipts will be sent to Coy HQ. at first opportunity.

3. The following men will be attached to No 2 Sec. for work on E battery positions:—
   Ptes Lowe. L.B.; Lishman E.W; James T; & Aspinall J.
   These four men will be returned to their Section on night of 27th inst.

4. No 3 Sec 175 M.C. plus 4 men attd as working Party will be relieved by 4 teams of 200 M.C. on night 23rd/24th. Tripods, Belt Boxes, S.A.A. & Tr. stores will be handed over and receipts obtained. On relief No 3 Section will march to DURROW CAMP, MORY. Guides will meet party at Coy HQ. 200 M.C. These guides will proceed to 200 Coy HQ with No 2 Section & wait there until relief is complete.

5. No 2 Section 175 Coy will come under orders of O.C. 200 Coy for Tactical purposes.

6. No 2 Sections limbers, after unloading gunkit, will report to O.C. No 3 Sec to convey gunkit to camp.

7. O.C. No 3 Section will report relief complete on arrival at 200 Coy HQ.

8. Hot meals will be provided by Coys, for No 3 Section on arrival in camp.

Copies 1 — Office
       2 — O.C. 200 Coy
       3 — 2/Lt Friend
       4 — 2/Lt Cradwell
       5 —   T.O.

7.
Liaison Officer will arrange for
one limber to arrive at 2/Lt Ferguson
Stations at 6 pm and one at the junction
of TANK AVENUE — RAILWAY RESERVE
at 6 pm to take Lt. Wilson's guns &
equipment back. Lt Ferguson
will provide guide for this number of
Stations. These two limbers will
proceed to 2/Lt Ferguson's HQ together
T.O will also arrange for two
limbers to be at U27d 10.10 to bring
back 2Lt Townsend & 2Lt Hawkes
guns & equipment at 6pm, and HQ
limber & cook cart to be at Coy HQ at 6pm

9.
All guides supplied by 177 Coy HQ
will return to Coy HQ on completion
of their task.

10.
Movement of Coy HQ & Transport
will be notified later

11. 177 Inf Bde will be notified relief
complete by wiring the word
DOVER.

26-2-18   E Needham
                                    Capt
Distributed to:
1 OMGC   8 Liaison Officer
2 177 Inf Bde   9 War diary
3 Transport Officer 10 175 Coy
                 11 Spare

SECRET

175 Machine Gun Company Operation Order No 29.

26-2-[?]

MAP: 1" REDOUBT SPECIAL SHEET.
51a SW.SE and 57c NW.NE 1/20,000.

I. THE 175 M.G.Coy WILL RELIEVE 177 M.G.Coy IN THE CENTRE SECTOR ON NIGHT 27/28 FEB.

II. FOUR GUNS No 2 SECTION AT PRESENT IN DOUTRON AT U26c & C26 WILL TAKE OVER POSITIONS AT PRESENT OCCUPIED BY 177 M.G.Coy AS FOLLOWS:— 1 GUN C3c29; 1 GUN C3c 2686.
1 GUN C3c35; 1 GUN C3c 42.
ON RELIEF THE FOUR GUNS 177 M.G.COY. WILL TAKE OVER POSITIONS VACATED BY No 2 SEC. 175 M.G.COY. THIS CHANGE OF POSITIONS WILL BE ARRANGED BETWEEN 2/LT FRIEND & SECTION OFFICER 177 M.G.COY.

III. 2 GUNS No 3 SEC. UNDER Lt GRADWELL WILL RELIEVE 2 GUNS OF 177 MGC SITUATED IN "STANHOPE REDOUBT" AT U27a.8075 & U27b.2075.   2 GUNS No 3 SEC. UNDER 2/LT ELFICK WILL RELIEVE 2 GUNS 177 COY IN POSITIONS AT C4c68 & C4c64
4 GUNS No 4 SEC. UNDER Lt FERRIE WILL RELIEVE 4 GUNS 177 COY AT U28a.91.   4 GUNS No 1 SECTION UNDER 2/LT EKINS WILL RELIEVE 4 GUNS 177 COY AT THE FOLLOWING POSITIONS:—
1 GUN "STATION REDOUBT" U27c7080
2 GUNS U27a.38, U27a.45; 1 GUN "TOWER RESERVE" U27b.48

IV. ALL GUNS, BELT BOXES, TRIPODS & EQUIPMENT WILL BE TAKEN INTO THE LINE.

V. RATIONS WILL BE DELIVERED NIGHTLY AS UNDER:-
No 1. SEC, No 4. SEC, & SUBSEC. No 3 SEC UNDER Lt GRADWELL. PER DECAUVILLE
No 2 SEC & SUBSEC. No 3 SEC. UNDER 2/LT ELFICK. ——— PER LIMBER
RATION PARTIES WILL MEET RATIONS AT 6 P.M. AT DUMA

VI. WATER CAN BE DRAWN FROM WATER TANK "RAILWAY RESERVE" U27a.5245

VII. ALL MAPS, INTELLIGENCE, TARGETS ENGAGED, WORK IN PROGRESS WILL BE TAKEN OVER.

VIII. COPIES OF RECEIPTS WILL BE SENT TO COY. H.Q. BY 8 A.M. 28TH INST.

IX. REPORTS. EXACT AS PREVIOUSLY.

X. GUN TEAMS WILL MOVE OFF AS FOLLOWS:-
1ST PARTY:— SUBSEC. No 3 SEC. UNDER Lt GRADWELL
No. 1. SEC UNDER 2/LT EKINS
THIS PARTY WILL MOVE OFF AT 5.15 P.M. AND REPORT AT 177 COY H.Q. WHERE GUIDES WILL BE PROVIDED.
2ND PARTY:— SUBSEC. No 3 SEC. UNDER 2/LT ELFICK
No 4 SEC. UNDER Lt FERRIE.
THIS PARTY WILL MOVE OFF 3/4 HR. AFTER 1ST PARTY AND REPORT AT 177 COY. H.Q. WHERE GUIDES WILL BE PROVIDED.

XI. 175 COY. H.Q. WILL CLOSE AT "DUAROW CAMP" AT 5.15 P.M. AND OPEN AT S.17b.25.65 AT 6.0 P.M.

XII. RELIEF COMPLETE WILL BE NOTIFIED BY WIRING WORD "OGUTA".

XIII. ACKNOWLEDGE.

DISTRIBUTION:— No.1. COPY. C.O.
2   "   ADJT.
3   "   O.C. No.1. SEC.
4   "   "   " 2
5   "   "   " 3
6   "   "   " 4
7   "   2/LT ELFICK
8   "   T.O.
9   "   177 M.G.C.
10 "   2ND M.G.C.
11 "   [?]
12 "   W.D.

www.ingramcontent.com/pod-product-compliance
Lightning Source LLC
Chambersburg PA
CBHW081424160426
43193CB00013B/2187